Lifting Every Voice

pedagogy and politics
of bilingualism

edited by

ZEYNEP F. BEYKONT

Harvard Education Publishing Group

Library of Congress Catalog Card Number 99-73661
ISBN 1-891792-01-6

Harvard Education Publishing Group
349 Gutman Library
6 Appian Way
Cambridge, MA 02138

Cover Design and Artwork: blondèl joseph
Editorial Production: Dody Riggs
Typography: Sheila Walsh

Dedication

*I dedicate my work on this book to
my soulmate and life partner*

Bruce Johnson-Beykont

*and to all those across the world who combine
teaching, research, and political activism
in their struggles for cultural and
linguistic democracy.*

Contents

Introduction

The linguistic composition of our public schools is rapidly changing.[1] Today, over three million students come from homes where Standard English is not the main language of communication. These language-minority students[2] join the educational system at different time points and with varied educational backgrounds. Some are born here or come to the United States when they are very young. An increasing number enter the public schools as teenagers: some having had years of rigorous schooling and others having received little or no formal education in their home countries. Whether U.S. or foreign born, we find variation in students' native language, culture, race, class, religion, economic resources, parental education, geographic mobility, and immigration histories.[3]

Upon entering school, most language-minority students are not proficient in English. While all young people meet the difficult tasks of schooling (such as learning to read, write, and understand the complexities of math, science, and history), language-minority students are challenged by the additional task of acquiring English as a second language and using it to learn academic content.[4] In order to participate in classroom activities and social circles, they must simultaneously acquire English oral fluency; use English for all school tasks; and exhibit grade-level performance. Exacerbating the difficulties, these young people often attend underfunded and overcrowded inner-city public schools where school failure is the norm even for native English speakers.[5]

Language-minority students face these academic challenges within a political context that defines their bilingualism as "problematic," "deficient," and "a sign of inferior intellectual and academic abilities."[6] The common identity struggles of childhood and adolescence are intensified for language-minority students soon after they discover that Standard English is the only language of power and prestige in the United States and other languages and dialects are devalued. Young people struggle to take pride in their native language while being pressured to abandon it and replace it with English. Developing a healthy ethnic identity is yet another challenge when students attend schools in which few teachers, administrators, school personnel, and historical figures in the school curriculum look like, speak like, or represent their home cultures. And finally, many language-minority students struggle to define a healthy racial identity in a society that lumps everyone into rigid categories of "White" and "Black."

Lifting Every Voice: Pedagogy and Politics of Bilingualism brings together essays on the complex political and pedagogical issue of language-minority education in U.S. public schools. In particular, this volume focuses on language-minority students in bilingual programs — those who receive some academic instruction in their native language. The book starts with the premise that bilingualism and academic excellence can be nurtured in bilingual classrooms when the necessary energy and supports for quality bilingual programs are made available. *Lifting Every Voice* thus moves beyond the simplistic question of whether bilingual programs are the best educational option for language-minority students and asks *how best* to address the varied strengths and needs of students *who choose to be* instructed in bilingual programs. The volume refocuses our attention on the political and pedagogical supports that are necessary to improve the quality of bilingual education throughout the nation.

As a multilingual researcher, practitioner, and activist in the field of language-minority education, I have compiled the essays in *Lifting Every Voice* based on a conviction that those whose lives are intimately linked to language-minority students should shape policy and pedagogical decisions in bilingual classrooms. As a nation, we have failed to tap into and learn from the knowledge base of classroom practitioners, researchers, community activists, and teacher educators — their work has been invisible, their knowledge base ignored, their insights misunderstood, and their success stories unavailable. People who are disconnected from the day-to-day realities of bilingual classrooms are leading the public debate. In order to improve our programs, and make sound policy and pedagogical decisions concerning the education of language-minority students, we must broaden the discussion. We must lift every voice.

Of course, bilingual programs do not operate in a political vacuum. In order to further explain the rationale for this volume, it is necessary to briefly examine present debates and language policy issues in the United States. Bilingual programs are under attack. Strong political and social forces have joined together in the English Only movement.[7] The English Only movement aims to adopt English as the official language of the United States and thereby protect the power and privileges enjoyed by native speakers of Standard English. Warning against the politically divisive potential of immigrant languages in the United States, leaders of the movement argue that bilingual services and schooling are communicating the wrong message — that people can survive without English skills. In order to give immigrants the incentive to learn English quickly, the use of other languages in government and public services should be banned. Public funds should not be spent on bilingual programs that are either "ineffective" in teaching English or sidetracked by the "competing" goal of teaching language-minority students in their native language.

The English Only movement has been particularly successful at the state level. By 1999, twenty-two states had adopted English as their official language[8] and passed laws that limit or ban bilingual schooling. Most notably, in 1998 California voted in favor of Proposition 227. This law bans bilingual education and reduces school services for language-minority students to one year of sheltered English instruction. While mixing children from different age and grade levels for English instruction is allowed, using students' native languages for educational purposes is strictly prohibited. In fact, under this initiative, parents can sue teachers who use any language other than English in classrooms. Proposition 227 has set a very negative precedent for similar initiatives to be introduced in other states and at the federal level.[9]

Why are bilingual programs under attack? Why is it that the English Only movement has gained such public support? In order to fully understand attacks on bilingual education, we need to look at the political, social, and economic context of the United States at this particular historical moment. The English Only movement has gained strength in the conservative political context of the 1980s and 1990s when many gains of the U.S. civil rights movement, such as affirmative action in the workplace and on college campuses, have been undermined. Attacks on bilingual education are closely linked to broader attacks on the civil rights gains of all people of color. The 1980s and 1990s have also been marked by a massive emigration from Asian, Pacific Island, Central Asian, South American, Central American, Middle Eastern, and African countries. Increasingly, public school classrooms across the country have enrolled language-minority students from cultural, racial, ethnic, and linguistic backgrounds that are notably different from those of European Americans. In a backlash, anti-immigrant sentiments have been translated into attacks on bilingual programs and other immigrant services.

Some Americans support English-only policies in schools because they are ignorant about second-language development in school contexts. Partly due to geographic isolation from the rest of the world and partly due to the status of English as an international language of communication, the U.S. population has remained largely uninterested in learning a second language.[10] Most people either do not have any experience learning a second language or recall frustrating experiences due to the generally poor quality of foreign language education in public schools. In the absence of any personal reference, the public readily buys into discredited folk theories about child bilingualism.[11] Such theories grossly underestimate the time it takes to develop the level of English proficiency that language-minority students need in order to succeed in mainstream classes without any native language support.[12]

Others endorse English-only policies in schools because they are afraid. There is a fear of losing the power and privilege that white, middle-class, and Standard English speakers have enjoyed in the United States. People of varied colors, with widely varied languages, cultures, and religions, are perceived as threats. There is also a fear that the new immigrants may resist assimilating into the American mainstream and may require that public schools provide more recognition and reinforcement of diverse languages and cultures. Last but not least, there is a fear that immigrants might take jobs away from native English speakers. Leaders of the English Only movement have seized upon all these fears and successfully injected myths and misconceptions about today's immigrants and bilingual education into the public debate. The current public debates often reveal more about unresolved questions concerning the role of minorities and minority languages in U.S. society than they reveal about effective methods for teaching English to language-minority students. Sadly, innocent children are suffering from the contradictions and growing pains of our society — a society that is demographically multilingual and multicultural, but ideologically monolingual and monocultural.

The examination of history is informative. The types of extreme educational measures recently adopted in California are reminiscent of other times in U.S. history.[13] In the late 1800s and early 1900s, the arrival of a massive wave of immigrants — largely from European but also from Asian countries — prompted a similarly negative public response. Bilingual programs that were actually common at that time were abolished and an English Only policy was adopted in public schools. Bilingual textbooks were burned and teachers were fired, brought to court, and convicted for explaining concepts in children's native languages. Students were punished for using their native languages in classrooms, cafeterias, and on playgrounds. They were left to sink or swim in all-English classes. With schools as English Only environments, generations of language-minority children grew up feeling ashamed of their native language, replaced it with English, and found themselves unable to speak to their grandparents, relatives, and sometimes even their parents.

It is a misconception that the immigrants of yesterday learned English quickly. Today's immigrants learn English much faster than ever before and replace their native language with English within two generations or less.[14] It is also a common misconception that the immigrants of yesterday succeeded in school even though they were instructed in mainstream classrooms with no special support. Most of them did not succeed in school. Vast numbers of language-minority students were relegated to special education or low track classes based on their performance on English tests before they were even given a chance to learn English.[15] A majority of these students eventually dropped out, or rather were "pushed out" of school.[16] The dropout rates of language-minority students were 80–90 percent in some districts.[17] However, an industrial economy was ready to absorb them with less than perfect English proficiency and less than a high school degree.

Nothing was done to change these abysmal educational circumstances until language-minority communities joined the civil rights movement and fought to obtain expanded language rights and bilingual services in schools. Civil rights legislation prohibited discrimination based on color, race, and national origin in federally funded programs, including schools. The Civil Rights Act of 1964, the Federal Bilingual Law of 1965, and the landmark Supreme Court case of *Lau v. Nichols* in 1974 set into law that educating language-minority students through a language that they do not comprehend is a violation of their civil rights. Due to their low proficiency in English, when educated in mainstream classrooms, language-minority students are denied access to a meaningful education. Similarly, other discriminatory practices were questioned, such as the disproportionate placement of these children in special education classes based on their performance on standardized English tests.

Districts were federally mandated to address the needs of language-minority students — both their need to acquire English as a second language and their need to learn appropriate grade-level content.[18] Schools had the option either to develop an alternative program specially designed for language-minority students or to supplement the mainstream program with some English-as-a-Second-Language (ESL) support. In essence, the federal bilingual law mandated that school districts take some affirmative educational measure to ensure equal educational opportunity for language-minority students, but it did not define exactly what an optimal program should look like. The bilingual law stated a preference for native-language instruction and provided some funding without prescribing the extent and nature of native-language use. In the absence of a specific formula, most schools avoided the use of native-language instruction and continued instructing language-minority students in mainstream classrooms with the addition of some ESL support. In fact, three decades after the federal bilingual law was first passed, approximately two-thirds of schools serving language-minority students do not offer bilingual programs.[19]

Other schools have chosen from among several bilingual program models — each with different academic and linguistic goals in mind.[20] One commonly used model, transitional bilingual programs, teach language-minority students in their native language for a few years while students are learning English. The program aims to quickly transition language-minority students into mainstream classes. A second model, maintenance bilingual programs, are longer in duration. Aiming to develop academic skills in both native language and English, maintenance bilingual programs do not transition language-minority students into mainstream classes until after the elementary school years. And a third model, two-way bilingual programs, teach native English-speaking and language-minority students in integrated classes bilingually and aim for full bilingualism for all students. A failure to clearly understand these varied program models and their differing goals has contributed to the confusion among parents, school personnel, and the general public regarding the expected pace of language-minority students' English development in bilingual programs.

There have been many challenges in the implementation of bilingual programs. One challenge is a shortage of well-trained bilingual teachers that has resulted in placement of native or fluent speakers of a particular language into teaching positions regardless of their prior training.[21] Another challenge is the lack of curriculum materials and books, especially for those languages that do not have a long-standing written literacy tradition. Furthermore, the academic and social integration of bilingual students has been a challenge, particularly when the larger school community views bilingual programs as a remedial service whose goals, philosophy, and implementation are either unclear or objectionable. In some cases, academic content and learning goals in mainstream and bilingual classrooms have been different due to estranged relationships between mainstream and bilingual staff within schools and lack of coordination between mainstream administrators and bilingual education departments within school districts.

The quality of bilingual programs has varied widely. Many well-designed bilingual programs have been extremely successful when they are implemented consistently across grade levels by well-trained teachers with the support of school administration and the larger school community and a focus on providing an academically challenging curriculum.[22] In these programs students receive the necessary academic, linguistic, and emotional support, stay in school, develop grade-level academic competencies and English skills,[23] and graduate with a positive sense of themselves, their home culture, and their native language. Other programs are bilingual only in name, with little consistency across grade levels, a substandard curriculum, teachers who are not bilingual, and an administration and a school community not supportive of native language instruction. Students in these programs are often rushed into mainstream classrooms prematurely, before having an opportunity to develop a strong foundation in their native language and in English, and subsequently fall behind academically. Undoubtedly, the variation in program quality has left bilingual programs open to criticism.

While the 1980s and 1990s have been a time of some program experimentation and innovation in schools, the federal vision of bilingual education has become increasingly conservative and narrow: remedial in focus, shortsighted in goals, and transitional in nature. At the federal level and in much of the public debate, bilingual programs are seen as a temporary special service for language-minority students — a somewhat small group of students who have a "problem," which is limited English skills, that needs to be quickly "fixed." No emphasis is placed on developing language-minority students' native language literacy skills. Rather, native language instruction is viewed as a "treatment" for language-minority students' "linguistic deficiencies," until they transition into English Only mainstream classrooms. Ironically, while nationwide school reform efforts are suggesting bilingualism as a high school graduation requirement for native English speakers, the primary outcome of language-minority education is defined as monolingualism in English. The differential treatment points to the extremely political nature of this issue.

Mirroring the narrow policy focus, large-scale evaluation studies have also judged the effectiveness of bilingual programs by how quickly students develop English skills and leave bilingual programs. In search of a magic formula — one "best" program model — many evaluation studies have asked such shortsighted questions as "What is the most effective program to teach English to language-minority students?" and "Are bilingual programs as effective as English-only programs?"[24] Not surprisingly, large-scale evaluation studies have been inconclusive because they tried to compare the short-term success of programs that have widely varied goals and different approaches to attaining those goals.[25] Focusing on how quickly students learn English, most evaluation studies have failed to document the enrichment aspects and long-term benefits of bilingual programs, such as full proficiency in more than one language, enhanced cognitive development, deeper cross-cultural understanding, expanded economic opportunities, and stronger community/school connections. The inconclusive results of large-scale evaluation studies have fueled the public debate.

As we enter the twenty-first century, policy discussions on bilingual education are both extremely politicized and too often blindly focused on the simplistic and misguided question of whether bilingual programs are the most effective educational option for language-minority students. These effectiveness debates are forcing teachers and advocates to put their energy into defending the very existence of our programs rather than engaging in more constructive dialogue, reflection, and sharing about what has worked in bilingual classrooms, under which circumstances, with which groups of students, and what more can be done to improve bilingual education.

The essays in *Lifting Every Voice* are particularly important at this historical juncture — with bilingual programs under attack, and myths and misconceptions about language-minority education holding prominence in a public debate led by mostly uninformed, misinformed, or opportunistic politicians and bureaucrats. The perspectives, testimonies, observations, and findings of teachers, community activists, teacher educators, and classroom researchers collected in this volume provide a window into the complex reality of bilingual classrooms. These voices illuminate the challenges and joys of educating students from a variety of ethnic, linguistic, and academic backgrounds. The authors demystify bilingual education based on concrete examples and provide a counterpoint to the often unfounded, distorted, and simplistic views of bilingual education that emanate from conservative political circles and currently dominate the public debate.

Lifting Every Voice is organized into three parts. Part One focuses on the power and significance of bilingualism for language-minority students from a cultural, pedagogical, and political perspective. In Part Two, authors share their research and practice-based experiences and insights in successful bilingual classrooms. Their nuanced discussion of what works, under which circumstances, and with which groups of students illustrates the complexities of teaching students with widely varied strengths and needs. Part Three then discusses the political, organizational, and programmatic supports that are necessary to better serve our language-minority students and to nurture their bilingualism.

In a democratic society, public schools should serve *every* child, not just a privileged few. Schools should develop the linguistic, academic, and cultural potential of *all* children. If the population in our public schools is changing, then our schools must also change. As you read the essays collected here, you will encounter practitioners, researchers, teacher educators, and community activists who speak loudly and clearly in support of this democratic ideal. These voices embody a spirit that embraces the linguistic, cultural, and ethnic diversity of all our students and trumpet a belief in the transformatory potential of public education in general and bilingual education in particular. At this propitious juncture in the history of bilingual education, we have a great opportunity to reflect on and build upon the many insights and lessons learned in the last three decades of rich experimentation in U.S. bilingual education. We have a great opportunity to use the impetus of nationwide educational reform efforts to improve curriculum standards and set higher learning goals in bilingual classrooms. We have a great opportunity to recommit ourselves to the equity ideal of public education and to making high quality bilingual schooling a reality for language-minority students.

Zeynep F. Beykont
Editor

Notes

1. The 1990 U.S. Census reported that over 329 languages are spoken in U.S. homes, including Spanish (72.9%), followed by Vietnamese (3.9%), Hmong (1.8%), Cantonese (1.7%), Cambodian (1.6%), Korean (1.6%), Laotian (1.3%), Navajo (1.3%), Tagalog (1.1%), Russian (0.9%), French-Creole (0.9%), and Portuguese (0.7%).

2. The terms *language-minority, linguistic-minority,* and *non-native speakers of English* are used interchangeably throughout this volume. These terms refer to all groups whose native languages are different from a country's official language(s), language(s) of power and prestige, language(s) of wider communication, language(s) of upward mobility, and/or standard dialect (Beykont, 1997a). In the U.S. context, in addition to being the language that is spoken by the majority of the population, Standard English is the language and the dialect of power, prestige, and upward mobility. Language-minority students in the United States come from homes where Standard English is not the main language of communication.

3. See Garcia (1998) for an extended discussion on student diversity.

4. See Wong Fillmore and Valadez (1986) for an extended discussion on academic and linguistic challenges that language-minority students face in our public schools.

5. Based on a representative sample of schools, the nationwide 1993–1994 survey concludes that language-minority students attend large urban schools with a large body of minority students receiving free or reduced lunch (National Center of Educational Statistics, 1997).

6. See Beykont (1994, 1997a) and Nielsen and Beykont (1997) for an extensive discussion on the favorable and unfavorable political contexts in which students develop bilingualism.

7. See Crawford (1992a, 1992b, 1995) for a comprehensive analysis and discussion of the English Only movement.

8. The states that adopted English as their official language include Alabama, Arkansas, Arizona, Arkansas, California, Colorado, Florida, Georgia, Iowa, Illinois, Indiana, Kentucky, Mississippi, Montana, Nebraska, New Hampshire, North Carolina, North Dakota, South Carolina, South Dakota, Tennessee, and Wyoming.

9. Already there have been several bills filed to reduce or cut federal support for bilingual education and remove the legislative preference for bilingual programs in the education of language-minority students. (Two examples are HR 3680 and HR 123.)

10. There are some exceptions to this pattern — a small group of elites who are motivated to cultivate their children's bilingualism in private schools so that they can find jobs in international business, diplomacy, and some language-minority parents motivated to teach their children the native language of their ancestry in community-based language programs.

11. See McLaughlin (1985) and Snow (1990) for a discussion on folk theories about child bilingualism.

12. See Beykont (1994), Collier (1992), Cummins (1989), and Ramirez, Pasta, Yuen, Billings, & Ramey (1991) for empirically based findings on the length of time that language-minority students need in order to develop grade-level English proficiency.

13. See Crawford (1995), Keller and Van Hooft (1982), and Paulston (1980) for extensive discussion on U.S. bilingual education history.

14. See Veltman (1983) and Wong Fillmore (1991) for qualitative and quantitative data on language loss in language-minority communities in the United States.

15. See Coleman (1966) for empirical findings.

16. See Padilla (1982) for a review.

17. See, for example, Massachusetts Association for Bilingual Education (1998) for examples from Massachusetts school districts.

18. See the memorandum released by the Department of Health, Education, and Welfare (May 25, 1970) to school districts with more than 5 percent language-minority students.

19. National Center for Education Statistics (1997) found that only one-third of schools serving language-minority students offer bilingual education.

20. See Beykont (1993, 1997b) for an extended discussion of bilingual program models that are specifically developed for language-minority students in the United States and across the world.

21. Less than 5 percent of teachers have an ESL or bilingual degree and less than 30 percent have had any training working with language-minority students.

22. See McLeod (1996) for a review of well-designed and successful programs.

23. See Beykont (1994, 1998) and Ramirez et al. (1991) for empirical findings.

24. See Meyer and Feinberg (1992) for a review of nationwide evaluation studies.

25. See Beykont, (1994, in press) for a detailed discussion of methodological flaws of evaluation research.

References

Beykont, Z. F. (1993). The choice of language policies and programs: A comparative view. In W. K. Cummings (Ed.), *Reaching peripheral groups: Community, language, and teachers in the context of development* (pp. 125–190). Buffalo: State University of New York.

Beykont, Z. F. (1994). *Academic progress of a nondominant group: A longitudinal study of Puerto Ricans in New York City's late-exit bilingual programs.* Unpublished doctoral dissertation, Harvard Graduate School of Education, Cambridge, MA.

Beykont, Z. F. (1997a). School-language policy decisions for nondominant language groups. In H. D. Nielsen & W. K. Cummings (Eds.), *Quality education for all: Community-oriented approaches* (pp. 79–121). New York: Garland.

Beykont, Z. F. (1997b). Refocusing school language policy discussions. In W. K. Cummings & N. F. McGinn (Eds.), *International handbook of education and development: Preparing schools, students, and nations for the twenty-first century* (pp. 263–283). New York: Pergamon.

Beykont, Z. F. (1998). Benefits of bilingual education on English reading skills. *NABE News, 21*(7), 5–6.

Beykont, Z. F. (in press). Research on bilingual education: Past, present, and future. *Cultural Circles.*

Coleman, J. S. (1966). *Equality of educational opportunity.* Washington, DC: U.S. Government Printing Office.

Collier, V. P. (1992). A synthesis of studies examining long-term language minority student data on academic achievement. *Bilingual Research Journal, 16*(1,2), 187–212.

Crawford, J. (1992a). *Hold your tongue: Bilingualism and the politics of English only.* New York: Addison-Wesley.

Crawford, J. (Ed.). (1992b). *Language loyalties: A source book on the official English controversy.* Chicago: University of Chicago Press.

Crawford, J. (1995*). Bilingual education: History, politics, theory, and practice* (3rd ed.). Los Angeles: Bilingual Educational Services.

Cummins, J. (1989). *Empowering minority students.* Sacramento: California State Department of Education.

Garcia, E. (1998, March). *Multilingualism in US schools: From research to practice.* Paper presented at the Reading and the English Language Learner Forum, Sacramento, CA.

Keller, G. D., & Van Hooft, K. S. (1982). A chronology of bilingualism and bilingual education. In J. A. Fishman & G. D. Keller (Eds.), *Bilingual education for Hispanic students in the United States* (pp. 3–22). New York: Teachers College Press.

Massachusetts Association for Bilingual Education. (1998). *The emperor's unraveling cloak.* Unpublished manuscript.

McLaughlin, B. (1985). *Second-language acquisition in childhood: Vol. 2: School age children.* Hillsdale, NJ: Erlbaum.

McLeod, B. (1996). *School reform and student diversity: Exemplary schooling for language minority students.* Washington, DC: National Clearinghouse for Bilingual Education.

Meyer, M. M., & Feinberg, S. E. (Eds.). (1992). *Assessing evaluation studies: The case of bilingual education strategies.* Washington, DC: National Academy Press.

National Center for Education Statistics. (1997). *1993–1994 schools and staffing survey: A profie of policies and practices for limited English proficient students. Screening methods, program support, and teacher training.* Washington, DC: U.S. Department of Education.

Nielsen, D. H., & Beykont, Z. F. (1997). Reaching the periphery: Toward a community-oriented education. In H. D. Nielsen & W. K. Cummings (Eds.), *Quality education for all: Community-oriented approaches* (pp. 247–267). New York: Garland.

Padilla, A. M. (1982). Bilingual education: Gateways to integration or roads to separation. In J. A. Fishman & G. D. Keller (Eds.), *Bilingual education for Hispanic students in the United States* (pp. 48–70). New York: Teachers College Press.

Paulston, C. B. (1980). *Bilingual education: Theories and issues.* Rowley, MA: Newbury House.

Ramirez, J. D., Pasta, D., Yuen, S. D., Billings, D. K., & Ramey, D. K. (1991). *Final report: Longitudinal study of structured English immersion, early-exit, and late-exit transitional bilingual programs for language-minority children.* San Mateo, CA: Aguirre International.

Snow, C. E. (1990). Rationales for native language instruction: Evidence from research. In A. M. Padilla, H. H. Fairchild, & C. M. Valadez (Eds.), *Bilingual education: Issues and strategies* (pp. 47–74). Newbury Park, CA: Sage.

Veltman, K. (1983). *Language shift in the United States.* Berlin: Moutan.

Wong Fillmore, L. (1991). When learning a second language means losing the first. *Early Childhood Research Quarterly, 6,* 323–346.

Wong Fillmore, L., & Valadez, C. (1986). Teaching bilingual learners. In M. C. Wittock (Ed.), *Handbook of research on teaching* (3rd ed., pp. 648–685). New York: Macmillan.

PART ONE

Power of Bilingualism

Bilingualism Is Powerful

Bilingualism is key for the survival and success of language-minority students. Culturally, bilingualism allows young people to stay connected with their community of origin and integrate with the English-speaking community. Politically, bilingualism enables language-minority students to develop a healthy identity, an authentic voice, and a positive self-image. Pedagogically, bilingualism enhances students' cognitive development and access to academic and career opportunities. In Part One of *Lifting Every Voice,* three community organizers — Brazilian parent liaison Heloisa Souza, Cape Verdean teacher educator Donaldo Macedo, and Chinese high school teacher Katy Kwong — discuss the power of bilingualism in reversing the school failure, alienation, and loss of self-esteem suffered by our students.

The cultural and linguistic significance of bilingualism for language-minority students becomes evident when we look at the alarming patterns of native-language loss in U.S. schools. In her essay, Heloisa Souza draws our attention to an often forgotten reality of immigrant communities — that many children replace their native language with English. She presents examples of several Brazilian children whom she has monitored over the years. These children entered school as monolingual Portuguese speakers and left school monolingual in English. In some cases, the children no longer share a common language with their parents, and almost invariably they cannot communicate with their grandparents and extended family in Brazil. English quickly replaces Portuguese for these immigrant students, particularly if their parents do not insist upon using Portuguese at home. The social memories and cultural knowledge that bond communities start to fade in the absence of a common language — driving a wedge between generations and causing dissolution of the younger generation's cultural values and identities. Souza urges parents and schools to take joint action to halt and reverse this native-language erosion. She emphasizes consistent use of the native language at home, prolonged bilingual instruction in schools, and a respectful and collaborative relationship between home and school, facilitated by school-based parent liaisons.

Souza points to an important distinction between the limited conversational vocabulary that children acquire quickly and the academic language skills that they need to succeed in mainstream classrooms. Policymakers, educators, parents, and the general public are confused about, and grossly underestimate, the time that it takes to develop the level of English proficiency that language-minority students need in order to succeed in mainstream classes with no native-language support. Acquiring the sophisticated vocabulary that is necessary in upper elementary grades and beyond to master complex academic material in English (such as literary allusion and photosynthesis) takes a long time. Souza warns both families and educators against rushing children out of bilingual programs based on their English conversational skills. Several children that Souza monitored who were prematurely placed into mainstream classrooms experienced academic failure, social isolation, and behavioral problems. However, Souza's success stories demonstrate that language-minority children do not have to lose their native language and give up their ethnic identity in order to gain proficiency in English, succeed academically, and integrate culturally.

It is undemocratic to impose English as the only language of instruction in schools when our students come from homes that speak 329 different languages and dialects. Focusing on the democratic power of bilingualism, Donaldo Macedo discusses the significance of native languages and English in language-minority students' lives. Proficiency in the native language enables young people to connect with their past, think critically, develop an authentic voice, and analyze the oppressive conditions that affect their communities. At the same time, proficiency in English allows them to participate in the mainstream, engage in dialogue across cultures, and contribute to transforming the current system that stratifies groups by language, class, race, and ethnic origin. Tracing the current attacks against bilingual education to a long history of English imposition in schools in U.S. territories, Macedo argues that attacks on bilingual education are most often rooted in a political agenda, even though it is claimed that the concerns are methodologically based.

Macedo maintains that English imposition in schools is a form of colonialism because it denies students' native languages, cultural histories, and life experiences, thereby preventing them from developing a critical perspective on social issues. In order to interrupt the harmful effects of English Only school policies, collaboration between researchers, educators, and community activists is necessary. Researchers can play an important role by contextualizing their study findings within the sociocultural realities of the students and communities that they are studying. Educators can perform the central task of building on the cultural and linguistic knowledge that their students bring to school and nurture bilingualism by teaching them English in addition to their native language. Community activists can serve the vital role of denouncing and organizing against attacks on linguistic rights and making clear the connections between the English Only movement and other efforts to relegate people of color and immigrants to subordinate status in U.S. society.

Practitioners who work day in and day out in bilingual classrooms know that there is a close connection between a student's native-language and second-language skills. Katy Kwong discusses the pedagogical power of bilingualism for her high school students from Mainland China, Hong Kong, and Vietnam who have nine years of prior formal education in Cantonese but low English proficiency. Kwong observes that the stronger her students' literacy skills in Cantonese, the more quickly they develop English literacy skills. With active teaching of similarities and differences between the two languages, Kwong finds that her students' skills in Cantonese transfer into English even though the writing systems of the two languages are different. If forced into mainstream classrooms, Kwong asserts that her students would not have the support they need for fully transferring what they know in Cantonese into English.

Kwong notes that in her bilingual classroom, learning continues apace because students understand the language of instruction. The shared language of communication allows her to carefully assess her students' academic strengths and weaknesses and to challenge each student at the appropriate conceptual level. With a focus on the academic content of instruction, Kwong is able to provide rigorous courses parallel to the ones taught in the college track. Kwong denounces the all-too-common practice of placing language-minority students into low-level mainstream classes based on their low English skills — a practice that denies students access to an academically challenging curriculum. Kwong argues that high-level courses must be given in students' native languages so that language-minority students receive the intellectual stimulation and life options that they deserve and are not relegated to an educationally deprived underclass.

Language Loss and Language Gain in the Brazilian Community: The Role of Schools and Families

I am a Brazilian immigrant and the mother of two children who have attended public schools in the United States. I have worked as a parent liaison and outreach worker for two urban school systems with large Brazilian populations. My job is to make sure that Brazilian parents learn their rights, understand the different programs that the schools offer, and make informed decisions about their children's education. An important part of my job entails testing Brazilian children in order to recommend a program that best meets their needs. I also explain to parents how the programs work in terms of children's first- and second-language development. Ultimately, the parents decide which program is best for their children. I then continue to work with these families to help them understand the school system and how they can support their children's academic growth. I also discuss with them issues regarding immigrant children's identity development.

In this chapter, I discuss twelve typical cases based on my personal and professional experiences with Brazilian families in the greater Boston area. The cases describe children's varied experiences in different programs and school systems, families' educational expectations from the schools, and schools' responses to parents' cultural and language backgrounds. Several cases illustrate how quickly children tend to lose their native language, as well as cultural ties and values, when placed in mainstream classrooms. Other cases show that children can become fully bilingual and bicultural if they attend bilingual classes for an extended period of time and if parents are consistent in speaking Portuguese at home. In order to contextualize the cases, I start with a brief history of Brazilian immigration to the United States.

Immigration History

Brazil was colonized by the Portuguese in 1500 and became an independent nation in 1822. Now the fifth-largest country in the world, Brazil covers 47.3 percent of Latin America. It is the world's eighth-largest economy and, with a population of 150 million, constitutes the largest Portuguese-speaking community.

Brazilian culture values close ties with family and community, and Brazilians are often described as loud, friendly, lively people with a passion for music, carnival, and soccer. The real picture would also describe them as a family-oriented people who do not like to move away from their relatives, friends, and community, and who tend to live within the region where they were born or grew up. There is no age at which children are expected to leave their parents' house; many live with their parents even after getting married.

Historically, Brazilians do not emigrate. The country is better known for receiving immigrants than for sending its people away. When slavery was abolished, Brazil gave land to and paid the traveling expenses for immigrants, mainly Italians, to settle there and work its vast territory. But in the 1980s, due to the disarray of the Brazilian economy, large numbers of Brazilians started to emigrate to the United States. At the time, Brazil was running a monthly inflation rate of 30 to 40 percent. These emigrants left in search of a better life: since they could not make a living at home, they planned to go to the United States, make money, and then return to Brazil. Many left their wives or husbands and children behind.

Brazilian government figures indicate that about 1,500,000 Brazilians — or one percent of the country's population — now live overseas. The United States is one major destination: 750,000 Brazilians reportedly live in the United States. Massachusetts has the third-greatest concentration, after New York and Florida. According to a Boston Archdiocese report, there were about 150,000 Brazilians living in the

Greater Boston area in 1993. The majority were in their twenties or early thirties, with kindergarten and elementary age children.

Brazilians continued to immigrate to the Boston area in large numbers despite the Brazilian government's efforts to control inflation and stabilize the economy in the 1990s. With the increase in their numbers and the rise in anti-immigrant sentiments since the 1980s, Brazilians have become politically and socially active in greater Boston. Local grassroots movements are pressing for language and cultural rights such as bilingual services in schools, hospitals, courts, etc., and government agencies are being forced to recognize the unique needs of this population.

Many Brazilians in the Boston area earned at least a high school degree before emigrating; some even attended one or two years of college. Others have neither a high school degree nor good literacy skills in their native language. In order to understand Brazilian students' educational backgrounds, it is important to examine how the Brazilian educational system works. Academically, it is more concentrated and demanding than the U.S. system. For instance, high school students must take three years of biology, chemistry, and physics. Students take algebra in middle school, and begin foreign language study in elementary school. Nevertheless, upon entering school in the United States, many Brazilian students are held back one grade because they are not proficient in English.

In Brazil, schools are an extension of home: teachers are called "aunt" or "uncle" and are invited to birthday parties and family dinners. Parents rely completely on teachers' decisions and expect the school to emphasize the family values that children learn at home. Brazilian parents in the United States send their children to school believing that they are being taken care of. These parents soon become frustrated when their children experience more violence in school than they do on the streets or are singled out as being hyperactive and poorly behaved, or when they themselves are accused of not being involved in or supportive of their children's education.

Unfortunately, new Massachusetts regulations for bilingual education leave it up to school districts to decide whether to hire paraprofessionals — that is, parent liaisons and bilingual field workers who know the system and the program options. Increasingly few educational systems have parent liaisons and bilingual field workers to advocate for language-minority parents and to keep them informed about school programs and their educational rights. Therefore, parents often make decisions without the support of someone who knows the system and the program options.

Many Brazilian parents want their children in bilingual programs for Portuguese speakers, but only a few understand what bilingual classes are, how they work, and what they can do for a child. Highly educated parents may prefer that their children attend mainstream classes. Some may even use English as the home language, assuming that their children will not lose Portuguese. When parents do realize that their children are losing their native language, it is usually too late to recover it, as the examples below indicate. These examples further demonstrate that schools and families must work together to help children add the new language, English, and the new culture, the American culture, without losing their native language and cultural ties.

1. Children lose their native language if parents do not use it consistently at home.

Sonia and Sylvia are two examples of children who have quickly lost their native language and cultural identity. They were born to Brazilian parents residing in the United States who have undergraduate degrees from a Brazilian university. The parents decided to send their girls to a mainstream classroom in a suburban school. Moreover, to better help the girls to integrate into American culture, they decided to live in a predominantly American neighborhood and speak only English at home, even though they are not proficient in English.

Now ages six and eight, Sylvia and Sonia cannot speak Portuguese nor relate to Brazilian culture. They do not identify themselves as Brazilians, and they get upset when their parents speak Portuguese together. Sylvia and Sonia cannot communicate with their relatives in Brazil. Worried that her girls have lost their Brazilian identity, ethnic roots, and family ties, Sylvia and Sonia's mother recently came to me for advice. Both parents now resent the fact that their children do not speak Portuguese or relate to their family back home.

Sylvia and Sonia lost their home language partly because their mother and father did not speak to them in Portuguese. By doing this they communicated the wrong message, essentially saying, "our language and culture are of no value." Sylvia and Sonia are now monolingual children; if they ever learn Portuguese it will be as a second language. What a tragedy it must be for these parents not to be able to communicate with their daughters in their own language. How hard it must be for parents to have to express their feelings in a foreign tongue. How sad it must be to be unable to sing lullabies or tell their daughters fairy tales using expressions that only exist in their native language.

Graca, on the other hand, is convinced that parents should speak their native language at home. A social worker at the Cambridge Hospital and the mother of six-month-old Sofia, Graca cannot think of communicating with her daughter intimately in English, even though that is the language she speaks with her Polish husband. The couple is committed to maintaining Portuguese as Sofia's first language and encouraging her connections to Brazilian culture.

Having close ties to the extended family and community is an important value in Brazilian culture. In Brazil, the sense of family is much broader than in the United States: friends, neighbors, and coworkers are considered family members along with the in-laws, grandparents, aunts and uncles, and other relatives. Therefore, Brazilian parents in the United States must use Portuguese consistently at home so their children do not lose it, and thus preserve their ability to communicate with the extended family back home. However, as the cases below indicate, use of the native language at home may not be enough to sustain a child's native language and cultural roots.

2. In addition to consistent use of native language at home, parents need to send their children to bilingual programs.

Maria's experiences illustrate the importance of continuous use of native language instruction. Maria can smoothly navigate both cultures and languages, a valuable asset that not many of us achieve. She did so with the help of her family and school. A third grader in an urban bilingual classroom, Maria was born in Boston eight years ago to Brazilian parents. Maria's parents graduated from college in Brazil, and both came to the United States without English skills. When Maria entered school at age four, she spoke only Portuguese and was assigned to a K1 bilingual class. By the time she finished first grade, she was writing and reading in both Portuguese and English.

During the family's first trip to Brazil to visit relatives, Maria's mother Jacqueline was amazed by how naturally her five-year-old granddaughter could switch between English and Portuguese. "From the moment she landed in Brazil, her Brazilianism (meaning the way Brazilians talk, gesture, use body language) showed strongly," Jacqueline related. "She spoke Portuguese without an accent, she knew the culture, she was familiar with the way we do and say things in Brazil." Jacqueline credits the bilingual program for helping her daughter make such an important transition so naturally. "It was so important for my family to be able to communicate with Maria. At the same time, the family connection strengthened my daughter's sense of who she is."

Last summer, Maria made her first solo trip to Brazil. "It wouldn't be possible if she didn't speak Portuguese and if she didn't feel part of my family and comfortable with my relatives down there," commented her grandmother. Although Maria's family has moved out of the school neighborhood, they have decided to keep Maria in the bilingual program until she graduates from the fifth grade.

My own daughter, Roberta, had an experience in a bilingual program similar to Maria's. My son Cesar was less fortunate because he was placed in an English-as-a-Second-Language (ESL) program. Roberta was eleven and Cesar was fifteen when we arrived ten years ago. They both came from private schools in Brazil and they had good academic skills in Portuguese. I had no information on bilingual classes: I just followed a school employee's instructions on how to get my children into school. My daughter was placed in a Portuguese bilingual class and my son in a multicultural ESL program at an urban school. I did not make this decision; I was told by a school department administrator that these were the best program choices for my children.

After a month or so, Cesar was able to start communicating in English. On the other hand, it took Roberta one year to launch her English. It took me about the same time to understand the concepts of bilingual education. Looking back, my daughter ended up learning English more thoroughly than my son and did not lose her Portuguese. Ten years, many readings, and many discussions after my daughter entered a U.S. school for the first time, I can fully evaluate what bilingual education did for her. It gave my daughter a sense of belonging, consistent and challenging academic support, and self-esteem that she would not have developed in a mainstream classroom. It kept her connected to me, to her father who did not speak English, and to her family and friends in Brazil. It enhanced her learning and helped her to understand who she was. Attending a bilingual program gave my daughter the chance to identify herself in a positive way with the language and the culture of her native country. At the same time, she was able to add a new language and culture. A fully bilingual and bicultural adult, she is currently enrolled at a university in Brazil and plans to continue her studies in the United States.

My son had a more stressful experience in ESL classrooms. The fact that he was conversant in English did not mean that he was proficient in the language. ESL classes did not give him a chance to keep improving his Portuguese writing skills, which would have translated into English writing skills. Today, he does not write perfect Portuguese or perfect English.

Cesar was fortunate to have good academic skills in Portuguese, and he came to the United States at an age when most of his cultural values were already established. He was also fortunate that my husband and I were committed to maintaining the home language and culture. We never spoke English at home and never cut ties with family and friends in Brazil. It helped him to make frequent trips to Brazil to revitalize the connection with his native language and culture. This is not the case for many Brazilian children here who are exposed mostly to the English language and to American culture, both of which have few similarities with the Brazilian. Young immigrants who have no chance to visit Brazil become frustrated because they are neither Americans nor entirely Brazilians, they cannot fully identify with either culture, and they do not belong to either culture. Furthermore, they experience academic difficulties because teachers often confuse their English language problems with learning disabilities, as in the case of Ricardo, Angela's youngest son.

Angela, the mother of six children, came to Boston ten years ago from northeastern Brazil to earn her Ph.D. Her youngest child was placed in a mainstream classroom in a suburban school system. "I thought that the most important thing for my children at the time was to get used to the system. I didn't think they needed bilingual education, I just thought they would do fine in school." Unfortunately, the transition was very difficult. Five-year-old Ricardo, who had not been taught reading and writing in Portuguese, was assigned to a mainstream kindergarten.

For six months, Ricardo rejected school. "He used to cry every morning; I forced him into school every single day," says Angela. When Ricardo started second grade, the teacher told his mother that he needed to be tested for special education placement. The second-grade teacher reported that Ricardo slept in the classroom, did not know letters and sounds in English, and did not want to study. Ricardo's first-grade teacher had never mentioned anything to the mother. "I don't know how he was promoted without knowing the alphabet," says Angela, adding, "I knew my son did not have a problem. At home, he knew by heart the tunes we played. He just needed more attention." Eventually Ricardo started making progress in his schoolwork. However, as the school concentrated on English, he rapidly forgot Portuguese.

As time went by, his lack of understanding of Brazilian culture started bothering his family. "He became too Americanized," his father, a university professor and musician, complained. At the time of the 1994 World Soccer Cup, the couple spent hours "teaching" Ricardo about Brazilian soccer "because all he cared about was American football," says Angela. Finally, after eight years of living in the Boston area, the family decided to go back to Brazil. Ricardo suffered when he entered school in Brazil; after three years there he still suffers from culture shock.

"Language is such an important reference," notes Renata, a linguist finishing her Ph.D. studies. When she came to the United States with her ten-year-old son Antonio, she made the decision to live in a suburban town with no bilingual program. Educated parents "do not get here and worry whether or not their kids will learn English. We assume they will," she says. Antonio arrived with strong, grade-level academic skills. Mother and son spoke only Portuguese at home. Antonio was assigned to a fifth-grade mainstream classroom, with some ESL help. "At the beginning he did not know what was going on," says his mother. "I had no participation in this decision and did not think I needed to participate," says Renata. By the time Antonio moved back to Brazil five years later, English was his dominant language. "His first year there was complicated. He was out of context, he did not know slang, he couldn't identify with his peers."

Now that the family has returned to Boston again, Renata has started teaching in a bilingual program. She believes that a strong bilingual program that teaches students through grade twelve is the best option to preserve language and cultural identity while adding English and comfort with the American culture. She also believes that parents should be involved in decisions regarding their children's education.

Too often, Brazilian parents do not get involved in these decisions because they assume that the system will make the best choice for their child or because they do not understand the program options. Unfortunately, however, schools may not be able to make the best decision without parents' involvement. The stories of Mario and Pedro illustrate that parents and schools need to work together to decide when a child should exit a bilingual program, as children's educational progress is inhibited if they exit a bilingual program too quickly.

3. Contrary to what some people say, second-language acquisition takes time. Some educational systems and parents are moving children out of bilingual programs too quickly.

Mario is an eleven-year-old fifth grader in an urban school. His father takes evening English classes and his mother can communicate fairly well in English. They are both high school graduates and they work as cleaners. Mario was eighteen months old when he landed in Boston with his parents. His first experience with school was a monolingual Head Start class. He started speaking English soon after enrolling in that school. At age five he was assigned to a Portuguese bilingual kindergarten class, where he continued in first grade. Then, when he went to second grade, his mother found out that he was in a mainstream classroom with some ESL help.

"They did not ask me if I wanted Mario out of the bilingual program," says his mother. "I thought that it was a bilingual class until I realized during a parent meeting that he was no longer in the bilingual program. I asked why my son had a monolingual American teacher and they told me he was not in the bilingual program." He had no Portuguese class in second grade, but they hired a teacher assistant who supposedly spoke Portuguese. She spoke the language poorly and sent home letters written in Portuguese that were full of mistakes.

Now Mario speaks Portuguese mixed with English. He reads Portuguese because his mother forces him to read a lot of Portuguese material, but he writes the language poorly. His mother is not pleased that English became her son's dominant language. She has a one-year-old daughter whom she wants in a bilingual program. Now she feels that she is better informed about her rights and can fight for them.

Like Mario, Pedro had a difficult educational experience when he was prematurely placed in a mainstream classroom. Pedro is now a sixteen-year-old ninth grader in a mainstream program in an urban school system. He left Brazil with his family — his parents and a younger brother — two years ago. He was in sixth grade in Brazil, a solid B student. When he arrived in the United States, Pedro had little or no English. He was assessed as a Step 1 student,[1] and was placed in a bilingual seventh-grade classroom. He attended bilingual classes for two years. When he graduated from middle school, teachers recommended that he move on to ESL3 classes. However, the family decided to place Pedro in a mainstream classroom. Three months into the school year, Pedro had failing grades in all subjects except physical education. "We tracked down the student's history and found out that he attended a bilingual program for two years and was a Step 2 student when he left," says Pedro's high school bilingual coordinator. "He needed to attend ESL3 classes. Instead, he was in regular English classes. He was doing poorly and showing his weaknesses. He was failing academically, he had an average of Ds, and all his teachers expressed concerns about his grades."

According to this bilingual coordinator, some families think their children are ready to be placed in mainstream classrooms after one or two years in a bilingual program. This common mistake shows how little people understand second-language development and the premises of bilingual education. He continues: "Children pick up language quickly, they may have fine English to communicate socially with friends, but they do not have enough English to perform academic tasks. Academically they are not ready to follow instruction in English."

Pedro's academic failures were reflected not only in his grades, but also in his behavior. He became aggressive and lost interest in school. He got in trouble for disturbing classroom instruction, and his mother was called to school several times to discuss his behavior. Pedro wasted one semester before he was tested and placed back into the bilingual program, where he is now doing well.

Unlike Pedro and Mario, Cecilia is typical of the many children who have benefited from staying in a bilingual program. Cecilia was a twelve-year-old seventh grader in Brazil when her family decided to immigrate to the Boston area. She did not know any English, had good grades in school in Brazil, and tested at her grade level. Both Cecilia's parents have a vocational high school diploma from Brazil and they did not know English when they came to the United States. "My mother is learning English," Cecilia says, but Portuguese is the consistent home language.

Cecilia was assigned to a seventh-grade bilingual class in an urban school system. Now fourteen and a ninth grader, she is still in the bilingual program and likes it. "I like it because I do not feel isolated and I am close to my Brazilian friends," she says. "Bilingual education is giving me a chance to maintain my Portuguese and learn English at the same time. I have a class in Portuguese that teaches me advanced grammar and writing. It teaches me how to speak good Portuguese. I would have forgotten Portuguese if I were not in the bilingual program. At the same time," she adds, "the program is helping me to learn English in the ESL classes."

4. School systems and administrators should be sensitive to families' cultural and language backgrounds and hire parent liaisons.

Rosa was a teacher in Brazil. She and her husband moved to the Boston area a year ago with their eleven-year-old daughter and their twin fifteen-year-old sons. The three children were assigned to bilingual classes. Rosa is active in school matters and always attends parent meetings at the school. Rosa knows that she is entitled to get all information from the school in both Portuguese and English. When she complained that her daughter's school sent letters in English only, the teacher said that they had run out of the Portuguese copies and offered to send the letters in Spanish. "Your mother can read Spanish, can't she?" she asked Rosa's daughter.

Rosa's experience is not an isolated case. Ignorance about languages and cultures is common in school systems. Once I strongly argued with the principal of an urban school with a Portuguese bilingual program that it would not be considerate to send Brazilian parents school letters written in Spanish. This principal was convinced that it did not make a difference "because Brazilians can usually understand Spanish."

Alberto, a community activist who helps Brazilian newcomers, once had a taste of how some school systems lack sensitivity to parents' culture and native language. He went to register his nephew for a bilingual program and was given school documents in English. When he reminded the assistant principal of his right to fill out papers written in his native language, he was told, "This is America. We speak English here." Unlike many immigrant parents, Alberto knew his rights and he demanded that the school comply with the bilingual law. The school then supplied him with forms translated into Portuguese.

In many cases immigrant parents do not know their rights and are not accustomed to questioning the school system. Consequently, they do not receive the services to which they are legally entitled. As the enrollment of children from different cultures increases, our schools must become more responsive to the needs and rights of all the families they serve. One way that schools can be responsive is by providing all school materials in parents' native languages. Another way is to hire parent liaisons from the community. Many of the cases I have presented illustrate the usefulness of having parent liaisons from the community who know the U.S. education system, as well as the language and culture of the community.

Conclusion

In this chapter, I have described twelve cases that illustrate the danger of Brazilian children losing their native language and cultural identity as they learn English. Furthermore, I have pointed to the unpleasant reality of Brazilian families losing ties to their own children. Based on my experience as an immigrant parent, a community organizer, and a parent liaison for two school systems, I have emphasized (a) the importance of consistent native language use at home; (b) the importance of sustained bilingual education; and (c) the importance of school systems being sensitive to parents' cultural and language backgrounds. When all these conditions are met, children can acquire English without losing Portuguese and can integrate into American culture without losing ties to Brazilian culture. Roberta's experiences, for example, demonstrate that the process of learning a second language and acquiring a new culture should not mean forgetting who we are.

Parents play an important role in promoting bilingualism and preventing their children from losing their native language. Most of the parents I have described here are highly educated. However, despite their educational background, these parents all faced the problem of their children losing their native language. In order to prevent this loss, families must use Portuguese consistently at home and support their children's education in bilingual programs. In my opinion, if Sonia and Sylvia's parents had spoken Portuguese at home and placed their children in bilingual programs, they would have better communicated to their children that their native language and culture have great value.

In addition, parents should know that, contrary to what is generally believed, second-language acquisition takes time. If Pedro's parents had not rushed him out of the bilingual program, he would not have failed academically. As Cecilia's and Maria's cases show, the longer a child stays in a bilingual program, the more likely she or he will be fully bilingual and bicultural. In my experience, the best programs support native language academic development to foster English development and involve parents actively in their children's education. In the current political context, parents must organize to advocate for access to prolonged bilingual instruction.

Schools also play an important role in preventing children's native language loss and promoting bilingualism. For example, Ricardo's and Antonio's loss of native language could have been prevented if the school system they attended had assigned them to bilingual programs. In Mario's case, he could have benefited from the bilingual program more fully if the school had not rushed him into mainstream classes. Moreover, schools can show their commitment to language-minority communities by hiring parent liaisons from the same language and cultural background as parents, and by providing parents with school documents in their native language. As Rosa's and Alberto's cases demonstrate, when schools do not respect parents' cultural backgrounds, parent-school communication is broken. The success of bilingual programs, and all educational programs, depends on parents and schools working together.

I cannot emphasize enough that learning a new language and acquiring a new culture should not mean losing one's native language and cultural identity. We should not have to forget who we are as we acquire a second language and a new culture. As Paulo Freire said, "We are our language and we are our culture." In Brazil, when our children get married, we say that we gain a new son or a new daughter and the family keeps on growing. When we immigrate, we should gain a new homeland, a larger family, and a new language and culture. But we should not have to lose the language and culture we already have.

Note

1. Students with low English skills are offered four levels of ESL support. If they have no English skills they are considered as Step 1 and are offered ESL1 classes. If they have some/limited English skills they are considered as Step 2 and are offered ESL2 and ESL3 classes. If they are close to proficient in English, they are considered as Step 3 and are offered ESL4 classes. Students who complete ESL4 classes are considered ready to be placed full-time in English monolingual mainstream classes.

Decolonizing English Only: The Democratic Power of Bilingualism

DONALDO MACEDO

> "So, if you want to really hurt me,
> talk badly about my language"
> — *Gloria Anzaldúa*[1]

The vicious attacks on people of color, the demonization of immigrants, the dismantling of affirmative action, and the assault on welfare programs for the poor are part and parcel of an unapologetic dominant ideology that was unleashed during the Reagan administration. It is the same ideology that has positioned itself against all public institutions, particularly those sectors that are perceived to serve mostly the poor and people of color, such as public education in urban areas.

Against a landscape of selective assaults on some public institutions, the bilingual education movement could not escape the wrath of the dominant ideology. However, the present attacks on bilingual education spearheaded by the conservative organization U.S. English should not be understood as a simple critique of methodologies. First and foremost, these assaults are fundamentally political. The denial of the political nature of the debate concerning bilingual education in itself constitutes a political action. It is both academically dishonest and misleading to point out some failures of bilingual education without examining the lack of success of linguistic-minority students within the larger context of the general failure of public education.

While conservative educators have been vocal in their attempt to abolish bilingual education because of, according to them, its lack of academic success and efficiency in teaching English, these same educators have conspicuously remained silent about the well-documented failure of foreign language education in the United States. In spite of the general failure of foreign language education in the United States, no one is advocating closing down schools' foreign language departments. Paradoxically, the same educators who propose the dismantling of bilingual education programs for linguistic-minority students, which have a higher probability of producing bilingual students, reiterate their support for foreign language education with the aim of developing bilingualism of native English speakers.

The English Only movement's position points to a pedagogy of exclusion that views learning English as the sum total of education itself for linguistic-minority students. What the movement's proponents fail to question is under what conditions English will be taught and by whom. For example, insisting on immersing linguistic-minority students in English-as-a-Second-Language (ESL) programs taught by untrained music, art, and social sciences teachers (as is the case in Massachusetts with the grandfather clause in ESL certification) will do little to accomplish the goals of the English Only movement.[2] Proponents of English Only also fail to raise two fundamental questions. First, if education in English alone can guarantee linguistic minorities a better future, as educators like William Bennett promise, why do the majority of Black Americans, whose ancestors have been speaking English for over two hundred years, still find themselves relegated to the ghettos? Second, if English is the most effective educational language, how can we explain why over sixty million Americans are illiterate or functionally illiterate? I argue in this chapter that the answers to these questions have nothing to do with whether English is a more viable language of instruction or whether it promises linguistic-minority students full participation in both school and society at large. This position would point to an assumption that English is, in fact, a superior language and that we live in a classless, race-blind society. I propose that the attempt to institute proper and effective methods of educating linguistic-minority students cannot be reduced simply to issues of language, but that it rests on a full understanding of the ideological elements that generate and sustain linguistic, cultural, and racial discrimination, which represent, in my view, vestiges of a colonial legacy in our democracy.

English Only as a Form of Colonialism

Many educators will object to my use of the term "colonialism" to characterize the present attack on bilingual education by conservative and many liberal educators. Some liberals will go to great lengths to oppose my characterization, rationalizing that most educators who do not support bilingual education are just ignorant and need to be educated. This is tantamount to saying that racists do not really hate people of color; they are just ignorant. While one cannot deny that they are ignorant, one has to realize nevertheless that ignorance is never innocent and is always shaped by a particular ideological predisposition. On another level, an attack on bilingual education or a racist act does not make the victims of these acts feel any better about their victimization.[3]

As a colonized person who experienced first hand the discriminatory language policies of Portuguese colonialism, I can readily see many similarities between that colonial ideology and the dominant values that inform the English Only movement. Colonialism imposes "distinction" as an ideological yardstick against which all other cultural values are measured, including language. On the one hand, this ideological yardstick serves to over-celebrate the dominant group's language to a level of mystification (i.e., equating learning English with being educated and measuring the success of bilingual programs only in terms of successful English acquisition) and, on the other hand, it devalues the other languages spoken by an ever-increasing number of students who now populate most urban public schools. The position of English Only proponents is not very different from Portuguese colonialism, which tried to eradicate the use of African languages in institutional life and, through its Portuguese-only educational system, to inculcate Africans with myths and beliefs concerning the savage nature of their cultures and languages.

If we closely analyze the ideology that informs the present debate over bilingual education and the present polemic over Western heritage versus multiculturalism, we can begin to understand that the ideological principles that sustain those debates are consonant with the structures and mechanisms of a colonial ideology, as described below:

> Culturally, colonialism has adopted a negation to the [native culture's] symbolic systems [including the native language], forget-

ting or undervaluing them even when they manifest themselves in action. This way, the eradication of [the] past and the idealization and the desire to relive the cultural heritage of colonial societies constitute a situation and a system of ideas along with other elements [that] situate the colonial society as a class.[4]

If it were not for the colonial legacy, how could we explain the U.S. educational policies in the Philippines and Puerto Rico? English was imposed as the only language of instruction in the Philippines, and the American textbook presented American culture not only as superior, but also as a "model par excellence for the Philippine society."[5] This type of miseducation was so prevalent that it led T. H. Pardo de Tavera, an early Philippine collaborator with the U.S. colonialists, to write the following letter to General Douglas MacArthur:

> After Peace is established all our efforts will be directed to Americanizing ourselves, to cause a knowledge of the English language to be extended and generalized in the Philippines, in order that through its agency we may adopt its principles, its political customs, and its peculiar civilization that our redemption may be complete and radical.[6]

It is this same complete and radical redemption that the United States hoped to achieve in 1905, when Theodore Roosevelt's commissioner of education in Puerto Rico, Rolland P. Faulkner, mandated that instruction in public schools be conducted in English, making Puerto Rican schools

> agencies of Americanization in the entire country, and where [schools] would present the American ideal to our youth. Children born under the American flag and the American soil should have constantly present this ideal, so that they can feel proud of their citizenship and have the flag that represents the true symbol of liberty.[7]

When we leave our colonial legacy unexamined, the choice of a methodology that denies students the option of studying their own language and culture becomes in reality a choiceless choice. Instead of becoming enslaved by the effectiveness discourse of the present bilingual educational reform that enhances the economic interests of the reformers while securing their privileged social and cultural positions, educators need to reconnect with the past in order to understand the colonial legacy that undermines our democratic aspirations. Although

Renato Constantino is writing about the colonial legacy in the Philippines, his thoughtful words are not only apropos, but also illuminating regarding our present historical juncture in education:

> We see our present with as little understanding as we view our past because aspects of the past which could illumine the present have been concealed from us. This concealment has been effected by a systemic process of mis-education characterized by a thoroughgoing inculcation of colonial values and attitudes — a process which could not have been so effective had we not been denied access to the truth and to be part of our written history. As a consequence, we have become a people without a sense of history. We accept the present as given, bereft of historicity. Because we have so little comprehension of our past, we have no appreciation of its meaningful interrelation with the present.[8]

Scientism as Neo-Colonialism

Oppressive dominant ideologies throughout history have resorted to science as a mechanism to rationalize crimes against humanity that range from slavery to genocide by targeting race and other ethnic and cultural traits as markers that license all forms of dehumanization. If we did not suffer from historical amnesia, we would easily understand the ideology that informed Hans Eysenck's psychological proposal that "there might be a partly genetic reason for the differences in IQ between black and white people."[9] It is the same historical amnesia that veils dangerous memories, keeping us disconnected from Arthur Jensen's "scientific research" and racist proposals.[10] One could argue that these incidents belong to the dusty archives of earlier generations, but I do not believe we have learned a great deal from historically dangerous memories, considering our society's almost total embrace of scientism, as characterized by the popularity of *The Bell Curve*, by Charles Murray and Richard J. Herrnstein.[11] It is this same blind acceptance of naive empiricism that is fueling the English Only movement's attempts to ban bilingual education in the United States.

By and large, the present debate over bilingual education is informed by the positivistic and management models that hide their ideologies in the false call for objectivity, hard data, and scientific rigor. A large body of critical literature interrogates the very nature of what they consider research. Critical writers such as Donna Haraway,[12]

Linda Brodkey, Roger Fowler, and Greg Myers have painstakingly demonstrated the erroneous claim of "scientific" objectivity that permeates all forms of empirical work in the social sciences. According to Brodkey, "Scientific objectivity has too often and for too long been used as an excuse to ignore a social and, hence, political practice in which women and people of color, among others, are dismissed as legitimate subjects of research."[13] The blind belief in objectivity not only provides pseudoscientists with a safe haven from which they can attempt to prevent the emergence of counterdiscourses that interrogate "the hegemony of positivism and empiricism,"[14] but it is also a practice that generates a form of folk theory concerning objectivity believed only by nonscientists. In other words, as Brodkey eloquently put it, "Any and all knowledge, including that arrived at empirically, is necessarily partial, that is, both an incomplete and an interested account of whatever is envisioned."[15] In fact, what these pseudo-scientists consider evaluation research can never escape the social construction that generated these models of analysis, from which the theoretical concepts are shaped by the pragmatics of the society that devised these evaluation models in the first place.[16] That is, if the results are presented as facts that were originally determined by a particular ideology, these facts cannot in themselves illuminate issues that lie outside of their ideological construction to begin with.[17] I would warn educators that these evaluation models can provide answers that are correct and yet without truth. A study that concludes that African American students perform way below White mainstream students in reading is correct, but such a conclusion tells us little about the material conditions with which African American students work in the struggle against racism, educational tracking, and the systematic negation and devaluation of their histories. I would propose that the correct conclusion rests in a full understanding of the ideological elements that generate and sustain the cruel reality of racism and economic oppression. Thus an empirical study will produce conclusions without truth if it is disarticulated from the sociocultural reality within which the subjects of the study are situated. For example, an empirical study designed to assess reading achievement of children who live in squalid conditions must factor in the reality faced by these children, as accurately described by Jonathan Kozol:

> Crack-cocaine addiction and the intravenous use of heroin, which children I have met here call "the needle drug," are woven

into the texture of existence in Mott Haven. Nearly 4,000 heroin injectors, many of whom are HIV-infected, live here. Virtually every child at St. Ann's knows someone, a relative or neighbor, who has died of AIDS, and most children here know many others who are dying now of the disease. One quarter of the women of Mott Haven who are tested in obstetric wards are positive for HIV. Rates of pediatric AIDS, therefore, are high.

Depression is common among children in Mott Haven. Many cry a great deal but cannot explain exactly why.

Fear and anxiety are common. Many cannot sleep.

Asthma is the most common illness among children here. Many have to struggle to take in a good deep breath. Some mothers keep oxygen tanks, which children describe as "breathing machines," next to their children's beds.

The houses in which these children live, two-thirds of which are owned by the City of New York, are often as squalid as the houses of the poorest children I have visited in rural Mississippi, but there is none of the greenness and the healing sweetness of the Mississippi countryside outside their windows, which are often barred and bolted as protection against thieves.[18]

An empirical study that neglects to incorporate in its design the cruel reality just described (and this is often the case in our supposedly classless society) will never be able to fully explain the reasons behind these children's poor performance. While pseudoscientists will go to great lengths to prevent their research methodologies from being contaminated by the social ugliness described by Kozol so that they can safeguard their "objectivity" in, say, their study of the underachievement of children who live in ghettos, the residents of these ghettos have little difficulty understanding the root causes of their misery, as described by Maria, a resident of the community:

If you weave enough bad things into the fibers of a person's life — sickness and filth, old mattresses and other junk thrown in the streets and ugly ruined things, and ruined people, a prison here, sewage there, drug dealers here, the homeless people over there, then give us the very worst schools anyone could think of, hospitals that keep you waiting for ten hours, police that don't show up when someone's dying . . . you can guess that life will not be very nice and children will not have much sense of being glad of who they are. Sometimes it feels like we have been buried six feet under their perceptions. This is what I feel they have accomplished.[19]

What Maria would probably say to researchers is that we do not need another doctoral dissertation to state what is so obvious to the people sentenced to live in this form of human misery. In other words, by locking children in material conditions that are oppressive and dehumanizing we are invariably guaranteeing that they will be academic underachievers. Once their underachievement is guaranteed by these oppressive conditions, it is then easy for such research studies as described in *The Bell Curve* — which, in the name of objectivity, are disarticulated from the political and social reality that shape and maintain these oppressive conditions — to conclude that Blacks are genetically wired to be intellectual inferior to Whites. Along the same lines, an empirical study that concludes that children who engage in dinner conversation with their families achieve higher rates of success in reading is not only academically dishonest, but also misleading to the degree that it ignores the class and economic assumptions that all children are guaranteed daily dinners in the company of their parents and other siblings. What generalizations can such a study make about the twelve million children who go hungry every day in the United States? What can a study of this type say to thousands of children who are homeless, who do not have a table, and who sometimes do not have food to put on the table that they do not have? A study that makes such sweeping and distorted generalizations about the role of dinner conversations in reading achievement says little about children whose houses are without heat in the winter, houses that reach dangerously cold conditions that led a father of four children to remark: "You just cover up and hope you wake up the next morning." If the father really believes the study results, he will suggest to his children, after they all make it through another freezing night alive, that they should have a conversation during dinner the next night, since it will be helpful in their reading development.

These questions make it clear how distorted empirical study results can be when they are disconnected from the sociocultural reality that informs the study to begin with. In addition, such distortion feeds into the development of stereotypes that, on the one hand, blame the victims for their own social misery and, on the other hand, rationalize the genetic inferiority hypotheses that are advanced by such pseudoscholars as Murray and Hernnstein.[20] What empirical

studies often neglect to point out is how easily statistics can be manip-
ulated to take away the human faces of the subjects of study through a
process that not only dehumanizes but also distorts and falsifies the
reality.

Fracturing Cultural Identities

Most conservative educators as well as many liberals conveniently embrace a form of "naive" empiricism in which scientism and methodological refinement are celebrated, issues of equity, class, cultural
identity, among other sociocultural knowledges "are subordinated to
the imperatives of efficiency and technical mastery, and [sociocultural
factors] are reduced to a minor footnote in the priorities of 'empirical'
scientific inquiry."[21] While the fields of bilingual education and English as a Second Language have produced a barrage of studies aimed
primarily at demonstrating the effectiveness of bilingual programs in
developing students' English skills, these research studies conspicuously fail to raise other fundamental questions: Does cultural subordination affect academic achievement? What is the correlation between
social segregation and school success? What role does cultural identity
among subordinated students play in linguistic resistance (a process
through which students consciously or unconsciously resist learning
the dominant language)? Does the devaluation of students' culture
and language affect reading achievement?

These questions are rarely incorporated in naive empirical studies,
which parade under the mantra of scientific "objectivity" in order to
deny the role of ideology in their work so as to prevent the development of counterdiscourses that interrogate these studies' major assumptions. As Paulo Freire would point out when these educators
claimed a scientific posture, "[They often] try to 'hide' in what [they]
regard as the neutrality of scientific pursuits, indifferent to how [their]
findings are used, even uninterested in considering for whom or for
what interests [they] are working."[22]

The censorship of political analysis in the current debate over bilingual education exposes the illusory and almost schizophrenic educational practice in which "the object of interpretation and the content of the interpretive discourse are considered appropriate subjects
for discussion and scrutiny, but the interests of the interpreter and the
discipline and society he or she serves are not."[23] The disarticulation
between the interpretive discourse and the interests of the interpreter

is often hidden in the false call for an objectivity that denies the dialectical relationship between subjectivity and objectivity. The false call for objectivity is deeply ingrained in a positivistic method of inquiry. In effect, this has resulted in an epistemological stance in which scientism and methodological refinement are celebrated while "theory and knowledge are subordinated to the imperatives of efficiency and technical mastery, and history is reduced to a minor footnote in the priorities of `empirical' scientific inquiry."[24]

The blind celebration of empiricism has created a culture in which pseudoscientists, particularly those in schools of education who engage in a form of naive empiricism, believe "that facts are not human statements about the world but aspects of the world itself."[25] According to Michael Schudson:

> This view was insensitive to the ways in which the "world" is something people construct by the active play of their minds and by their acceptance of conventional — not necessarily "true" — ways of seeing and talking. Philosophy, the history of science, psychoanalysis, and the social sciences have taken great pains to demonstrate that human beings are cultural animals who know and see and hear the world through socially constructed filters.[26]

The socially constructed filters were evident when California voters passed a referendum banning bilingual education. While school administrators and politicians were gearing up to disband bilingual programs, data from both the San Francisco and San José school systems showed that bilingual graduates were outperforming their English-speaking counterparts.[27] This revelation was met with total silence by the media, proponents of English Only, and political pundits. In fact, throughout U.S. bilingual education history, whenever the empirical data provided by researchers such as Zeynep Beykont, Virginia Collier, David Ramirez, and Jim Cummins[28] demonstrate linguistic-minority students' success in bilingual programs, the data are either ignored or buried in endless debate over research design. This is where the call for objectivity and scientific rigor is subverted by the weight of its own ideology.

Because most educators, particularly in schools of education, do not conduct research in the "hard sciences," they uncritically attempt to adopt a neutral posture in their work in the social sciences, leaving out the necessary built-in criticism, skepticism, and rigor of the hard sciences. In fact, science cannot evolve without a healthy dose of self-criticism, skepticism, and contestation. However, a discourse of critique and contestation, for example, is often viewed as contaminating "objectivity" in social sciences and education. As Freire would argue, these educators "might treat [the] society under study as though [they] are not participants in it. In [their] celebrated impartiality, [they] might approach this real world as if [they] wear 'gloves and masks' in order not to contaminate or be contaminated by it."[29]

The metaphorical gloves and masks represent an ideological fog that enables educators to comfortably fragment bodies of knowledge so they can conduct their research among children who live in Mott Haven, for example, to determine their phoneme-grapheme awareness disarticulated from the material conditions of Mott Haven as described by Jonathan Kozol, in which children are locked in a chain of oppressive and dehumanizing circumstances that invariably guarantee that they will be academic underachievers.

By reducing the reading principles or the acquisition of English, for instance, to pure technicism (i.e., phoneme-grapheme awareness), these educators can easily disarticulate a particular form of knowledge from other bodies of knowledge, thus preventing the interrelation of information necessary to gain a more critical reading of the reality. These metaphorical "gloves and masks" enable educators to engage in a social construction of not seeing, which allows them willfully not to understand that behind the empirical data there are always human faces with fractured identities, dreams, and aspirations. The fracturing of cultural identity usually leaves an indelible psychological scar, experienced even by those subordinated people who seemingly have "made it" in spite of all forms of oppression. This psychological scar is painfully relived by Gloria Anzaldúa:

> *"El Anglo con cara de inocente nos arrancó la lengua"*[30] [The Anglo with the innocent face has yanked out our tongue], thus sentencing colonized cultural beings to a silenced culture.
>
> *Ahogados, escupimos el oscuro. Peleando con nuestra propia sombra el silencio nos sepulta.*[31] [Drowned, we spit darkness. Fighting with our very shadow we are buried by silence.]

The fragmentation of bodies of knowledge also prevents us from making the linkages necessary to understand that the "yanking out" of linguistic-minority students' tongues is not only undemocratic but is also reminiscent of colonial policies, as recounted by the Native American writer Joseph H. Suina, in his article "And Then I Went to School,"

> My language . . . was questionable from the beginning of my school career. . . . Speaking it accidentally or otherwise was a sure reprimand in the form of a dirty look or a whack with a ruler.[32]

"And then I went to school" expresses a common experience in the United States, where bilingualism and multiculturalism are under a constant assault by the Western cultural commissars. We conveniently fall into historical amnesia, forgetting the English reeducation camps designed primarily to yank out the tongues of Native American children, who were taken from their parents and sent to boarding schools with the primary purpose of cutting them off from their "primitive" languages and "savage" cultures. While we forget the dehumanization of Native American children in these schools, we nevertheless proudly denounced the reeducation schools created by communist governments as examples of human rights violations. "And then I went to school" is, however, not forgotten by Suina:

> School was a painful experience during those early years. The English language and the new set of values caused me much anxiety and embarrassment. I could not comprehend everything that was happening but yet I could understand very well when I messed up or was not doing well. The negative aspect was communicated too effectively and I became unsure of myself more and more. How I wished I could understand other things as well in school.[33]

Whether we feel the pain of Gloria Anzaldúa's tongue being yanked out, whether we connect with the pain and embarrassment Joseph Suina experienced in U.S. schools, or whether we listen to African author Ngugi's lament for the loss of the Gikuyu language, these experiences undeniably share one common feature — colonization:

> We therefore learnt to value words for their meaning and nuances. Language was not a mere string of words. It had a suggestive power well beyond the immediate and lexical meaning. Our appreciation of the suggestive magical power of language was reinforced by the games we played with words through riddles, proverbs, transpositions of syllables, or through nonsensical but

musically arranged words. So we learnt the music of our language on top of the content. The language, through images and symbols, gave us a view of the world, but it had a beauty on its own. The home and the field were then our pre-primary school but what is important for this discussion, is that the language of the evening teach-ins, and the language of our work in the field were one.

And then I went to school, a colonial school, and this harmony was broken. The language of my education was no longer the language of my culture.[34]

If we closely analyze the ideology that informs the present debate over bilingual education and the present polemic over the primacy of Western heritage versus multiculturalism, we can begin to see and understand that the ideological principles that sustain those debates are consonant with the structures and mechanisms of a colonial ideology designed to devalue the cultural capital and values of the colonized.

It is only through a full understanding of our colonial legacy that we can begin to comprehend the complexity of bilingualism in the United States. For most linguistic-minority speakers in the United States, their bilingualism is not characterized by the ability to speak two languages. There is a radical difference between a dominant speaker learning a second language and a minority speaker acquiring the dominant language. While the former involves the addition of a second language to one's linguistic repertoire, the latter usually provides the minority speaker with the experience of subordination in speaking both his or her language, which is devalued by the dominant values, and the dominant language that he or she has learned, often under coercive conditions. Both the colonized context and the asymmetrical power relations in terms of language use in the United States create, on the one hand, a form of forced bilingualism, and on the other what Albert Memmi appropriately calls a linguistic drama:

In the colonial context, bilingualism is necessary. It is a condition for all culture, all communication and all progress. But while the colonial bilinguist is saved from being walled in, he suffers a cultural catastrophe which is never completely overcome.

The difference between native language and cultural language is not peculiar to the colonized, but colonial bilingualism cannot be compared to just any linguistic dualism. Possession of two languages is not merely a matter of having two tools, but actually means participation in two physical and cultural realms. Here, the two worlds symbolized and conveyed by the two tongues are in conflict; they are those of the colonizer and the colonized.

Furthermore, the colonized's mother tongue, that which is sustained by his feelings, emotions, and dreams, that in which his tenderness and wonder are expressed, thus that which holds the greatest emotional impact, is precisely the one which is the least valued. It has no stature in the country or in the concept of peoples. If he wants to obtain a job, make a place for himself, exist in the community and the world, he must first bow to the language of his masters. In the linguistic conflict within the colonized, his mother tongue is that which is crushed. He himself sets about discarding this infirm language, hiding it from the sight of strangers. In short, colonial bilingualism is neither a purely bilingual situation, in which an indigenous tongue coexists with a purist's language (both belonging to the same world of feeling), nor a simple polyglot richness benefiting from an extra but relatively neuter alphabet; it is a linguistic drama.[35]

An excellent example of how our society treats different forms of bilingualism is reflected in our tolerance of certain types of bilingualism and our lack of tolerance of others. There is a great deal of tolerance for the various degrees of bilingualism of foreign language teachers and professors, which range from speaking the foreign language with a heavy American accent, to a serious lack of mastery of the foreign language they teach. Nevertheless, these teachers, with rare exceptions, have been granted tenure, have been promoted within the institutions they teach, and, in some cases, have become "experts" and "spokespersons" for various cultural and linguistic groups in our communities. On the other hand, if bilingual teachers are speakers of a subordinated language who speak English as a second language with an accent, the same level of tolerance is not accorded them. Take the case of Westfield, Massachusetts, where, in response to the hiring of a Puerto Rican teacher, "about 400 people . . . signed a petition asking state and local officials to ban the hiring of any elementary teacher who speaks English with an accent"[36] because, according to the petitioners, "accents are catching."[37] Clearly, empirical studies that neglect to fully investigate this linguistic drama and treat bilingualism as mere communication in two languages invariably end up reproducing those ideological elements characteristic of the communication between colonizer and colonized. These naive empirical studies inevitably recycle old assumptions and values regarding the meaning and usefulness of the students' native language in education. The notion that education of linguistic-minority students is a matter of learning Standard English still informs bilingual programs. For the notion of the education of linguistic-minority students to become meaningful, it has to be situated within a theory of cultural production[38] and viewed as an integral part of the way people produce, transform, and reproduce meaning. Bilingual education, in this sense, must be seen as a medium that constitutes and affirms the historical and existential moments of lived culture. Hence, it is an eminently political phenomenon, and must be analyzed within the context of a theory of power relations and an understanding of social and political production and reproduction. Bilingual education programs in the United States have, in fact, existed within a de facto neocolonial educational model. In this case, such experiences are rooted in the interest of individual and collective self-determination. It is only through a cultural production model that we can achieve a truly democratic and liberatory educational experience.

While the various debates in the past two decades may differ in their basic assumptions about the education of linguistic-minority students, they all share one common feature: they all ignore the role of languages as a major force in the construction of human subjectivities. That is, they ignore the way a language may either confirm or deny the life histories and experiences of the people who use it.

The pedagogical and political implications of English Only programs for linguistic-minority students are far-reaching and yet largely ignored. These programs, for example, often contradict a fundamental principle of reading, namely, that students learn to read faster and with better comprehension when taught in their native tongue. In addition, the immediate recognition of familiar words and experiences enhances the development of a positive self-concept in children who are somewhat insecure about the status of their language and culture. For this reason, and to be consistent with the plan to construct a democratic society free from vestiges of oppression, a bilingual education program should be based on the rationale that such a program must be rooted in the cultural capital of subordinate groups and have as its point of departure their own language.

Educators must develop radical pedagogical structures that provide students with the opportunity to use their own reality as a basis for literacy. This includes, obviously, the language they bring to the classroom. To do otherwise is to deny linguistic-minority students the rights that lie at the core of the notion of a democratic education. The failure to base a literacy program on the minority students' language means that the oppositional forces can neutralize the efforts of educators and political leaders to achieve the decolonization of schooling. It is of tantamount importance that the incorporation of the minority language as the primary language of instruction in the education of linguistic-minority students be given top priority because it is through their own language that linguistic-minority students will be able to reconstruct their history and their culture.

I conclude that the minority language has to be understood within the theoretical framework that generates it, that its ultimate meaning and value has to be understood through the assumptions that govern it, and that it has to be understood via the social, political, and ideological relations to which it points. Generally speaking, the issue of effectiveness and validity often hides the true role of language — in this case the role of Standard English in maintaining the values and interests of the dominant group, White middle-class America. In other words, the issue of the effectiveness and validity of bilingual education becomes a mask that obfuscates questions about the social, political, and ideological order within which the minority language exists.

In this sense, students' language is the only means by which they can develop their own voice, a prerequisite to the development of a positive sense of self-worth. As Henry Giroux elegantly states, the student's voice "is the discursive means to make themselves [the students] 'heard' and to define themselves as active authors of their worlds."[39] The authorship of one's own world also implies the use of one's own language, and relates to what Mikhail Bakhtin describes as "retelling the story in one's own words."[40] To tell a "story in one's own words," according to Vaclav Havel, not only represents a threat to those conservative educators who are complicit with dominant ideology, but also prevents them "from concealing their true position and their inglorious modus vivendi, both from the world and from themselves."[41] Simply put, proponents of the English Only movement and other educators who are willing to violate linguistic-minority students' democratic rights to be educated in their own language as well as in English work primarily to preserve a social (dis)order that, according to Jean-Paul Sartre, "sanctions misery, chronic hunger, ignorance, or, in general, subhumanity."[42] In essence, educators who refuse to transform the ugliness of human misery, social injustices, and inequalities invariably become educators who, as Sartre so poignantly suggested, "will change nothing and will serve no one, but will succeed only in finding moral comfort in malaise."[43]

Conclusion

During a conference in which I attempted to unmask the dominant ideological mechanisms involved in the present assault on bilingual education, a woman approached me and said, "Thank you very much for your courage to say things that many of us are too afraid to say." Taken by surprise, I did not know how to respond, but I managed to make a point with the following question: Isn't it ironic that to speak the truth in a democracy, at least one's own truth, one must have courage to do so? She squeezed my hand and politely said good-bye. After she left I began to think that what I should have told her is to advocate for the democratic rights of bilingual students and to denounce the inequities that shape their (mis)education, "it is not necessary to be courageous; it is enough to be honest."[44] To be honest would require that we denounce those reactionary educators who believe that bilingual education "is highly contentious and politicized . . . and [that] there is a lack of clear consensus about the advantages and disadvantages of academic instruction in the primary language in contrast to early and intensive exposure to English."[45] To be honest would also require that we denounce the research industry that makes a living by pointing out the "lack of clear consensus" in the bilingual debate without providing alternative pedagogies that would effectively address the specificities of needs among linguistic-minority students, while the same research industry remains complicit with the very oppressive structures responsible for the poverty and human misery that characterize the lives of a large segment of linguistic-minority students who go to inner-city public schools. To be honest would require, for example, that reactionary educators be made to understand that what Latinos need is not "basic" research, as these educators claim. What Latinos need is social justice and educational equity and classroom-based research that documents educational practices that bring about social justice and educational equity. To be honest would require that reactionary educators acknowl-edge the existence of the intimate interrelationship between society's discriminatory practices and the "savage inequalities" that shape the (mis)education of linguistic-minority students. This would invariably point to the political nature of education, which reactionary educators call "politicizing" education.

Condemning the politicization of education serves to muffle rig-orous academic debate about both the grievances and the educational needs of linguistic-minority students. Only through a thorough de-construction of the ideology that prevents linguistic-minority stu-dents' sociocultural reality from becoming an area of serious inquiry can, for example, educators who want to falsely take politics out of ed-ucation learn that it is erroneous to think that "speaking a nonstan-dard variety of English can impede the easy acquisition of English lit-eracy by introducing greater deviations in the representation of sounds, making it hard to develop sound symbol links."[46] This posi-tion makes the assumption that standard dialects are monolithic and show no phonological variations. Such a posture is sustained only by a folk theory believed only by nonlinguists. Anyone who has been ex-posed to the Boston dialect notices that its speakers almost always drop the phoneme /r/ in the final position, as in *car*, yet middle-class speakers of such dialect have little difficulty linking the dropped pho-neme /r/ and its respective grapheme representation. This form of folk theory is possible due to the present excess in positivism, whereby numbers are elevated to an almost mythical status, which in turn dis-misses other fundamental factors that have important pedagogical im-plications yet remain largely ignored.

Perhaps more than the mere ability to link sound and symbol in English, factors such as linguistic and cultural resistance play a greater role in the acquisition of Standard English. bell hooks painfully ac-knowledges that Standard English, far from being a neutral tool of communication, is viewed by most African Americans as the "oppres-sor's language [that] has the potential to disempower those of us who are just learning to speak, who are just learning to claim language as a place where we make ourselves subject."[47] In learning the "oppressor's language," we are often forced to experience subordination in speak-ing it. Upon reflection, bell hooks states that "it is not the English lan-guage that hurt me, but what the oppressors do with it, how they shape it to become a territory that limits and defines, how they make it a weapon that can shame, humiliate, colonize."[48] The shame, humiliation, and colonization that nonspeakers of dominant Standard English feel in their relationship with English have a great deal more to do with the lack of reading success in Standard English than with the mechanical struggles they face in making sense of sound-symbol links due to unavoidable phonological variations found in all dialects, including Standard English. The nature of the nonstandard variety does not determine the subordinate students' inability to learn the ABCs, which in turn warrants that these students be taught "how to learn." These students have little difficulty learning what the chief of psychiatry at San Diego's Children's Hospital rightly describes as the "more relevant skills of the DBSs (drive-by-shootings)"[49] and other survival skills, which are vividly and painfully mastered by any student whose reality is characterized by violence, human misery, and despair.

To be honest would require that we reconnect with history in order to learn from the thousands of Chicano high school students who, in 1968, walked out of their respective schools in Los Angeles as a protest against their miseducation. They walked out to demand quality education, cultural dignity, and an end to cultural violence. The passion, courage, and determination those Chicano students demonstrated will serve us well again as we attempt to refigure how best to educate linguistic-minority students. Their courage, passion, and determination energized educators, political leaders, and community activists to coalesce to address the urgent needs that Chicanos and other linguistic-minority students were facing then. The needs of linguistic-minority students are, in a sense, greater today, given the added vicious assault on bilingual education. For this reason, teachers, parents, researchers, and community members need to coalesce again with the same determination not only to provide quality education to linguistic-minority students, but also to work aggressively to dismantle the social and cultural fabric that informs, shapes, and reproduces the despair of poverty, fatalism, and hopelessness.

By incorporating linguistic-minority students' cultural and linguistic processes into forms of textual, social, and political analysis, educators will not only develop the means to counter the dominant attempt to impose English as the only educational practice, but they will also equip themselves with the necessary tools to embrace a pedagogy of hope based on cultural production. Cultural production takes place when specific groups of people produce, mediate, and confirm the mutual ideological elements that emerge from and affirm their cultural experiences. These obviously include the languages through which these experiences are reflected and refracted. Only through experiences that are rooted in the interests of individual and collective self-determination can we create democratic education. Cultural production, not reproduction by imposing English, is the only means through which we can achieve a true cultural democracy. In this sense, bilingual education offers us not only a great opportunity to democratize our schools, but "is itself a utopian pedagogy."[50] By the very fact that it is a utopian pedagogy, according to Paulo Freire,

> it is full of hope, for to be utopian is not to be merely idealistic or impractical but rather to engage in denunciation and annunciation. Our pedagogy cannot do without a vision of man [and woman] of the world. It formulates a scientific humanist conception that finds its expression in a dialogical praxis in which the teachers and learners together, in the act of analyzing a dehumanizing reality, denounce it while announcing its transformation in the name of the liberation of man [and woman].[51]

Notes

1. Gloria Anzaldúa, *Borderlands: The New Mestiza* (San Francisco: Spinsters/Aunt Lute, 1987), p. 207.
2. The Massachusetts Department of Education allowed teachers in other disciplines, particularly English, to teach ESL without any required training. This waiver was recently changed and all ESL teachers must now undergo a certification process.
3. The apologetic stance of some liberals concerning the so-called ignorance of those educators who blindly oppose bilingual education is not surprising, since classical liberalism, as a school of thought and as ideology, always prioritizes the right to private property while relegating human freedom and other rights to mere "epiphenomena or derivatives." A rigorous analysis of thinkers such as Thomas Hobbes and John Locke will clearly show that the real essence of liberalism is the right to own property. The right to private property could only be preserved through self-conservation. This led Liubomir Tadic to pose the following question: "Isn't conservatism a more determinant characteristic for liberalism than the tendency toward freedom?" (Mihailo Markovic, Liubomir Tadic, Damko Grilic, *Liberalismo y Socialismo: Teoria y Praxis* [Mexico City: Editorial Grijalbo, 1977], p. 19). He concluded that owing to this ambiguity, liberalism is always positioned ideologically between revolution and reactionarism. In other words, liberalism vacillates between two opposing poles. It is this liberal position of vacillation that, on the one hand,

propels many liberals to support bilingual education and, on the other hand, to object to the linkage between the attack on bilingual education and colonial language policies.

4. Geralso Navas Davilla, *La Dialectica del Desarrollo Nacional: El Caso de Puerto Rico* (San Juan: Editorial Universitaria, 1978), p. 27.

5. Renato Constantino, *Neocolonial Identity and Counter-Consciousness* (London: Merlin Press, 1978), p. 66.

6. Constantino, *Neocolonial Identity*, p. 67.

7. Maria M. Lopez Lagunne, *Bilingualismo en Puerto Rico: Actitudes Sociolinguisticas del Maestro* (San Juan: M.I.S.C.E.S., Corp.,1989), p. 17.

8. Constantino, *Neocolonial Identity*, pp. 66–67.

9. H. Eyzenck, *The IQ argument: Race, Intelligence, and Education* (New York: Library Press, 1971).

10. Arthur R. Jensen, "How Much Can We Boost IQ and Scholastic Achievement?" *Harvard Educational Review, 39* (1969), 1–123.

11. For an example of scientism, a process that makes a claim to science but is, in reality, antiscientific, see Richard J. Herrnstein and Charles Murray, *The Bell Curve: Intelligence and Class Structure in American Life* (New York: Free Press, 1994).

12. For a comprehensive and critical discussion of scientific objectivity, see Donna Haraway, "Situated Knowledges: The Science Question in Feminism and the Privilege of Partial Perspectives," *Feminist Studies, 14* (1988), 575–599.

13. Linda Brodkey, *Writing Permitted in Designated Areas Only* (Minneapolis: University of Minnesota Press, 1966), p. 10.

14. Brodkey, *Writing Permitted,* p. 8.

15. Brodkey, *Writing Permitted,* p. 8.

16. Roger Fowler et al., *Language and Control* (London: Routledge & Kegan Paul, 1979), p. 192.

17. Greg Myers, "Reality, Consensus, and Reform in the Rhetoric of Composition Teaching", *College English, 48* (February 1986), pp. 2, 104–174.

18. Jonathan Kozol, *Amazing Grace: The Lines and the Conscience of a Nation* (New York: Harper Perennial, 1996), p. 4.

19. Kozol, *Amazing Grace*, p. 39.

20. Herrnstein and Murray, *The Bell Curve.*

21. Henry A. Giroux, *Theory and Resistance: A Pedagogy for the Opposition* (South Hadley, MA: J.F. Bergin, 1983), p. 87.

22. Paulo Freire, *The Politics of Education: Culture, Power, and Liberation* (Westport, CT: Bergin & Garvey, 1985), p. 103.

23. Freire, *The Politics of Education*, p. 103.

24. Giroux, *Theory and Resistance*, p. 87.

25. Michael Schudson, *Discovering the News: A Social History of American Newspapers* (New York: Basic Books, 1978), p. 6

26. Schudson, *Discovering the News,* p. 6.

27. "Bilingual grads outperform others in 2 districts," *San Diego Union Tribune,* July 8, 1998, p. 143.

28. Zeynep F. Beykont, *Academic Progress of a Nondominant Group: A Longitudinal Study of Puerto Ricans in New York City's Late Exit Bilingual Programs*, Diss., Har-

vard Graduate School of Education, 1994; Virginia P. Collier, "A Synthesis of Studies Examining Long-Term Language Minority Student Data on Academic Achievement," *Bilingual Research Journal, 16* (1992), 187–212; James Cummins, "The Role of Primary Language Development in Promoting Educational Success for Language Minority Students," in *Schooling and Language Minority Students: A Theoretical Framework,* ed. California State Department of Education, Evaluation, Dissemination and Assessment Center, California State University (Los Angeles: Author, 1981); David J. Ramirez, "Executive Summary," *Bilingual Research Journal, 16* (1992), 1–62.

29. Freire, *The Politics of Education,* p. 103.

30. Anzaldúa, *Borderlands,* p. 203.

31. Anzaldúa, *Borderlands,* p. 203.

32. Joseph H. Suina, "And Then I Went to School," in *Linguistic and Cultural Influences on Learning Mathematics,* ed. Rodney R. Cocking and Jose P. Mestre (Hillsdale, NJ: Lawrence Erlbaum Associates, 1998), p. 298.

33. Suina, "And Then I Went to School," p. 297.

34. Ngugi Wa Thiong'o, *Decolonizing the Mind: The Politics of Language in African Literature.* (Portsmouth, NH: Heinemann Press, 1986), p. 11.

35. Albert Memmi, *The Colonizer and the Colonized* (Boston: Beacon Press, 1967), p. 107.

36. Alan Lupo, "Accentuating the Negative," *Boston Globe,* March 4, 1992, p. 19.

37. "Humanities 101, Westfield Style," *Boston Globe,* March 3, 1992, p. 16.

38. I use the term *cultural production* to refer to specific groups of people producing, mediating, and confirming the mutual ideological elements that merge from and reaffirm their daily lived experiences.

39. Henry A. Giroux and Peter McLaren. "Teacher Education and the Politics of Engagement: The Case for Democratic Schooling," *Harvard Educational Review, 56* (August 1986), 213–238.

40. Mikhail Bakhtin, *The Dialogic Imagination,* Trans. C. Emerson and M. Holquist (Austin: University of Texas Press, 1981), p. 294.

41. Vaclav Havel, *Living in Truth* (London: Faber and Faber, 1989), p. 42.

42. Jean-Paul Sartre, "Introduction," in *The Colonizer and the Colonized,* Albert Memmi (Boston: Beacon Press, 1967), pp. xxiv–xxv.

43. Sartre, "Introduction," p. xxvi.

44. Amilcar Cabral, *Return to the Source* (New York: Monthly Review Press, 1974), p. 16

45. Catherine E. Snow, M. Susan Burns, and Peg Griffin, eds., *Reading Difficulties in Young Children* (Washington, DC: National Academy Press, 1998), p. 29.

46. Snow, Burn, and Griffin, *Reading Difficulties,* pp. 27–28.

47. bell hooks, *Teaching to Transgress* (New York: Routledge, 1996), p. 168.

48. hooks, *Teaching to Transgress,* p. 168.

49. Saul Levine, "On Guns and Health Care, The U.S. Caves In to Force," *San Diego Union Tribune,* August 12, 1993, p. 11.

50. Freire, *The Politics of Education,* p. 57.

51. Freire, *The Politics of Education,* p. 57.

Bilingualism Equals Access: The Case of Chinese High School Students

KATY MEI-KUEN KWONG

When people inquire about my profession, they are often surprised and fascinated with the answer: I am a Cantonese bilingual high school teacher. Besides the fact that many people do not have the slightest idea what a bilingual teacher actually does, they are surprised to find out that I would choose this field over engineering, which was my college major. To be honest, I did not choose this field. Bilingual education chose me. The calling to work as a Cantonese bilingual teacher in the public school system that I graduated from — in Malden, Massachusetts — was simply irresistible.

During the past twenty years, the demographics of Malden have changed tremendously. The city's residents used to be mostly Irish, Italian, Jewish, and Scandinavian. When my family arrived here with the first wave of immigrants from Hong Kong in 1979, there were only a handful of Chinese American families in town and no bilingual program in the schools. Since the 1980s, there has been an influx of immigrants from Asia, as well as from South America and the Caribbean. Today, about 30 percent of Malden's population is minority, 20 percent of these being Asian Americans. The city now has the third-largest Chinese population in Massachusetts. In order to meet the needs of a growing number of immigrants, the Malden Public Schools established its Bilingual Department in 1986. I assumed a teaching position soon thereafter.

Throughout my eleven years of working as a counselor and teacher in elementary, middle, and high schools, and in adult education, I have observed the pedagogical benefits of bilingual education for language- minority students of all ages. In this chapter, I share my observations of these benefits for the high school population. In particular, I focus on the educational experiences of Cantonese speakers from Mainland China, Hong Kong, and Vietnam — students whose native languages use writing symbols different from English letters.

As a high school teacher, most of my students are new arrivals with at least nine years of formal education in their respective home countries. Some speak both Mandarin and Cantonese.[1] In other words, some are already fluent in two languages before they arrive in U.S. schools. In terms of their academic skills, many of my students are proficient in reading and writing the Chinese language. Some have studied English as a foreign language before; however, none of them is proficient in English. In areas such as math and science, these students often surpass their American counterparts. I also have students with learning challenges, low literacy skills, a lack of formal education, or an interrupted education due to war or financial constraints in their country of origin. These students have the greatest difficulty in acquiring English and in completing high school in the United States.

The Cantonese transitional bilingual program in my high school currently serves about thirty-five students. The program offers content courses such as math, science, and social studies in Cantonese. As the only teacher in the program, I teach all of these content courses. My students also take English-as-a-Second-Language (ESL) classes, and as their English proficiency improves, they begin to be partially mainstreamed — that is, they take some content classes with monolingual English teachers and some with me. Since I am the only Cantonese bilingual teacher in the high school, most of my classes have to be multilevel.[2] Thus it is not unusual for me to teach algebra and geometry to two different groups of students in my classroom within the same time period. For students who have low literacy skills in their native language and have other academic gaps, the school has created basic skills and literacy courses. In these courses, teachers help strengthen students' basic math, reading, writing, and science skills.

Pedagogical Benefits of Bilingual Education

In my experience, bilingual education for high school students has many pedagogical benefits, regardless of the students' previous academic preparation. Students with high, medium, and low academic skills in their native language all benefit from bilingual education. These benefits include transfer of native language skills into English, quicker acquisition of English, continuation of content learning, easier teacher-student communication, appropriate levels of academic challenge, learning special skills for future employment, development of a healthy cultural identity, and easier adjustment to the host country. The table on page 46 lists these benefits and outlines the differences between monolingual and bilingual programs. The text that follows describes these dimensions of difference in greater detail.

Transfer of Previous Skills

In bilingual classes, students have the opportunity to improve their Chinese literacy skills, which can then be transferred into English. In my experience, the more literate students are in the written Chinese language, the more quickly they develop English literacy skills because they can transfer what they know in Chinese into English. If they already have strong skills in Chinese, it is still an advantage to continue to develop native language literacy skills, as those can be transferred into English as well. Students who begin with low reading and writing skills in Chinese will have the same difficulties in English. For example, a broken Chinese sentence will be translated into a broken English sentence, especially since both languages have the same basic sentence structure. Such limited literacy in the native language also inhibits students' learning in other ways. For example, these students will have difficulty when they attempt to look up the meaning of an English word in an English-Chinese dictionary if they do not recognize the Chinese character. Thus, highly developed Chinese literacy skills are essential in my high school students' acquisition of English literacy skills.

The transfer of skills from Chinese into English does not happen automatically. I actively teach the similarities and differences between the two languages. For instance, the writing styles of Chinese and English are extremely different. Chinese people tend to write in circles

PEDAGOGICAL BENEFITS OF BILINGUAL EDUCATION

	Bilingual Program	English Monolingual Program
Transfer of Previous Skills	• Continue to develop higher level native language literacy and academic skills	• Stop developing native language literacy and academic skills
	• Native language skills will transfer into English	• No support for transferring native language skills into English
	• Learn English faster	• Learn English slowly
	• Active teaching of similarities and differences between languages	• Lack support in deciphering similarities and differences between languages
Understandable Instruction	• Learning continues because students understand the language of instruction	• Learning is delayed until students acquire English
	• Teacher and student have a common language of communication	• Teacher and student do not have a common language of communication
	• Lower level of frustration for teachers and students	• Higher level of frustration for teachers and students
Academic Challenge	• Engage in appropriate level of academic curriculum	• Engage in lower level of academic curriculum
	• Translation skills can be taught	• Student's native language skills are not utilized
Emotional Benefits	• Easier student adjustment to the new environment	• Students lack support in adjusting to the new environment
	• Teachers, peers, and historical figures act as role models	• Lack role models among teachers and peers
	• Students can develop a healthy bicultural identity and take pride in their native language	• Experience difficulty in developing a healthy bicultural identity
	• Validation of previous cultural and immigrant experience	• Lack validation of previous cultural and immigration experiences
	• Connection to peers with similar immigration experiences	• Isolation from peers with similar immigration experiences

and never in a direct manner. English writing, however, is extremely direct and clear-cut. In most cases, one need only read the first sentence of each paragraph to understand a piece of English writing. I need to make these rules clear and teach the differences across the two languages so that students will learn to use proper English in academic and non-academic settings. I also point out differences between the languages by highlighting typical mistakes that a Chinese speaker makes in English, such as the use of plurals, articles, and tenses. My students are also learning special skills, such as translation. The ability to translate from English to Chinese and vice versa improves students' metalinguistic awareness, strengthens their understanding of the structure of both languages, and develops translation skills that they may use in a future career.

In monolingual classrooms, Chinese students' English acquisition is slower. First, Chinese students placed in monolingual classrooms lack the opportunity to practice the Chinese academic language skills that they bring to school. This inhibits their chance to develop higher level native language skills, which could subsequently be transferred into English. Furthermore, these students do not receive the necessary guidance and support in deciphering the similarities and differences between Chinese and English. Without such support and explicit instruction, transfer of Chinese language skills into English is hampered and English acquisition is slowed.

Understandable Instruction

Instruction in the native language allows immigrant students to continue learning without interruption. In bilingual classrooms, learning continues because students can comprehend the instruction. I have students entering my bilingual class as late as June who can immediately dive into the curriculum because they understand the language of instruction. In mainstream classrooms, however, learning shuts down until a student is proficient in English. Are students supposed to wait until they acquire enough English to allow academic learning to continue? If instructed in their native language, students can continue to be challenged intellectually and learn new content while also acquiring English.

Furthermore, teaching and learning are much easier for both students and teachers when they share a common language. It is frustrating for teachers and students when they cannot communicate. It is extremely difficult for students to be put in a mainstream class in which the language of instruction is English — a language that they cannot understand. I often hear horror stories from my newly arrived students about their experiences in monolingual classrooms, where they sat clueless and frustrated. It is equally difficult for a teacher to deliver a lesson and expect learning if her students are unable to understand what is being discussed in class. In a bilingual classroom, where students and teacher have a common language, students can actively participate in class discussions, and both teacher and students can concentrate on the content of the lesson.

Academic Challenge

In a bilingual class, students can engage with more appropriately challenging academic material. Without a bilingual program, my students would be immediately placed in low-level, content-based ESL courses. Such courses are designed for students from many language groups to use their acquired knowledge, in math for example, to learn English. Unfortunately, ESL teachers are often not trained in the content area, so that classes lack academic rigor and substantive challenge. An even worse scenario is when a bilingual or ESL content class is not available; students are then placed in low-level monolingual English classes due to their lack of English skills. Their academic development is thus interrupted, and in the absence of a challenging curriculum, many students are turned off by school. In many cases, students' lack of English skills is the sole reason they are kept from placement in college preparatory classes, vocational programs, and school-to-career programs. If the goal of education is academic development, then students should continue to be challenged academically in bilingual classes while they are developing English.

Our bilingual classes provide equitable education because students can be taught the same curriculum that is used in mainstream classes. I can challenge my students at their respective academic levels, whether they have previously received low-, middle-, or high-level preparation. For example, I have begun to offer a college preparatory math program at Malden High School for bilingual students who have a high level of academic preparation. These students are intellectually challenged daily in high-level math while they continue to improve their Chinese language skills and acquire English. I engage them in the same research projects and upper level curriculum that is provided in the mainstream classes. For students with less preparation in math, I offer a lower level course that is still more intellectually challenging than the mainstream math course they would otherwise have to take due to their lack of English skills. Unless society's aim is to create and maintain an underclass — a group of students who are doomed to work, for example, as unskilled labor in Chinese restaurants or electronics factories — Chinese (and other non-English-speaking) students should be given the opportunity to continue to learn in bilingual classes.

Emotional Benefits

In addition to achieving academic objectives, a bilingual program has emotional benefits for students. Bilingual classes can help newcomers adjust to their new environment and develop a healthy bicultural identity by providing role models, including teachers, peers, and the historical Asian American figures we study. With the help of role models, students learn to incorporate aspects of American culture without losing their Chinese identity.

As a bilingual and bicultural person, I provide a role model for my students as they struggle to incorporate the American culture into their Chinese cultural identity. My bilingual classes are also a safe haven for newcomers as they adjust to their new country. As a bilingual teacher, I can listen to students' adjustment problems, offer guidance, and validate their previous cultural and current immigration experiences. Peers in the class can also help each other because they are coping with similar immigration experiences. Each time a new student joins my class, the other students immediately welcome him or her into our extended family. In mainstream classrooms, our students do not have any of the support systems necessary to help them adjust to their new environment.

I also use a curriculum that explicitly addresses the literature on Asian Pacific American identity, racism in America, and contributions of Asian Pacific Americans to the United States. This curriculum demonstrates how other Asian Americans have coped with cultural identity issues. In monolingual classrooms, our Chinese students lack the necessary guidance, support, and role models to develop a healthy bicultural identity. They are expected instead to replace their cultural identity with a new American identity.

Conclusion

All of our students deserve the highest quality bilingual education. After many years of teaching Chinese immigrant students, I can attest to the fact that all of my students benefit from bilingual education for the following reasons: their existing native language academic skills transfer to English; they continue to learn rather than having to wait until they are proficient in English; they are challenged intellectually at their respective academic levels; and they find emotional support and cultural role models in bilingual classrooms. As their bilingual teacher, I understand that my role is much more than what the job description suggests. I have to be their parent, friend, counselor, cultural mediator, and, perhaps most importantly, their advocate in the school system and beyond. I work to make sure that my students get the highest quality bilingual education and are not doomed to a low-level, English Only curriculum that denies them access to the college-track and a variety of career choices. All students deserve these educational and career options.

In order to provide quality education for all children, we need to focus on the characteristics of good educational programs: offering instruction in a language that students can understand; providing teachers who can communicate with students and act as positive role models, supporting and guiding children's identity development; and teaching an academically challenging curriculum. Educational programs designed for either monolingual English speakers or language-minority students should have these same characteristics. A good bilingual program meets these criteria: it allows for transfer of native language skills, understandable instruction, appropriate academic materials and challenging curriculum, as well as an easy adjustment and a healthy bicultural identity. Hence, a good bilingual program is the most appropriate educational program for language-minority children. If we believe in equity in education, then we as educators must go beyond the confines of our classroom, to build community support and to advocate for quality bilingual education.

Notes

1. Mandarin and Cantonese are two spoken Chinese languages. A Mandarin and a Cantonese speaker would not be able to understand each other when talking, but can communicate in the written form of the Chinese language.
2. The school would not hire another teacher unless we had more than twenty-five students in each time period. In order to address the needs of all students, I must offer multilevel courses within the same time period.

PART TWO

Practice of Bilingualism

Nurturing Bilingualism in Classrooms

Good teaching practices that nurture bilingualism look different in different contexts. Given the widely varying needs, strengths, and educational histories of language-minority students, there is no single recipe for good teaching practice in bilingual classrooms. There is, however, a central principal — that bilingualism flourishes when teachers incorporate the resources, histories, and experiences of language-minority students and their communities into the curriculum. Exemplary bilingual classrooms disprove the misconceptions that have stigmatized language-minority students and their communities and debunk the myth that language differences are language deficiencies. In these classrooms, students' native languages, communities, and cultural backgrounds are recognized as essential resources for learning and teaching.

Across the nation there are countless examples of excellent classrooms that support the bilingualism of language-minority students. The everyday work of practitioners is, however, seldom visible and their knowledge base unavailable to educators, policymakers, and the general public. In Part Two of *Lifting Every Voice,* authors share their research- and practice-based experiences, insights, and observations in successful bilingual classrooms that serve varied groups of students. Examples are purposefully drawn from bilingual programs with varied designs, philosophies, and goals. Bilingual teacher Mohamed Farah, teacher/researcher Berta Berriz, and classroom researcher Cynthia Ballenger present their observations and research on successful teaching practices in classrooms with Somali high school students, African American and Latino elementary school students, and Haitian middle school students, respectively. Next, educational researchers Jim Cummins and Dennis Sayers report on innovative uses of global computer networks in maintenance and transitional bilingual classrooms with Latino and African American students. Finally, classroom researcher

Evangeline Stefanakis focuses on best practices in the assessment of bilingual students.

The authors emphasize the importance of building on students' native language and their prior personal and cultural knowledge and experiences, and of engaging students with an interesting, pertinent, and challenging curriculum. These chapters give a sense of the student diversity in our bilingual programs — in native language, dialect, culture, age, communication style, prior academic preparation, first- and second-language literacy skills, and immigration history — and illustrate how thoughtfully chosen teaching strategies can successfully address the varied strengths and needs of our students in specific contexts.

One dimension of student diversity is manifest in the differing immigration experiences and varying levels of formal education that students have received prior to their arrival in the United States. Mohamed Farah discusses his experiences in teaching Somali high school students who immigrated to the United States as teenagers with little or no formal education experience due to ongoing civil war and upheaval in Somalia. In his quest to teach this group of students — who lack not only English skills and grade-level content knowledge, but also literacy skills in their native language — Farah focuses first on supporting and raising students' basic literacy skills and content knowledge in Somali. Despite the fact that academic materials in Somali are scarce, he finds that use of students' native language is the most effective teaching resource for his classroom. Of course, students must master English, but they should not have to wait to start learning content (e.g., math, science, and history) until they acquire English proficiency. Farah maintains that, when taught through Somali, his students can concentrate on the content, their conceptual development is not inhibited, and they learn more quickly. Another crucial curricular resource is the wealth of personal and cultural knowledge and experiences that his students bring to the classroom. In order to link his students' prior knowledge to academic knowledge, Farah uses daily free-writing activities, community-based research projects, and a process writing approach.

Students' languages, dialects, and cultures constitute other dimensions of diversity in bilingual classrooms. Berta Berriz shares her insights on teaching academic English and promoting a healthy identity among African American and Latino/a students in her third-grade two-way bilingual classroom. Berriz emphasizes three principles of her teaching. First, because learning happens in relationships, she uses co-operative learning, team teaching, and cross-cultural learning experiences that enhance teacher-teacher, student-student, teacher-student, student-community, and teacher-community relationships. Second, she incorporates cultural arts activities such as portraiture, visual arts, music, and stories into the curriculum, which validates each student's history, brings family culture into the classroom, and helps students make the connection between home and school. Third, she uses personal writing activities — including autobiographical writing, journal writing, and publishing for real audiences — that enable students to develop academic writing skills based on their personal stories. In addition, Berriz capitalizes on the varied languages and dialects in her classroom by guiding students to compare and contrast the similarities and differences between Standard English, Standard Spanish, "Spanglish," and Black English.

Just as there are ways to teach academic English without demeaning other dialects and languages in the classroom, there are also ways to teach science by building upon rather than denigrating students' varied cultural styles of communication and experiences with scientific phenomena. Cynthia Ballenger describes her research in a multigrade Haitian Creole/English transitional bilingual classroom that implements an inquiry-based science curriculum driven by students' own questions. The Haitian students in this middle school class have received varied amounts of formal education in Haiti and have been in the United States for less than three years. While the students are mostly taught using Haitian Creole, the science textbooks are in English. In this classroom, the teacher considers students' native languages, playful ways of talking and joking, and culturally based interaction styles as resources for learning. He organizes the class so that students can engage in extended discussion, exploration, and questioning of their own and each other's personal theories and observations concerning complicated scientific concepts, such as metamorphosis. Ballenger concludes that this science class is successful because children are able to comprehend and participate in discussion of complex concepts using their native language and cultural communication style and because the classroom organization allows students to draw on their everyday experiences.

In addition to cultural communication style, students in bilingual classrooms also vary in literacy skills in their native language and in

English. Global learning networks provide opportunities for students with varying degrees of bilingual skills to participate in cooperative projects with sister classes in geographically distant locales. Jim Cummins and Dennis Sayers discuss examples drawn from one cross-cultural network, De Orilla a Orilla, that has established collaborative projects between classrooms across the world in many languages on various subjects, including geography, language arts, and math. When working on a topic such as proverbs in different cultures, students in bilingual classrooms use both their languages to exchange research findings and compare cultural and linguistic knowledge in their exchanges. Families and communities can be an integral part of these projects as reservoirs of cultural and linguistic knowledge and as actual participants in long-distance cooperative activities. Teachers have an opportunity to find teaching partners around the world who share an interest in a topic and then collaboratively plan and implement innovative projects with the support of electronic mail and computer-based conferencing. Cummins and Sayers present three case studies that illustrate the potential of cooperative network projects in developing students' first- and second-language literacy skills, validating oral histories and cultural traditions of communities, reducing ethnic and racial tension in peer relations, and contributing to the critical thinking skills and political clarity that young people need to participate in a cultural democracy.

In the final essay in Part Two, Evangeline Stefanakis shares her research on best practices in assessing language-minority students. Stefanakis argues that assessing a diverse group of bilingual learners requires collecting information on students' skills and knowledge from a variety of people, including family members and school personnel; in a variety of settings, such as classroom, playground, and home; and with a variety of formal and informal assessment techniques, such as observations, interviews, standardized tests, and student portfolios. In order to reverse the disproportionate referral of language-minority students to special education classes, Stefanakis recommends a sociocultural framework for teachers' classroom assessment that centers on who the child is, where the child comes from, what the child knows, and what the child needs to learn. Her framework suggests a shift from a sole focus on what a child can learn by him/herself to what a teacher and a child can accomplish together, and from a focus on what is wrong with the child to what is wrong with the learning environment.

Reaping the Benefits of Bilingualism: The Case of Somali Refugee Students

MOHAMED HASSAN FARAH

A number of Somali high school students have come to the United States as refugees in the last few years, fleeing civil war, anarchy, and famine in their native country. The ongoing unrest in Somalia has disrupted their young lives: horrible things have happened to them and their families; losing their chance for an education is just one of their losses. Thus, the majority of Somali students entering the school system either have little or no prior schooling or have large gaps in their formal education.

Somali students present a challenge to the school system. What are the best ways to educate these young people? Some of them have had formal education and can read and write in Somali, but lack English skills (these we designate "nonliteracy students"). Others lack not only proficiency in English, but also literacy and academic skills in their native language (these we designate "literacy students"). While it is clear that literacy and nonliteracy Somali high school students have distinct academic needs, it is also clear that providing one program for all of them is not optimal for anyone's academic development. Both literacy and nonliteracy students need to learn English, and both groups need to learn content in their native language. Literacy students, however, also need to develop basic literacy and academic skills in Somali.

Students from Somalia are only one of several language groups that present this particular challenge to public schools in the United States. Students coming from many parts of the world enroll in the public schools with similar gaps in their educational background. As a result of a legal challenge filed by parents and language rights activists, my school system has started to address the unique needs of all literacy students. In response to the court mandate, for example, English High School started a program specifically designed for Somali literacy students. In addition to daily English-as-a-Second-Language (ESL) classes taught by ESL teachers, these students also receive content-area instruction in Somali by bilingual teachers, which emphasizes basic literacy skills and content learning. I am responsible for teaching this group of students reading, writing, math, history, and science using their native Somali as the language of instruction. In this chapter I focus on instructional practices that I have found to be effective with Somali literacy high school students. I hope the lessons I have learned are applicable to literacy students from other language groups. In order to introduce my students, I first discuss the sociohistorical background of the Somali community and their immigration and education history.

Immigration and Education History of the Somali Community

The Somali people are often described as one of the few homogeneous groups in Africa. They share one language, Somali; one culture, Somali Muslim; and one religion, Islam. In this regard they can be described as being one tribe. But in reality, the Somali tribe is divided into numerous clans and subclans. In the rural areas, most of these clans are nomads who follow their animals, such as camels, sheep, and goats, from one pastureland to another. Historically these clans were independent from one another and often fought over limited resources such as water and pastureland, even though the traditional law system, or *Heer* as it is commonly known, delineates how to use these resources and how to resolve conflicts that arise from sharing them.

Somalia was fully colonized by two European powers, Britain and Italy, from the turn of the century until 1960. The colonizers destroyed the existing educational system that was based on religion and Somali culture. They also abolished the traditional Heer system of government based on the authority of elders in the community, which had worked well for the Somali people. Colonial governments replaced the Heer with an alien centralized system of government. After gaining independence from Britain and Italy in 1960, many politicians took advantage of the clan system and abused it for their personal political gains. For example, it was not uncommon for politicians to call upon their clan to vote for them during election time, promising in return a share in the "national pie" in the event that they were elected to parliament or became a cabinet minister. Such abuse resulted in a series of corrupt civilian governments until 1969, when a group of military officers overthrew the civilian parliamentary government, citing corruption and nepotism in government and declaring that democracy had not worked in the nine years since independence.

It is generally agreed that one of the good decisions the military made soon after it came to power was to establish the Somali Language Commission. The first mandate of this commission was to adopt an appropriate script for the hitherto unwritten Somali language. The second one was to write all school textbooks, up through high school level, in the Somali language. The commission adopted the Latin or Roman script to write the Somali language in 1972.[1] The official choice of a common script throughout the country changed the educational landscape of Somalia. Before, the medium of instruction in schools was Arabic, English, or Italian, depending on where one attended school. Many Somalis, including myself, who went to school before this change had to take courses in different languages at different levels in our schooling. For example, in elementary school I took all my courses in Arabic, and I became literate writing the Arabic script from right to left. Then, at the intermediate and secondary levels, the language of instruction changed to English. After high school, some of my friends attended the Somali National University, where the medium of instruction in some academic departments was Italian. I was spared this because I enrolled at the College of Education, where courses were taught in English. These stories illustrate how confusing it was for students before a common script was adopted and mandated as the medium of instruction for all Somali education up through the secondary level. They also explain why parents of our Somali students might have been educated in any one of these languages and may or may not be proficient in English or literate in Somali.

While the military government is credited with some wise decisions, including those in the areas of language and education, they made many decisions that were widely debated and criticized. For example, by the mid-1970s, the military regime had built one of the strongest armies in sub-Saharan Africa (exceeded only perhaps by that of apartheid South Africa). This military buildup encouraged Somalia to go to war with Ethiopia to regain the Ogaden region — a region that is populated by ethnic Somali and had been transferred to Ethiopia during colonial times by Britain and Italy. After capturing much of the land in a very short period, the Somali army was pushed out of the region by a coalition of communist forces led by the Soviet Union and including troops from Cuba and South Yemen. Somalia fell into major disarray after this defeat. Unhappy with the results, some senior army officers unsuccessfully tried to topple the military government.

Following the war and the failed coup, the military government began to misuse the clan system to an even greater extent. In order to gain and maintain loyalty, government officials awarded jobs and contracts only to members of their respective clans. Such actions led the country to its present chaos. In the mid-1980s, opposition groups organized armed resistance along clan lines to oust the military dictator who had ruled the country with a firm hand since 1969. After the fall of the military government in 1991, the opposition groups then splintered along clan lines and became clan factions with several "warlords" controlling different regions of the country and vying for ultimate power. The armed groups had succeeded only in their primary objective of removing the dictator from power. They could not form a stable government nor bring stability to the country because they did not have or could not agree upon a common agenda for ruling Somalia and restoring civil life. In fact, they have repeated the vicious cycle of corruption, nepotism, and competition among the clans seeking to grab power at any cost.

After 1991, Somalia fell into deep anarchy and total chaos. No one was safe from the brutal militias of the so-called warlords, who ransack the country with impunity and spare no one from their ruthless craft of indiscriminate killing, raping, looting, and destruction of property. Many Somalis fled war and famine in their country and sought refuge in the neighboring countries of Kenya, Ethiopia, and Djibouti. Living conditions in the refugee camps were not easy. The Somali refugees found a harsh environment in which they struggled daily to procure the minimum essentials of food, water, fuel wood, shelter, and clothing. Education for their children was not an option. After a few years of refugee experience in these camps, many families were fortunate enough to obtain visas for resettlement in the United States.

That is how many Somalis arrived in major U.S. cities and towns. Somali young people and their families had to adjust to yet another unfamiliar country, with a new language and culture to learn. Upon arrival in the United States, many Somali students were fifteen years of age or older. They came here either having missed a significant portion of their schooling years or not having attended school at all. Some of them were able to read and write in Somali but were behind in other academic areas and spoke little English. Others were not able to read and write in Somali and were also behind in academic areas and English. In my city, they were assigned to English High School — the designated school for newly arriving high school age students coming into the system.

As soon as the students were enrolled at the school, the gravity of their academic needs became very obvious. It was not their fault that their country had been in turmoil for so long. It was not their fault that their schooling experiences were interrupted and they had not received a proper education. The question then became how best to educate these youngsters within the school system. In order to formulate an appropriate educational plan, an initial diagnostic test was administered to determine these students' academic and literacy skills in both Somali and English. After analyzing the test results, the students were divided into two groups: literacy and nonliteracy students. The nonliteracy students were those who could read and write in Somali but demonstrated low English skills. The literacy students were those students who had suffered large gaps in their schooling, had low English skills, and additionally had little or no literacy skills in their native language, Somali.

The need for native language instruction in content areas for both literacy and nonliteracy students was evident from the low test scores. Student knowledge of content-area subjects such as science, math, and social studies was often at grade five or lower. Somali students had a long road ahead of them to acquire the grade-level academic skills necessary to graduate from high school. For the purpose of this chapter, I will focus on the educational needs of and the educational plan developed for my literacy students, who have the burden of enrolling in high school while not being able to read and write in either English or Somali.

Educational Plan

The overall goal of the Somali literacy class at English High is to instruct all Somali students with low native language literacy skills in one classroom, providing them instruction in two primary areas: teaching of content (math, science, social studies), as well as reading and writing in Somali by a bilingual teacher; and English instruction by an ESL teacher. Students also choose one elective from among art, dance, or gym, and take it with mainstream students. These elective classes serve the purpose of integrating bilingual students into the general student population in the school.

Native language instruction is important for my Somali students, as they learn a lot more when I present academic material in their native language. They learn more quickly because they are not struggling with understanding the language. Instead they are able to concentrate on the content and continue to develop academic skills. Appropriate academic literature in the Somali language is both scarce and very hard to find, so Somali teachers generally translate from the English texts for each of the subjects they teach. This translation activity distracts teachers from the more important activity of inspiring and teaching students. However, it is necessary if students are to complete the required courses for high school graduation. For example, one requirement for high school graduation is a U.S. history class. Last year I taught that course to a group of Somali seniors and juniors in their native language. In that class, we were able to concentrate on the content and cover much of the U.S. history curriculum without being hampered by the language. In the end, my students and I were surprised by how much they had learned about the history of their adopted country. This is knowledge that will help them function as informed U.S. citizens for the rest of their lives. At the same time, the class is a high school graduation requirement. I believe that many of my students would not have been able to graduate last year had we not covered this class in Somali.

These students also take ESL classes. There is no question that Somali students need to learn English, the language of their new country, but we cannot wait to teach them history, science, and math until they learn English. They are already behind in their academic skills and have a lot of catching up to do. They need to learn a vast amount of content matter in addition to acquiring English. The bilingual approach allows a balance between teaching ESL and content matter, so that they learn English without sacrificing academic development. Over time, as students acquire more and more English, they transfer skills that they gained in Somali into English.

Promising Strategies for Native Language Literacy Development

My students bring with them a wealth of knowledge and experiences. The starting point of my writing, history, science, and math lessons is my students' prior knowledge and experiences. First, I want to get to know my students intimately, to build close connections with them. I have students who have lost parents and family members in the war and endured other traumatic experiences. When I, as their teacher, take interest in and validate their experiences and bring their positive experiences into the classroom, students are motivated to learn. I can then build on their knowledge and experiences to design my curriculum. For example, one of our regular classroom activities is journal writing. Every morning, students freewrite in their journals. The journals are private, and I promise students that I will not share their journal with anyone else. They often write about their experiences during the war, in refugee camps, and as immigrants in the United States. At an emotional level, it helps them to write about difficult experiences. At an academic level, they learn to express themselves through writing. I can then build on their reflections and expand the general discussion of these topics, such as immigration or the civil war in Somalia, in the classroom.

Community-based projects also provide a good avenue to build on students' prior knowledge and experience. These projects have been very effective in teaching my Somali literacy students. I begin by having students identify a research question of interest to them. We use graphic organizers to structure and record large- and small-group brainstorming sessions, which help students develop a set of research questions. Students then carry out research projects in the community. For example, this year we want to find out about services available in the community. Students developed a questionnaire, on which they will follow up by going out to the community to conduct interviews. They will later compile responses to their interview questions.

After collecting and compiling the data, I use a process writing method (Calkins, 1986; Johnson & Roen, 1989). This method encourages my students to write drafts, edit, revise, and eventually publish research reports based on their readings, field trips, and interview findings. This method entails five steps. First, we use prewriting activities that kindle students' thinking and imagination. Students brainstorm, freewrite, use graphic organizers, and meet with the teacher in a private conference. They have to organize the information in an outline form. Second, I ask my students to start writing without worrying about grammatical mistakes. At this stage, students organize the information they have gathered into a written draft and determine if they need to collect more information. Third, students solicit feedback from their peers, make changes, revise, and rewrite their report based on peer feedback. They provide samples of their writing to me and to their peers, use response groups, and confer with me for tips on revising. At the next stage, students proofread, copyedit, and fine-tune their writing. Students use checklists, read their works aloud, and set up an editing table for peer review of their writing. Finally, the reports are ready to be shared with a wider audience. Students read their final product to the class, and then compile their writings in a booklet. At the end of the school year, students will self-publish their works in order to share them with their peers, parents, and community members.

These community-based projects involve students in intensive literacy and academic activities on topics that capture their interest. They also help students practice important skills such as formulating their own questions, developing a questionnaire, identifying interviewees, and conducting, compiling, and analyzing interviews. Furthermore, students develop a political awareness of the conditions of their community in the United States and learn about the services available to them. Community leaders are invited into the classroom, and students take field trips to community centers to learn more about the local issues that concern the community. Similar projects can be conducted on other topics, such as aspects of U.S. culture and history. These projects enable students to develop full and healthy connections with both the Somali community and the U.S. community.

Conclusion

Somali students have waited a very long time to get a good education. It was not their fault that they did not attend school in their home country or in refugee camps. Now that they are here, they should not have to wait any longer to get the education they have missed. While they are struggling to acquire English as a second language, they should be given the opportunity to simultaneously gain basic literacy skills in their native language and learn academic content in the Somali language. My students have such an opportunity now at English High School.

Three factors contribute to the success of our program: (a) a balance between native language support and English support that allows students to catch up with academic content quickly and transfer knowledge and skills gained in the native language into English; (b) an instructional approach that builds on students' prior knowledge and experience and uses community-based research projects and process writing activities to develop academic and literacy skills in the native language; and (c) community involvement and support for the program.

In our literacy program, students are able to study some core subjects that are required for graduation in their native language. When taught in their native language, students are able to catch up in a relatively short period of time with the years of academic content that they have missed. Our program also emphasizes teaching of basic Somali literacy skills. These basic literacy skills build the foundation necessary for English acquisition. At the same time, they are learning English in ESL classes taught by native English speakers who are experienced in working with bilingual students.

The community-based projects that I use in my classroom are based on the philosophy that good education builds on students' prior knowledge and experience. We focus on issues of concern to students, constructing a relevant curriculum that strengthens students' reading, writing, and research skills. These research projects provide a window onto U.S. history and culture, as well as the Somali history and culture. Community involvement is an essential aspect of these projects, involving everyone from parents and relatives to activists. The end products, such as student reports on services available in the city, are valuable to both the students and the community.

Finally, any discussion of our educational program for Somali students must describe the crucial role played by parent and community advocacy. In fact, the special programs for Somali and other literacy students only exist because of the dedication and advocacy of parents, teachers, and community activists. As mentioned earlier, the city's immigrant communities brought the particular educational needs of their literacy and nonliteracy high school students to the attention of the school district. Supported by the legal expertise of META (Multicultural Education, Training, and Advocacy), a community-based organization, parents and activists advocated for separate classrooms for literacy students so that instruction could be targeted to meet these particular students' needs. Based on a court ruling, literacy students from several immigrant communities won the right to have their own educational programs designed for them. The Somali literacy program was started as a result of this case.

Though in the United States for a relatively short period of time, the Somali community has become familiar with the educational system and program options for their children. For example, there is significant Somali involvement in parent organizations. Active parents have formed a Somali parent action committee and they are also members of a citywide parent association that links parents from many cultures and language groups. Moreover, one Somali parent is a member of the executive committee of the citywide group and another is a member of the Bilingual Task Force that advises the school system on bilingual education reform issues. Active parents also inform other parents on their rights and on how they can get involved in their children's education.[2] One challenge has been to educate Somali parents about the differences between bilingual education and ESL-based approaches. As a result of parents' community outreach efforts, many in the Somali community now understand the benefits of bilingual education for their children and actively support their teachers and schools.

I believe that my students deserve the best. That is why I am always searching for new and better ways to teach. I have learned three basic lessons in my experience with this particular group of Somali literacy students. First, I have learned that my students possess a great deal of unprocessed knowledge and experience that needs to be validated, used, and expressed in a positive way. As their teacher I need to help students make connections between what they already know and what they need to learn. The best way to help students make these connections is by teaching them in their native language, building on native language oral skills. Second, I have also learned that a process writing approach is effective with my students. The beauty of process writing is that it allows students to express their experience and content knowledge through writing without initially worrying about grammatical mistakes. They then work with their peers, with me, and on their own to correct, revise, and develop their composition. Of course, in the end our goal is that students learn to write very well and produce high-quality academic writing in two languages. And third, I have learned that the community is vital to the success of the program. Community support and advocacy have built and sustained our programs at English High School. Just as importantly, the community enriches and deepens our curriculum through participation in our students' community-based projects and by encouraging and recognizing the academic achievements that our students exhibit through our public presentations. The success stories involving Somali students who have come through our program and earned a high school diploma despite the large gaps in their educational backgrounds give us hope. The promise of education is becoming a reality for our community and students.

Notes

1. Primarily for economic reasons, the Somali Language Commission (Guddiga Af-Soomaaliga) chose the Roman script over the Arabic, the Osmania, or the Gadaburi scripts. The latter two were invented by prominent Somali scholars, Osman Kennadid and Sheikh Abdulrahman Sheikh Nur, respectively.

2. Our students often lack academic support at home because many Somali parents have had gaps in their own education. Although parents provide the necessary emotional support, they are not able to provide the necessary academic supports. Furthermore, parents are not in a position to help their children if they are not familiar with the school system in this country. Many parents are also kept from being fully involved in the education of their children because they do not speak English. It helps greatly when schools systems provide personnel who can work with parents and explain their educational options in their native language. In the absence of parent liaisons who can provide parents with the necessary information, it falls on other parents and bilingual teachers to explain the premises of bilingual education and how parents can support their children's academic development. On my part, I have reached out to many parents to gain their cooperation in helping their children succeed in school.

References

Calkins, L. (1986). *The art of teaching writing.* Portsmouth, NH: Heinemann.

Johnson, D., & Roen, D. H. (1989). *Richness in writing: Empowering ESL students.* New York: Longman.

Raising Children's Cultural Voices: Strategies for Developing Literacy in Two Languages

BERTA ROSA BERRIZ

How can teachers create a learning environment that honors the diverse family cultures of students within a racist society? Further, how can teachers develop literacy in two languages within a standards-driven curriculum that dictates what each student needs to learn, regardless of cultural and linguistic differences? I work with my colleague Ramona in a large urban school system in Massachusetts. Our journey as teachers is grounded in our search for answers to these questions within our two-way bilingual program classrooms, in which native speakers of Spanish and English are taught in integrated classes in both languages.

As third-grade teachers, we are committed to quality education for inner-city youth and hold the highest expectations for our students. Our students are African Americans and Latinos whose family cultures differ significantly from mainstream U.S. culture. Thus they move between two cultural worlds — their home culture and the mainstream culture. Becoming familiar with these two worlds is a developmental process with a double edge: our students must strengthen their sense of pride in their family culture while at the same time building skills to succeed in mainstream culture. Part of the work of our bicultural classrooms is to live and re-create our own cultures within an integrated learning environment.

We experiment with various approaches to promote students' academic development in two languages and affirm their cultural identity within a two-way bilingual program. We use a team approach to create a consistent learning environment in which we model cross-cultural respect and cooperation for our students as we learn and teach together from different points of view. Our teaching combines use of the arts and a strong emphasis on writing within a web of relationships essential to our bilingual and bicultural classroom, which includes the teacher, the teacher team, the students, their families, and our community. The arts become tools that celebrate the cultural identity of our students, develop their cultural voices, and strengthen their connection with their family and community. Writing links children's personal experiences to academic learning. This weave of symbols from family cultures and the community becomes the foundation for the development of dual literacy within a standards-driven curriculum. Our program enables students to interact with academic language on their own terms from a position of strength and pride. We also count on the curricular involvement of our students' families and communities.

A Story from Our Two-Way Bilingual
Third-Grade Classroom

It's Tuesday morning in our two-way bilingual third-grade classes. *Eramos de una visión . . . la música de su corazón* is playing softly as the children write in their morning journals. Ramona, my teaching partner, and I are talking about the day in the doorway between the Spanish and English classrooms. Then it is time for morning circle. The *chékere* — a beaded gourd instrument — calls us to order. Each child says their name and the group responds and echoes. Echoes of names bounce back around the circle as we play the whispering name game. Yismilka/Yismilka, Rodney/Rodney, Maria/Maria. Frederick says Federico with a nervous smile. The game stops: Federico has changed his name over the long weekend.

"Federico, let me tell you a story of how I lost my name in third grade." I tell Federico and the class this story:

My name is Berta . . . Berrrrrr-ta. I was born in La Habana, Cuba. When I was in third grade my family moved to this country. I spoke no English. The folks at the school spoke no Spanish. Sadly, not one of my twelve blond, blue-eyed, third-grade guardian angels could say Berta. *"Bbbbbbb-eeeeee-rrrrrrrrrr . . . como tren, ferrocarril, tigre: rrrrrrrrrr . . ."* Not one. I decided that I had to teach my new classmates how to pronounce my name. I gave lessons during recess and after school. I recited the rhyme: *"Erre, con erre cigarro, erre con erre barril, rapido corren los carros sobre las lineas del ferrocarril."*

The teacher told me that I must change my name to something Americans could pronounce easily: Bertha. But there is no *thuh* sound in our Spanish. We are Cubans, we are not a colony of Spain, we do not use the royal lisp. I had to practice *th-th-th-th*, and discovered, instead, *zzzzzz* — another sound not found in Cuban Spanish.

At lunch the second week of school, I eyed the tray of grilled American cheese sandwiches and the white milk without sugar — food I could not eat. I was gagging at the prospect of swallowing that bland white stuff all at once — the food stuck in my throat, like the name they wanted me to adopt: Ber-thz-thz-thz . . . Ber-zzzz-a. Not my name, not my name! I lost my name, my spirit.

Frustrated and disappointed, I compromised by calling myself "Bert" while reluctantly answering to "Bertha." Without the support and encouragement of teachers and other adults, it took me ten years to reclaim my name, and with it my Cuban identity. But at eighteen years old I declared proudly, for all to hear: *¡No! Me llamo Berta. ¿Te gusta? Berta.*

"So Federico, I tell you this story so that you never give up your name. Keep on, Federico!" "Federico" we whisper back. The ritual call and response of names settles. Others around the circle share stories about their names, nicknames, and namesakes. Miguel was named after his father's favorite uncle. Marilyn carries the name of her great-grandmother who was an important matriarch. Kevonia was called Kiki by her sister, and now everyone calls her Kiki. Joshua has his father's name and his sister the name of their grandmother, who is still in Puerto Rico. Each name is a thread in the weave of the family heritage, regardless of the immigration route.

Chairs from the circle get shuffled back to the desks clustered in small groups. Students are in charge of much of the organization of the day. Rodney walks over to get the materials for his group. Maria is the "checker" this week. She pulls out the group's clipboard and begins to check for homework from each member of her group. Josymir, the group librarian, is collecting books signed out from our popular multicultural classroom library. I am going over last night's word problems with Jamar and Robert. The teachers' desk serves as a resource materials area. The agenda for the day, homework, schedules, and announcements are posted. The resource teacher joins us. The language arts class begins. Teaching within dual-language programs, we have found an inclusive structure for quality urban education.

The purpose of this chapter is to bring you into our classroom and share with you some of our successes. It is written in three parts. The first part describes the two-way bilingual program structure. The second exposes three principles that guide our teaching: (a) learning happens in relationships, (b) the arts develop students' cultural voices, and (c) writing is a gateway to literacy. The final part includes my reflections on best classroom practices.

Two-Way Bilingual Program Structure

In our program, the language of instruction is separated by classroom. There are two classrooms with one teacher for each language. I always use English in my classroom and Ramona always uses Spanish in hers. Two groups of students spend an equal amount of time in each language, rotating between Spanish and English classrooms biweekly. Each class group has a mix of students who speak Spanish or English as their native language. Students are becoming bilingual to varying degrees, depending on how long they have been in the two-way program. Teachers speak only one language, while students may use either language as they are acquiring the new language.

The language immersion in our classrooms is supported by team teaching. The team spends time coordinating the development of the curriculum so that it develops sequentially. We do not repeat teaching content. Students follow the development of ideas in one language at a time. For example, a child may start the math investigations unit on patterns in Spanish and finish it in English. In other cases, an entire unit will be presented in one language and then we move to studying the next unit in the other language. In each classroom, students who are at ease in both languages are resources to their peers in the learning process. Both languages are used as a tool for students to explore and interact with their world.

The integration of students from diverse cultural and linguistic backgrounds is achieved through cooperative learning groups. We do not believe in tracking or ability grouping. Children learn and play together with their peers, many of whom are neighbors in their community. Learning together, they are protected from the harm that segregated student groupings may cause to their spirit and ability to learn. In our child-centered classrooms, the children are language resources for one another. We take care to group students with mixed abilities in each cooperative group. For example, social studies curriculum includes building skills for cooperative learning, cross-cultural understanding, and conflict resolution. Each group will have members who are strong in English, Spanish, reading, writing, drawing, and so on. In our collaborative learning environment, differences are good and necessary for the success of the challenging work of learning in two languages. While there are many principles contributing to the effectiveness of our program, in the following pages I will focus on three that guide our work in the third-grade two-way bilingual program.

Learning Happens in Relationships

The most human aspect of learning is that it happens in a web of relationships with valued peers and ideas within the wider scope of the community. As classroom teachers we envision a web of relationships that creates a sense of belonging and inspires learning. The weave begins with a team of teachers comfortable with their cultural identities. These teachers then collaborate to create and manage a consistent structure and curriculum that respectfully engages children in cross-cultural learning experiences. Working in cooperative groups, students are engaged in the active exchange of ideas and experience producing a new cultural bounty. Children learn within this weave of relationships in our classrooms.

As a teacher, my intention is to orchestrate this web of relationships so that I value the knowledge that students bring while expanding upon it and presenting new challenges. When a classroom teacher is comfortable with her cultural identity, she can more easily inspire a sense of belonging for her diverse students. It is easier for me to know what questions to ask my students about their culture because I have gone through the process of affirming my own cultural identity. Being comfortable with my own cultural identity helps me to be more open to the cultures of others. I do not perceive other cultures as a threat to my own. For this reason, I believe that a cornerstone for student success in a bilingual-bicultural classroom setting is the teacher's relationship to her own cultural identity. As Cynthia Ballenger writes, "I do believe that teachers need to try to open up and to understand both our own assumptions and the cultural meaning that children from all backgrounds bring to school" (Ballenger, 1992, p. 207). Having comfort with and confidence in her personal cultural identity enhances a teacher's ability to nurture the cultural identity of diverse students.

A strong teaching team models the behaviors and attitudes essential to building a supportive learning environment. One primary feature of our instructional team that contributed to our strength was desire: we wanted to work together. Though we had known each other for a relatively short time, Ramona and I had *una afinidad, una simpatía* (an affinity) around our creative pedagogical styles. We both delight in the *chispa* (spark) of our Spanish-speaking Caribbean heritage and honor our students as our own. Our team is also rich in language resources; we each could teach in our strong academic language. When we began teaching together, we made an honest assessment of our strengths and divided areas of leadership. Two periods a week were set aside for planning and looking at student work. In reality, our dialogue was continuous and as open as the doors between our classrooms. Our two classrooms became one learning community where each teacher contributed her strengths to the process.

We also broadened our safety net of supportive relationships by participating in a study group with other teachers. The Becoming Bicultural Study Group was a two-year project. During the first year we read and discussed *Other People's Children* by Lisa Delpit and *Culture and Difference* by Antonia Darder. Our goal was to design a classroom-based research project that would enable us to reflect on our practice vis-à-vis the bicultural issues involved in the education of our students. The challenge as we saw it was to honor the family culture of our students, whether Latino or African American, while enabling them to adapt successfully to mainstream culture. Our meetings with other teachers were opportunities for critical thinking. They became our "watering holes" for encouragement and professional support.

Our relationship to our students' community and its cultural and linguistic knowledge is also important. Both Ramona and I want our learning community to inspire a sense of belonging in the children and a classroom environment that honors our students' backgrounds. For immigrant children, the loss of home makes the maintenance of cultural identity a matter of study and practice. For example, when we do not know the names of the creatures or the plants from our countries of origin, we gather natural science books, folktales, and songs that contribute to our research. After a while we can name birds: *el múcaro, el guaraguao, el pitirre*. In a bilingual and bicultural classroom, literacy is a form of cultural production. The stories from the oral tradition, dances, games, songs, riddles, textile arts, and festivals are all rich resources for cultural learning. It is a sense of belonging, of being wanted and important, that inspires students to participate in cross-cultural production.

"In this class you can learn Spanglish, African American English, Standard English, and Standard Spanish."

This story happened during a homework check in English language arts class. The homework was about verbs in the past tense. Rhonda's homework was questioned by Josefina. She wrote: "The girl had went around the corner in her homework. I wrote the girl had gone." In context Josefina was using the correct Standard English tense. Rhonda was referring to African American English. The students' teacher did not know how to deal with this discussion and she brought it to my attention. I in turn brought the question to the class. Out of the responses we created a language game with our homework assignment. "If you're really good in our class," I said, "you can learn four languages here: African American English, Spanglish, Standard English, and Standard Spanish. How many people here speak one of these languages?" We laughed and enjoyed a lively discussion comparing the similarities and differences among the four languages. We highlighted the creative nature of Spanglish, the African cultural roots of African American English, and the structure, rules, and academic importance of the standard languages. Finally, we were able to work through most of the verb tenses in the homework assignment in four languages. Once the children felt validated in their own language they could offer their expertise to the success of our class in four languages. As they felt at ease with their talk in our classroom, their written language blossomed.

The way we welcome our students and build close relationships with them enables them to learn better. Ramona sets the stage for this sense of belonging for our students in this way: third graders are lined up by the door of their new classroom on the first day of school. Ramona hugs each one as they enter and says, *"Tu eres mio"* (You are mine). This cultural gesture communicates to the children that they belong and that they are wanted.

A central welcoming piece at the beginning of the year is a blank world map. Students go home on the first day with an enlarged map of their state or country of origin to fill with illustrations and locations of family stories, celebrations, and memories of first days at school. This Family Map project opens a year-long series of family interviews on varied topics, such as "What is sound?" "What are the names of rocks and minerals in your country/neighborhood?" "What advice would you give your child to keep for their future?" The story maps bring to the classroom the first portraits of the families that make up our community. Soon, immigration routes, bright hummingbirds, tropical islands, and pictures of dinner tables adorn our world map. I remember the excitement of the first time that all of my students memorized their addresses with certainty. It was as if knowing their place in the world gave meaning to the street where they lived. The world map reminds me of how important it is for the success of our students to consider the whole before its categorical parts. This opening geographical exploration enables students to find their place in the big picture of the world and begins to establish a sense of belonging to our learning community.

Within our classroom walls we attend to beauty, color, and diverse cultural visual representation. Our bulletin boards celebrate our students' cultural art, and our classroom exhibits actively encourage students' relationship to their cultural backgrounds. Developing biculturalism in our Latino and African American students involves enculturation experiences for children with their own culture within the classroom. This work can be both scholarly research and renewing practice. For example, students learn stories from their own cultural backgrounds, or our classroom celebrations may include family recipes. It is important for the socialization process to include opportunities to interact successfully with the mainstream culture and develop critical awareness of that culture, as well as Standard English. For instance, we may visit a local university aerodynamics lab as part of our science unit on flight. We may compare and contrast Standard English and varied English dialects. We may participate in content analysis of media advertising, while checking for bias and stereotypes expressed about people of color in this country. The analysis takes the sting out of the intended demeaning media message and gives children the tools to control its effect.

Children's relationships with one another augment their learning, much as cooperative learning builds on the sense of belonging. Our students belong to each other, to the class, to their families, and to the community. Students must be taught many skills that are necessary for successful cooperative learning projects such as taking turns, giving ideas, encouraging, and listening, which are not commonly part of students' competitive learning experiences. Each week students participate in cooperative games and challenges that may focus on one or more skills. For example, one week students may seem to be having difficulty taking turns. During morning circle that week, students may play "Count to Ten" — a cooperative game that teaches taking turns. Our circle discussion then highlights the strategies students use to improve their ability to take turns. Cooperative skills also form part of the academic work in the group self-evaluation at the end of each cooperative experience. In every content area, students bring knowledge to the cooperative group work of problem-solving. For example, in a science class, groups were asked to contribute their discoveries to the question, "What is sound?" Family interviews contributed some answers and ideas: "Sound travels in waves." "You can feel the vibrations sound makes." "Sound travels through air and you can hear it under water." Such family knowledge contributes to the success of cooperative problem-solving. Each cooperative group then had to make a musical instrument from the materials supplied in their sound box. The experiments were designed to highlight various properties of sound.

As students articulate what they have learned, they are encouraged to appreciate individual differences. Maria tapped the bowl with water and saw the ripples bounce on the surface. Jose thought that the ripples must be the vibrations his father talked about during the prior night's homework interview. Joshua drew the poster illustrating their discovery. Natashia thought of other words for vibration and included some Spanish ones that her classmates came up with, like *timbre*. Positive peer interactions are an important feature of structured cooperative learning. Students credit other group members for their contributions, and the assignments illustrate how each member contributes to the group's success. Students discover, grasp, and understand new information, and then talk, teach, and write about it. Language in the science class has immediacy and meaning. Annette, one of our third-grade students, described a photograph of her cooperative group working during the science class:

> This picture is important because Robert, Franchesca, and I are working together. We are friends and brothers and sisters. I like the picture because we are a team from different places. We are coloring a paper together for science. This team likes science and math.

In order to maximize language learning, we make connections across disciplines whenever possible. For example, the sound theme weaves through math stories about rhythm in multiplication. In the language arts class, children use illustrated student-made books to re-tell the *Ayapá* story about how the drum got its echo. In these ways, students gain new words in their second language while deepening academic language based on shared learning experiences in the classroom.

In summary, when immersed in a theme, active learning in cooperative groups engages the whole child. In this fashion, students come to embrace ways of collaborating in order to gain new knowledge. This is particularly evident in an environment that inspires a sense of belonging and encourages diverse cultural expression. Fostering a sense of belonging, nurturing personal identity, and establishing high expectations facilitate the relationships that are essential to the learning process for our students (Delpit, 1995).

I have described how teachers with a strong sense of cultural identity can enhance student learning by cultivating relationships inside the classroom and with the surrounding community. These relationships humanize learning and form a foundation for literacy development through an integration of arts and writing. The next section describes the role of the arts in literacy development in two languages.

The Arts Develop Students' Cultural Voices

The arts give voice to the whole child. In our bilingual, bicultural classroom, the expression of students' cultural voices through the arts is the foundation for literacy development. Student voice "represents unique instances of self-expression, through which students affirm their own class, culture, racial and gender identities" (Giroux, 1988, p. 199, quoted in Darder, 1991, p. 66). Third grade is a critical year for children in developing a strong sense of identity, cultural voice, and pride in their family heritage, and in making connections between schooling and future work in the community (Kunjufu, 1995). Varied forms of cultural production, like portraits, stories, music, and textile arts, bring family culture into our classroom. Classroom knowledge can only have meaning if it is connected to everyday life. The arts in turn connect the work of the classroom to the world outside the school.

In our classroom, self-expression through portraiture plays an important role in positive identity formation and literacy development in two languages. "Claiming Our History and Our Future" is our year-long arts-based community service learning project, in which students create self-portraits, family portraits, and community portraits. These portraits, based on students' identities, generate critical comparisons of art across cultures and throughout the ages. Students create, display, and view their art in their community. In conversations with community artists, students can see that their issues and struggles with making art can lead to making a contribution to the community.

Self-portraits are symbolic representations of how a child sees herself and the world. In an artistic sense, self-portraits initiate a conversation from the child's point of view with her learning community. This conversation is based on a symbol system that comes directly from the child's own worldview, the familiar place from which she can articulate art and language more easily. As a child creates a self-portrait, she spends time imagining what colors and symbols represent her well. This happens much in the same way that language develops; we create the symbols that articulate what we want to say. Portraiture supports identity formation by broadening the child's personal vocabulary of self-expression.

Local artists have presented ways of creating self-portraits to our students. Two artists/educators, Francisco Mendez-Diez and Johnetta Tinker, introduced the group to the techniques of portraiture. Francisco and Johnetta taught basic art techniques, such as ways to mix colors or to use the canvas and the brush, while the museum provided quality art materials — canvas, acrylic paints, and brushes. Francisco's lessons were always in Spanish; Johnetta taught in English. They led small groups on gallery walks that focused on self-portraits from Spanish- and English-speaking cultures. Student artists worked in acrylics, clay, plaster of Paris, cloth, collages, and printmaking. They gained an insider's perspective on the realm of art and art making while increasing their expressive vocabulary.

Family portraits give students the opportunity to articulate their family's beauty and to connect the family with the classroom learning environment. It is important that children see that their home languages and cultures are valued in school. The reflection of family in the classroom creates a safe place where children can take the risks that are necessary in the learning process. For example, Maria draws a sketch of her mother and sister playing by the river in Puerto Rico. This sketch will gain texture and color in cloth for Maria's family quilt square. As she carefully cuts the pieces of cloth, she proudly tells her friend the story of her favorite family outing. Her family portrait joins the others in an artistic affirmation of the resources each child brings to our learning.

A sculpture project, Stepping into the Future, produces another family portrait that incorporates family values into our classroom. Students bring in their parents' old shoes to use in creating a collage about what they want to be when they grow up, complete with business card designs. Parents' advice to their children is written on paper plaques that are also embedded in these fantastical sculptures, such as what Sr. Feliciano said to his daughter: *"El dia de mañana*, you will need to connect with folks from different cultures and languages if you want to make a difference."

Community portraits provide an opportunity for students to describe the world they see around them and place themselves in it — to expand the classroom walls to include a real-world arena for learning. These explorations in art take us out of the classroom and into the neighborhood. MYTOWN — Multicultural Youth Tour of What's Now — has helped us to take our show on the road. Denise Thomas and Karilyn Crocket, the young directors of this community-based organization, have designed tours of public and private art in Massachusetts. On the public art tour they took us to see the mural at Villa Victoria, a housing development in the city. There they held a scavenger hunt, requiring that students find familiar objects in the mural and share stories of their significance. The mural included symbols that students could recognize and name. Collectively, students could articulate a great deal about the meaning of the community art piece that expressed something important about their cultural and family histories. At a nearby church, students created their own murals based on themes about their own lives — family foods, games they play, clothes they wear, and important people in their lives past and present. Later, writing about their mural designs formed part of their autobiographies.

MYTOWN's private art tour took us to meet artists whose work was on display at an exhibit in the Harriet Tubman House — a local social service agency. Our students met artists who were creating murals, using textiles, and telling their own view of the world through art. One of the most exciting aspects of this field experience was the students' enthusiasm — their questions whirled around the gallery rooms. They spoke personally with the curator, impressing us with their earnest focus and outspoken self-expression.

We display student art in various community and school venues. As students display their art, they analyze it in relationship to the different art forms in the community. Our students' art was on exhibit in a gallery at a local fine arts museum, but sadly, only one family ventured into the museum to view the show. This lack of attendance speaks to the museum's accessibility. In contrast, when students later had an opportunity to present their work at the school, the exposition was well attended by parents, students, and community members.

In addition to self, family, and community portraits, cultural arts such as storytelling bring our students' family cultures into direct relationship with literacy development. Personal stories and stories from the diverse cultures in our community form the content of our storytelling arts program. The program includes the teachers' preplanning session with the artist, weekly planning and development with other teachers, one professional development workshop for the entire staff, and one school-wide performance by the resident artist. Recently, with funding from the Massachusetts Cultural Council, our students participated in a twelve-session storytelling curriculum with Derek Burrows, a Massachusetts Folk Arts Fellow. Our third-grade students learned storytelling techniques that encourage audience participation and effective communication. All components of the program are conducted in Spanish and English. The storytelling curriculum is designed to enhance second-language acquisition, personal identity, and cross-cultural understanding. Students develop their awareness of their own cultures and gain an appreciation for cultural differences as they listen to one another. While participating in traditional tales, games, songs, personal stories, and other cultural arts, students practice the language skills necessary to succeed in a two-way bilingual education program. Students work in pairs or small groups to select stories, which they memorize through drawing a sequence of images from the stories. Students practice retelling the story and giving each other feedback. Movement gestures and call-and-response are two delightful storytelling skills that enhance their efforts. It is often difficult for the student storytellers to learn their stories and strengthen their performances, and working in groups eases the anxiety of being on stage. Eventually, each storytelling group schedules performances in classrooms throughout the school. Students document their gigs with photographs, but their smiles and body language tell the real story.

Through the storytellers we found that the Caribbean stories culturally connect African, English-speaking, and Latino cultural groups. These stories represent a fertile ground for building bridges among people from these varied cultural and language backgrounds, like our students in the two-way bilingual program.

In sum, our third-grade students find their cultural voice and develop literacy in two languages through their involvement with the arts. They learn to value multiple aspects of culture and language. Andrea, one of our students, wrote in her final evaluation:

> Culture is what you belong to. There are many skills I have learned through studying about my culture. I learned that a good interview should have questions that are not straight yes or no answers. You can express what you know about a culture by story-telling. All of the things that I have learned make me feel very special and lucky. It makes me feel like I belong somewhere and that I can do many things and learn new ones. Now, I feel that I'm not isolated. I feel happy that I can meet new cultures.

The quotation above indicates that students proclaim their place in the world as they create portraits and tell stories in their own voice. As Antonia Darder explains, "The development of voice and social empowerment go hand in hand as bicultural students peel away the layers of oppression and denial, undergo a deconstruction of the conditioned definitions of who they are, and emerge with a sense of their existence as historically situated social agents who can utilize their understanding of their world and themselves to enter into dialogue with those who are culturally different" (Darder, 1991, p. 69). Building on students' knowledge of family cultures, we can strengthen their academic abilities and literacy development in two languages.

Writing Is a Gateway to Literacy

Writing, the creation of symbol on a page, is an important step toward literacy. In our classrooms, writing accompanies the arts in the development of biliteracy. Artistic expression and writing are connected in that they are both symbol systems. In the process of making art, a child spends time with images before they take on shape, color, and texture in an art piece. In the same way, writing requires that a child spend time with ideas and bring them out in conversation before they take shape in a manuscript. Both forms of self-expression, arts and writing, have common requisites: a safe place to explore, a personal place to move from, and a community place to share both the process and the message. Many of the writing activities in our third-grade classrooms are based on art projects.

Autobiographical writing, journals, and publishing are three major components of our writing program. Autobiographical writing builds on a personal story and develops academic knowledge of Standard English.[1] Journals provide a safe place to express personal concerns, try out new ideas, and have exchanges in writing with the teacher. Publishing promotes effective communication through writing for general audiences.

Autobiographical writing is key to the positive cultural identity formation of children who have been inhibited by negative immigration experiences or racism. Student autobiographies are developed over the course of the year and represent self-discovery, family history, and future dreams. Autobiographies encourage children to reconnect with family stories and name the values in those stories that sustain them. It is significant that the experts on this writing assignment are also the protagonists. Yismilka's words from the introduction to her autobiography exemplify both depth in self-expression and quality writing in her second language:

> I see the world as a dark place. If people depended on helping and saving, we could make a vast difference. The world is a good place to grow in. If we stick together the large difference can take us to an incredible blossom.

We use "sheltering" strategies to enhance the quality of autobiographical writing. One sheltering language development strategy highlights students' prior knowledge in conversations held before writing. For example, sheltering for autobiographical writing may include building descriptive language through talk about family pictures or drawings. In the process of writing their autobiographies, students talk to their classmates about the family pictures. Using oral language, children elaborate with detail as they develop descriptive language for their written life stories. These ideas can be graphically organized for further development around a central theme. Word banks organized on large chart paper by categories — such as nouns (names), verbs (actions), adjectives (descriptions), or by topic — such as colors, feelings, textures, or geographical locations — are always on display and are added to by students as their vocabulary expands. Sheltering strategies also include the use of repetitive phrases such as "I know that it is a *piñata* because . . ." Students are asked to repeat the phrase and fill in as many descriptions of a piñata as they can. Invented spelling, oral dictation, and illustrated response to questions are also part of sheltering strategies for students who are beginning to develop literacy.

Another strong support for good autobiographical writing is simply discussing with students the criteria for evaluating a writing piece. For example, students were preparing artist statements for a schoolwide exhibit that would form part of their autobiographies. In writing, they had to describe the scene that was represented on their family quilt square. The best artist statements would meet the task (stay focused), use a variety of sentence structures, use details, use descriptive language (including smells, colors, adjectives, adverbs), and use good basic mechanics (spacing, margins, indentations, capital letters, spelling, and punctuation). We used a sample quilt square and generated lists of words that would visually describe the art piece by categories such as colors, textures, background, and foreground. The second part of the assignment required students to describe the art-making process. In preparation, they dictated a list of actions involved in making their quilt square. The list generated a repetitive pattern of sentences: "I chose the color . . . because it . . ." Clarifying the assignment, using visual cues, generating lists of words, and using repetitive language patterns are sheltering strategies that enable second-language learners to write effectively. These student-generated lists are resources for the whole class as they compose. The words and ideas have been experienced orally, visually, dramatically, and in writing. This allows for reciprocity between students and teachers. Both players are participants in the learning process and vocabulary development.

A variety of genuine writing experiences is woven throughout our day by the frequent use of journals, which accompany many of our classroom activities: morning journals, math journals, science journals, end-of-the-day journals — though different in content, all these journals provide a safe place for students to try out ideas. I respond to the journals regularly. The personal nature of these exchanges allows me to build friendships with my students and a sense of trust. The interactive morning journal opens the day with a personal dialogue and is written in freestyle. Poems or illustrations may be the communicative symbol system on any given morning. There is something peaceful and gentle about morning journal time. While music plays softly, children sit quietly at their desks and make their transition from home to the work of school as they read and respond to my comments. Both reading and writing form part of our written conversations. The following is a poem from a student's morning journal:

Shhhhh.
Listen! to the sound
Higher than the ground
We are black,
We are white
they are not so tight.
We are Puerto Rican,
We are Dominican,
We are Chinese,
We are Cuban,
We will hold hands and stand.
We are Japanese,
We are Indian,
We are together forever.
Together forever.
(from *I Am Black* by Myeshia)

End-of-the-day journals are strictly academic in nature. A special book with a beautiful cover and quality paper is purchased for this purpose. At the end of the day, one student leads the class in a discussion that generates three main ideas that were learned during the day. Three other students write these in complete sentences on the board. The day closes as students enter their summary of the learning for the day in their end-of-the-day journal. Content-area journals, such as literature-response and math journals, also provide a review and confirmation of the main ideas covered in a lesson or unit.

Our many forms of journaling are important tools for written communication, review, and documentation of academic gains. In telling, writing, and presenting themselves to the world, students realize reciprocity in learning — that is, that students are also teachers.

Bringing student writing to real-world audiences through publishing or the Internet also promotes effective communication skills. One such publication project over the Internet resulted when third and fifth graders in our school worked together on math stories in their math journals, writing stories about their everyday lives with numbers. News about a bilingual Internet exchange project called De Orilla a Orilla inspired our students. A group of teachers in New York, California, and Puerto Rico were facilitating exchanges between Spanish and English bilingual students through the Internet. Students wanted to participate even though we did not have Internet access in the class-room.

Our students' math journals contain stories and describe ways of thinking about math. They write, for example, about how they solved a problem, and include real-life math stories. They enjoyed their math journals and wanted to share them with other students. We decided to participate in De Orilla a Orilla by using the Internet connection on my computer at home. Students prepared the following announcement for the project on the Internet:

Math Journals Take Us across Grades and across Cyberspace

Warm Greetings from Chilly Boston:

We are students in third and fifth grade classes in a two-way bilingual program in Greater Boston. You might be wondering what it means to be a two-way bilingual program (two x bi = multi?). We are African American and Latino kids who are learning about one another's cultures and languages. We study math, science, and social studies in Spanish and English. In math class we have been keeping a math journal and writing math stories with the ideas we are discovering in math class.

Here are some ideas we have been writing about:

The Community We Have Multiplied

In math class we were multiplying, multiplying, multiplying. We read Anno's *Mysterious Multiplying Jar.* We wrote our own versions of the Multiplying Jar set in our own communities. Would you like to write with us? Please send us your stories and let us know if you would like to read ours.

I sent the message from my computer at home. A few weeks later, I printed the responses and brought them into class. Although the exchange was difficult to maintain without classroom access to the Internet, this collaboration across grade levels strengthened the writing for both groups as they presented their work to an international audience. The literacy circle is complete when children take what they have learned in the classroom and use it in their experiences with the outside world.

Another example of student publishing was preparing student stories in book form for the classroom library. Including quality student writing in the multicultural library inspired children to write their own versions of stories that were popular with the class. One reading group was reading science fiction with animal characters. Their favorite was *Catwings* by Ursula LeGuin. This story takes place in an urban setting; the wings saved the cats from a terrible fate. Stories sprouted from our students about urban animal families with liberating anatomy. Final edited versions were included in the library for classmates to read.

To summarize, as classroom teachers we emphasize varied ways of developing literacy through writing. Autobiographies, journals, and publishing projects encourage children to express themselves through writing. Second-language learners benefit from sheltering strategies to support the development of their academic language. Children write to be read when their work is validated through publishing.

Reflections on Best Classroom Practices

How have we created a learning environment that honors the diverse family cultures of students living in a racist society? How have we developed literacy in two languages within a standards-driven curriculum? I will attempt to answer these questions, and in so doing, reveal the pedagogical character of our approach to teaching in our two-way bilingual third-grade classroom.

The first thing we do is to make sure that our students feel loved, welcome, and respected. We use physical gestures and personal stories to make it clear to our students that "this classroom is yours and you are mine."

We take care to call the children by the names that were given to them by their families. We know that it is not easy to hold on with pride to our lifeline of family, culture, and language if we belong to any group that is undervalued in these United States of America. We also know that without this, learning will be inhibited.

Students are encouraged to contemplate the strengths, joys, and nurturing experiences of their family life in order to represent it in their beautiful art works. But we don't stop there. Their family voice is imprinted on maps, math journals, science experiments, and future plans. And we don't stop there, either. Our students not only have to know very well where they live and where they are from, they must also know where that is in the world.

We use artistic strategies to develop voice in our students. Portraits and storytelling help us to get to know our students. We want to get to know their thinking and offer them many venues for expressing themselves: self-portraits, family portraits, community portraits, masks, murals, autobiographies, and poetry. Paulo Freire and Donaldo Macedo say it this way: "Understanding the oppressed's reality, as reflected in the various forms of cultural production — language, music, art — leads to a better comprehension of the cultural expressions through which people articulate their rebelliousness against the dominant" (Freire & Macedo, 1987, quoted in Darder, 1991, p. 90). We nurture resistance to the dominant culture through art projects that strengthen positive identity formation.

We find strong connections between art, oral language, writing, and reading that support both first- and second-language learning. Bringing student work before real-world audiences is a key motivational factor in every case of cultural production. Certainly there are other factors that are critical to the effective education of our students. However, this chapter highlights the classroom teacher's power to use instructional strategies that develop children's abilities to learn while developing dual literacy.

Our pedagogy is clearly structured upon the human need for relationship. We teachers are unified in our expectations for our students. Our consistency is unshakable, and this serves as a model for students in their cooperative groups. Our work did not evolve in isolation. The children see that we are supported by the families and community-based agencies involved with our curriculum. We have found that our sphere of influence within our school is strengthened by the community involvement in our classroom.

We are convinced that learning truly happens in relationships, and thus insist that our students learn in relationships within and beyond the classroom. Schools systematically respond to cultural differences with traditional policies, such as tracking and ability grouping, that adversely affect children's ability to learn (Massachusetts Advocacy Center, 1990). We count on the involvement of families and our community and see collaboration among teachers, students, families, and the community as the foundation for accelerating student achievement. We can create a learning environment that honors the diverse family cultures of our students within a racist society through this web of relationships.

These, then, are answers to the questions that opened this chapter, questions that inspired the creation of our two-way bilingual third-grade program. It is the brief beginning of a program that we have developed over a two-year period. It is an experiment of hope for the development of our multilingual and multi-ethnic community. The vision that drives our teaching is to play a part in transforming our fragmented society so that the future citizens of Boston know and value one another as allies with cultural and linguistic resources.

Note

1. Autobiographical writing meets the systemwide standards for language arts. What is not included in the standards is an approach that helps second-language learners to develop literacy.

References

Anno, M. (1983). *Anno's mysterious multiplying jar*. New York: Philomel Press.

Ballenger, C. (1992). Because you like us: The language of control. *Harvard Educational Review, 62*, 199–208.

Cummins, J. (1986). Empowering minority students: A framework for intervention. *Harvard Educational Review, 56*, 18–36.

Darder, A. (1995). *Culture and difference: Critical perspectives on the bicultural experience in the United States*. Westport, CT: Bergin & Garvey.

Darder, A. (1991). *Culture and power in the classroom*. Westport, CT: Bergin & Garvey.

Delpit, L. (1995). *Other people's children: Cultural conflict in the classroom*. New York: New Press.

Dentzer, E., & Wheelock, A. (1990). *Locked in/locked out: Tracking and placement practices in Boston public schools*. Boston: Massachusetts Advocacy Center.

Ferdman, B. (1991). Literacy and cultural identity. In M. Minami & B. P. Kennedy (Eds.), *Language issues in literacy and bilingual/multicultural education* (pp. 347–371). Cambridge, MA: Harvard Educational Review.

Freire, P. (1991). Adult literacy process as cultural action for freedom. In M. Minami & B. P. Kennedy (Eds.), *Language issues in literacy and bilingual/multicultural education* (pp. 248–265). Cambridge, MA: Harvard Educational Review.

hooks, b. (1994). *Teaching to transgress: Education as the practice of freedom*. New York: Routledge.

Kunjufu, J. (1995). *Countering the conspiracy to destroy Black boys*. Chicago: African American Images.

Nieto, S. (1992). *Affirming diversity: The sociopolitical context of multicultural education*. New York: Longman.

Ogbu, J. (1987). Variability in minority responses to schooling: Nonimmigrants vs. immigrants. In G. Spindler & L. Spindler (Eds.), *Interpretive ethnography of education* (255–278). Hillsdale, NJ: Lawrence Erlbaum Associates.

Rivera, R., & Nieto, S. (Eds.). (1993). *The education of students in Massachusetts: Issues, research and policy implications*. Boston: University of Massachusetts, Boston, Mauricio Gaston Institute.

Resources

Museum of Fine Arts Artful Adventures Program
Francisco Mendez-Diez and Johnetta Tinker
Education Department, Avenue of the Arts
465 Huntington Avenue
Boston, MA 02115-5523
617-369-3303

MYTOWN—Multicultural Youth Tours of What's Now
Denise Thomas and Karilyn Crocket
554 Columbus Avenue, 4th Floor
Boston, MA 02118
617-536-8696

Pleasant and Company Publications
(Publishers of the Addy Books)
P.O. Box 620991
Middleton, WI 53562-0991
608-836-4848

Primary Source-Social Studies and Global Education
Anne Watt and Anna Roeloffs
P.O. Box 381711
Cambridge, MA 02238
617-923-9933

Thompsons Island Outward Bound
Experiential Education and Cooperative Challenges
Boston Harbor Islands
Boston, MA 02127
617-328-3900

Teaching For Change/Networks on Educators on the Americas
P.O. Box 73038
Washington, DC 20056
202-238-2379
necadc@aol.com

Books on Cooperative Learning and Conflict Resolution

Spencer Kagan
Cooperative Learning: Resources for Teachers
Kagan Cooperative Learning
P.O. Box 5589
San Clemente, CA 92674-5589
800-266-7576.

William J. Kreidler
Elementary Perspectives: Teaching Concepts for Peace and Conflict
Educators for Social Responsibility
23 Garden Street
Cambridge, MA 02138

Karl Rohnke
Silver Bullets: A Guide to Initiative Problems, Adventure Games,
    Stunts and Trust Activities
Project Adventure
P.O. Box 100
Hamilton, MA 01936

Bilingual in Two Senses[1]

CYNTHIA BALLENGER

I n this chapter, I explore the learning that took place in a science classroom of immigrant Haitian children. In general, these children did not arrive in the United States with a strong background in science, and their families did not have the opportunity to receive a great deal of formal schooling before leaving Haiti. In examining what these children have to offer to a science curriculum and to views of learning, I consider two pedagogical premises that were central in their classroom: 1) the use of the students' first language, Haitian Creole, provided an easier way for them to communicate and was a resource for their learning; and 2) the students' own everyday experiences with scientific phenomena — and their interpretations of these experiences — played a central part in developing their science knowledge.

Haitian Creole is a language that has not had a long association with formal schooling. It originated among slaves brought to Haiti from different places in Africa, whose only common language was the French of the colonizers. Few scientific papers have been written in Haitian Creole, although there are an increasing number of literary works in the language. One might assume that Haitian Creole lacks the technical vocabulary, the precise language needed in serious talk about science.

Furthermore, talk in science is generally regarded as highly specialized, quite different from the ways of thinking and knowing that are part of less formal experiences. Problems arise when teachers attempt to include in the curriculum the voices and experiences and interpretive frameworks of all their students, particularly students whose background does not include regular schooling. Such students also often lack the out-of-school educational experiences and ways of talking that many educated families are able to provide (Ballenger, 1997; Heath, 1983; Snow & Ninio, 1986). These students may seem to have enormous gaps in their knowledge. To many teachers they don't even seem able to speak precisely or "correctly," and their view of a topic may seem impossibly wide or confused. Many educators feel that the science classroom is the least conducive to the mixing of approaches, experiences, and points of view that occur when the voices of diverse students are raised (Hudicourt-Barnes, 1999).

To counter this view, I have analyzed pieces of two all-class science discussions and part of an interview with one child, all on the topic of insect growth and development. I hope to give a sense of the many forms of participation — such as jokes, arguments, personal references, religious opinions — that these students bring to these discussions. I also hope to show that, while these various ways of talking are not typically considered important components of learning science, in this case the students use both the syntax and the everyday genres of participation of their first language to build on and extend their knowledge of insects and metamorphosis.

Language Issues

The science classroom I discuss in this chapter is one in which children with vastly differing exposure to science participated in an inquiry-based science program driven by their own questions about the world, within parameters set by the teachers, such as ant biology and pond ecology (Ballenger, 1997; Rosebery, Warren, & Conant, 1992; Warren & Rosebery, 1996; Warren, Rosebery, & Conant, 1994). The students were in from the fifth through the eighth grade and all spoke Haitian Creole, which was the primary language of their science work, although the texts used were usually written in English.

The questions the students asked were pursued in small groups of students, who did library research and developed "hands-on" observational and experimental procedures to answer their questions. Because the questions came from the students, the teachers did not always know the answers or even, at times, exactly what the student meant. Thus, discussions in this classroom had little of the default format identified by various researchers as typical of U.S. classrooms in which teachers pose the questions and evaluate the replies; rather, the teacher's attention was necessarily focused on the question itself and on what the questioner wanted to express. This focus on the student's intentions opened up a new structure of participation. Students spoke to other students, for example, and what was acceptable as a contribution to the discussion expanded to include jokes and stories, arguments and personal theories. Students were able to draw on knowledge, experiences, and conversational styles from many areas of their lives.

Thus, in this classroom, science learning was supported by bilingualism in two senses: first, students spoke in their first language, in this case Haitian Creole, as they developed their English ability; second, and of equal importance, students were able to draw upon their familiar, everyday ways of characterizing, organizing, theorizing, and arguing about the phenomena of the natural world as they developed less familiar ways that are strictly associated with science. I argue that using their first language was of tremendous benefit to their thinking in both senses. Their deep knowledge of Haitian Creole and their facility with its syntax and vocabulary allowed them to refine distinctions and to express subtle nuances of meaning. The use of their own questions as curriculum led them into familiar storytelling and argument styles, grounding the curriculum in "their voices and lives," and thus enlarging and elaborating on the areas of contact between what they knew about the world and what they wanted to know about science.

One might ask, Where does such an entry point lead? When scientists talk, their discourse is often highly formal, remote from personal experiences and the stories told about it. The relationship between words seems almost more important than the relationship between the experience and the word for it. As Halliday and Martin (1993) claim, "Technical terms organize the world in a different way than do everyday ones. . . . [They] imply taxonomies which organize reality differently to common sense" (pp. 205–206). These students are starting from personal experience and everyday ways of talking. Further, it is often said about children who speak a Creole language, and those who speak nonstandard dialect as well, that their language doesn't contain the ability to speak technically, to use scientifically precise terms, that there's something always nonformal about the way they express things since these languages have rarely been used in academic conversation and writing. One purpose of this chapter is to explore the way these students use their first language — in both senses — in developing scientific ways of exploring and presenting ideas.

The Participants

The students in my study had been in this country less than three years and had received varying amounts of schooling in Haiti. Some had gone to schools in which they had received a French-style education, while others had gone to school only irregularly in underfunded schools in which the teachers were educated only a few years beyond their pupils.

The teachers were all members of the Chèche Konnen Center,[2] where they had been meeting for a number of years with other teachers who had concerns about some of their bilingual students and their success in science (Warren & Rosebery, 1995). This group had developed an interest in what were called "science talks," which are discussions in which student talk is primary. The teacher often follows the students' sense of topic and their way of making connections. In many cases the teacher is surprisingly quiet (see Gallas, 1995, for her account).

The Setting

This is a transitional bilingual classroom, so the children are typically in it for three years or less. However, models of language use in bilingual classes — transitional, immersion, etc. — never seem to me to address the particularities of real classrooms. There are three teachers in this classroom. Pat is an ESL teacher who's primarily responsible for the seventh and eighth graders. She speaks only rudimentary Haitian Creole, although she is learning more. She addresses some of the latest arrivals in Creole as best she can, hoping they will understand her. Students who might otherwise choose to speak Creole often address Pat in English so she will understand. Sylvio is primarily responsible for the fifth and sixth graders. He speaks Haitian Creole, fluent English, and a number of other languages. Laura is the science teacher. She is a monolingual English speaker at this point, although she has various connections to the Haitian community. Her involvement in the science curriculum in this classroom is beyond her ordinary responsibilities.

The science talks typically take place in Haitian Creole because the three teachers feel that the students are best able to express their ideas in their native language. Sylvio is usually in charge of them for the entire class. However, this varies with circumstances. For example, most science texts that they use are in English, and the discussion around these texts sometimes continues in English as well. The students, for their own reasons, at times choose English.

Metamorphosis

This science talk took place after the class had spent some weeks watching mealworms move through stages of metamorphosis. On this day the students are working their way through a text on the subject. The text is in English. The students are reading the English, then discussing what they have read paragraph by paragraph in Creole. Manuelle, after reading what a huge amount the larvae eat before they turn into pupae, asks somewhat rhetorically: Why, if people eat and eat they don't change their skin, they don't transform, the way insects do? Sylvio, the teacher, asks the students to comment on her question. They put the book away and a science talk ensues. I will tell the story of this science talk; the full transcript is in the appendix.

After Manuelle asks why people don't change if they eat a huge amount, one child reminds her that our skin does peel.

Manuelle replies, "But we don't transform."

Fabiola says, "God did not create us like insects"; she evidently means that's why we don't transform.

Raoul brings in basketball: "If you play basketball, you get dirty; when you bathe, your skin comes off with the dirt." He is suggesting that we do, like the larvae, change our skin.

Marianne responds to this claim: "It's not all people who do that." She gets up to demonstrate how slowly some people walk, implying that they don't play hard and get all dirty and then change some of their skin while bathing.

Joel says that he has learned on television that your skin rubs off inside your clothes.

Stefan, a new student, makes a general declaration: "People and animals aren't the same thing." He agrees with Fabiola perhaps, in thinking that God didn't make us like that.

Jean-Charles then addresses his response to Manuelle's initial question:

> "Manuelle, skin changes. It's like, the larva, when it was inside the egg, you, like when you were inside your mother's stomach. It's like when you were a little baby. When you were born, when you were a little baby, you had hardly any hair. Didn't that change? Don't you have hair?"

At this point the kids explode. Manuelle says not all babies are born without hair. Marianne wants to distinguish growth from change: "You grow, you don't change," she tells Jean-Charles. Jean-Charles responds to Marianne on the question of change versus growth, saying, "When you were a baby, your eyes were closed." His implication is that they clearly aren't closed anymore, thus she *has* changed. Joanne appeals to the teacher as she points out that Manuelle now and Manuelle as a baby do not look the same — Manuelle has changed. Manuelle stands up to exclaim, "Do I change my skin like this, *vloop vloop?*" pretending to unzip her skin and climb out of it.

Analysis

I see this conversation as a negotiation over what the term *change* might mean in the context of making sense of experiences with insects.

Manuelle's first question combines both changing skin and changing form in metamorphosis. As the children at first focused on changing skin, Manuelle reminded them that she was also thinking of transformation, change of form. In the end, with her "*vloop vloop,*" one doesn't know if she is referring only to the movement of a larva out of a whole skin, or if she also has some view of movement — from, say a pupa to a beetle — included in her idea of vloop vloop. In any case, she takes the position that there are differences between what these insects do and what humans do — she doesn't think it's the same.

The skin-change question has led some children to claim the opposite. They have learned that humans do slough off their skin playing basketball, as Raoul suggests, or inside their clothes or from sunburn, and so they argue that in this case human processes and insect processes are the same — humans change skin and so do insects — we all do.

Jean-Charles represents the broadest usage of *change*. He says, "Manuelle, skin changes" as his opening claim. He then goes on to give an example that is not skin change, but a change of form: the larva is like the embryo. He then adds growing hair, another sign of change, which, he seems to be claiming, is comparable in some way to the changes of metamorphosis. He points out to Joanne, when she challenges him by saying we grow, we don't change, that her eyes are open now, and they probably weren't at birth. Jean-Charles seems to want to use *change* to refer to any number of differences and developments, such as height, more hair, and open eyes, as well as the development from a larva to a pupa, from embryo to newborn. According to Jean-Charles, all animals change over time, insects and humans. He seems to see metamorphic change, changing skin, and hair growth as all essentially the same.

There are a number of critiques of this broad usage. First, there are Stefan and Fabiola, who don't seem to think people and animals should be compared. In some sense the whole discussion is a response to this point of view, but a discussion on a biological plane that asks in what ways they can be compared.

Both Manuelle and Marianne first point out that the examples Jean-Charles and some of the others are giving are not true without exception; not all people play basketball, not all babies are born without hair, the way — and this part is implicit, unarticulated by the girls — all mealworms move through skin change and metamorphosis. Their work with mealworms has focused on finding a pattern in their skin changes: at what size, at what age, and how many? The two girls evidently have a sense that change as they want to use it in relation to mealworm growth refers to a sequence that is inviolable, a pattern that is secure and doesn't vary with individuals.

Manuelle critiques the broad usage of change on another front, however, when she argues that changing skin as she sees it is "*vloop vloop*," the way a larva gets out of an old skin, not the way old skin gradually is replaced among human beings. As she demonstrates, larva skin is replaced all of a piece.

These students are asking, Is there more than one kind of change? Will one word do, or do we need more than one? What distinctions should they make if we do? The students are negotiating what distinctions matter in this context. Certainly Jean-Charles is right in saying we all change; in some contexts it might even be appropriate to talk about the metamorphosis of a young child into an adult. But what are the crucial features of change in this conversation, with these intentions? The crucial features vary depending on what you want to figure out. In their attempt to understand their mealworms' life cycle, and to understand it in some relation to their own, they have created a need to sort out a particular version of what matters in insect and human development.

Metamorphosis is, as they have suggested, a series of distinct stages; it is not a kind of change that is noticeably gradual and continual. It follows a reliable pattern — it does not differ by individuals like hair growth might, or the ability or desire to play basketball. The students are getting at the basis for the use of the terms *grow* and *develop* in biology, the former with its reference to continuous change and the latter with its reference to reliably patterned transformation from one discrete stage to the next.

Kinds of Participation

Science talks vary and teachers use them in different ways, but this kind of conversation is not unusual. What we see here is that the children are bringing their everyday reasoning, their ways of talking and making sense into contact with the issues in science that they are exploring. They are using their familiar ways of talking as a resource to help them as they think. The students with little schooling background participate fully as much as those with strong academic backgrounds. Let me note a few of the features of this science talk:

- Students are speaking in their first language, a Creole language not known for its scientific vocabulary.
- Sylvio hears Manuelle's question, which could easily be heard as a joke, as serious, and stops what he is doing so that the group can address it in a science talk. He presumably does not get through his plan for the day because he does this instead.
- Sylvio's main function is to facilitate student turns. This is not all he does in teaching science, but it is what he generally does during science talks.
- The students talk to each other and in a manner that is more associated with social situations outside of school. There are jokes and

disagreement, and references to religion as well as basketball, bathing, and old people. There are physical demonstrations, dramatic enactments of ideas, such as Manuelle's "*vloop vloop*," or Marianne's slow old people.

This conversation demonstrates how the children's everyday ways of talking and thinking support multiple ways to begin to talk about growth and development. Their familiarity with each other and their deep knowledge of their first language allowed them to joke and tease, on the one hand, and to probe meanings and imagine change in insects and in people on the other. I don't see these everyday ways of talking and theorizing as being in opposition to scientific ways, or even as fully distinct from them. They clearly seem to be resources that support deep intellectual engagement.

Jean-Charles

These students have taken some first steps into scientific discourse in this discussion, but how far will their jokes and their loose metaphors lead them toward a truly scientific usage and outlook? To consider where this discourse leads as they continue their work with insects, I will focus on one child, Jean-Charles, and on the particulars of his use of language in science.

Jean-Charles is a thin, bespectacled Haitian boy who was in fifth grade during the previous conversation. His older brother Raoul is also in this multigrade bilingual classroom, and Jean-Charles appears to rely on him somewhat, perhaps because they arrived together from Haiti and lived with an aunt for a number of months before their father was able to join them. Their mother didn't manage to come until the following year.

Jean-Charles comes from a religious family. The two boys are at church several nights a week, where Jean-Charles plays the drum. They are respectful and diligent at school; both boys speak very softly. Jean-Charles is a fairly solemn child, not a storyteller or a joker like many of his classmates. It frequently takes him a long time to begin to speak, and the class often has to wait while he formulates his thoughts. He is always the last child ready to move on, no matter what the activity. His desk is a catastrophe. He is considered to have difficulty organizing language both in English and in Haitian Creole, and has been referred to special education for this problem. His drawings, on the other hand, are admired by his classmates. They are very detailed, full of shading and texture. He was one of a small number of students granted scholarships to the local art college one summer. He is considered by his teachers to be a gentle boy, perhaps too gentle, one who often won't defend himself even when provoked. The other boys like him nevertheless, and even the more aggressive, outspoken ones seem to enjoy his company.

I include this description partly to point out that Jean-Charles is considered a special education student, and to give a sense of the varied and difficult experiences he has had. These features lead many of us to expect less from such a child. I will claim that, within the context of this classroom, where many approaches and experiences are considered relevant, Jean-Charles is a fully capable science student who in fact shows signs of innovative ways of thinking and of using both Haitian Creole and English. Further, I think the details of his expression show us more clearly than most general statements what it might mean to develop a scientific view.

Interview Text

In the discussion, if you remember, Jean-Charles was proposing a very broad use of the term "change," which covered everything from the stages of development to the growth of hair and the opening of eyes. Here he is describing a beetle. I will include the Creole because I want to make a point about how he is using the grammar of his first language to help himself distinguish the kinds of change in the phenomena in front of him:

> *Li gen yon pakèt de chanjman. Premye chanjman an se lè l te ti bebe li vin gran epi, dezyèm chanjman an li vin toumen yon pupa. Twazyèm chanjman an epi li vin tounen yon beetles.*

> It has a whole bunch of changes. The first change is when it was a baby it got bigger, then the second change it turned into a pupa. The third change it turned into a beetle.

Jean-Charles is saying that the beetle goes through a lot of changes. The larva grows, then it gets bigger. And then, after a certain period, it turns into first a pupa and then a beetle. He calls all these phenomena *chanjman* (changes), reminiscent of his use in the conversation of a broad definition of change that includes everything from metamorphosis to growing hair. But here he seems to be making a distinction he didn't make before. I am particularly impressed by the words he chooses to make this distinction, which may be a newly acquired or newly relevant distinction for him in this context:

vin(i) gran means *become big,* and he uses this for growth.

Vin(i) tounen includes the idea of becoming (vini) and of turning into or transforming (tounen), and this he uses for *change to another form.*

He uses *vini* as a part of both meanings and changes the second term to distinguish the kinds of becoming. There are other Creole words he could have used: he could have used *grandi* (grow) for "larva," *transfôme* (transform) for "turn into" — *transfôme* is what Manuelle used to begin the conversation we explored earlier, and *grandi* was used by Joanne and others in that conversation. But by including *vini* in both phrases, he preserves a sense that, while both "become," one becomes big and one becomes something else. The sense of contrast as well as of similarity is represented iconically in the phrases he chooses — one common to both phrases, one different. Having sorted these kinds of change into two terms that he perhaps once regarded as essentially the same, he chooses by the words he uses to mark the sense that they are both aspects of the same thing.

Haitian Creole happens to have in its syntax the capacity to place many verbs next to each other in what are known as serial verb constructions; thus Jean-Charles can say *vini tounen,* literally "become turn into," which sounds quite odd in English. I would suggest that Jean-Charles makes use of this capacity of Creole syntax to explore his developing sense of aspects of change.

As a result of its historical usage, Haitian Creole may not contain a great deal of technical terminology in biology but, like any language, the potential for clarity is there. Languages are enormously flexible tools, and there seem to be few limits to the ways in which someone who is thinking hard can find to make them work.

Later in the same interview Jean-Charles, of his own volition, switches into English and, in speaking about ants, he uses the English terms *grow* and *develop* to work further with these same two aspects of change:

the eggs develop, um, they, the eggs become, um grow, the eggs growing bigger bigger bigger bigger til it's um develop and when it's finished it could be a queen or a worker.

Here he again develops a creative use of terminology, this time in English, to distinguish the types of change he sees within the processes of one organism. He starts by saying the eggs develop, then backtracks to say they grow, which they don't, although the larvae inside, which can be seen, do. The eggs [or actually larvae] grow "bigger, bigger, bigger." This they do "till it's um develop and when it's finished it could be a queen or a worker." When he uses "develop" here he is concerned with radical changes of form. He uses what must for him be a past participle "develop[ed]," focusing on the over-and-doneness of the change; he marks this again in the next phrase, "when it's finished." Thus he doubly marks the sense that the focus in development is on the endpoint. This latter was Manuelle's *"vloop vloop"* point — some growth is continuous, other growth is over and done with. In contrast, when he is referring to continuous growing he uses a present participle with a comparative and repeats the comparative three times: "growing bigger bigger bigger." The focus here is clearly on the sense of the continuousness, not on the endpoint, and the sense of ongoing process is almost onomatopoetically presented here with the repetitions of bigger. Again we have the sense from the way he puts these terms together that, in English, as in Creole, Jean-Charles is particularly interested in his sense of the way these terms contrast with each other, the distinctions that they make together. He began, during the whole-class discussion, articulating a rather undifferentiated view of growth; now he has these two aspects of growth, central ones for biology, existing in some sort of defining contrast.

As Halliday and Martin stated above, in science, words and concepts exist in relation to each other — scientific terms are seen as part of frameworks of explanation, which contribute to the definition: you can't understand tension without compression and a theory of forces is implicit in fully understanding them both. The full significance of the terms *invertebrate* and *vertebrate* may require a sense of the place of each within evolutionary history. I think Jean-Charles is using, first of all, the language he knows best, Haitian Creole, and then English, as a tool to map out the territory of growth and development in a similarly broad conceptual landscape. He has, I would suggest, some distance from these terms — he is aware of them as terms in relation to each other, with definitions that he seeks to refine. He has moved from an unexamined everyday usage to a view that suggests an awareness of language itself. He is labeled a special education student, a bilingual student who has particular difficulties with language, and yet he is demonstrating a creative and subtle way of working with words and thought.

Using their first language in both senses, these students have opened up a concept and explored the requirements for its differing use in a particular area of science. Although I have shared final data on only one student, I suggest that in many ways, many of these students have developed a view of growth and development, and a way of expressing it, that we would regard as an important part of scientific thinking and scientific language.

Conclusion

These students were in a bilingual classroom where they worked in science using their first language. If these students were in a content-based ESL class or a mainstream class with teachers who did not speak Haitian Creole, the conversation would undoubtedly have been much more limited. In a mainstream classroom it is frequently the case that the second-language speakers do not participate at all. If only for reasons such as these, native language use is crucial for teaching.

Of course, by itself native language use is but one characteristic of good bilingual science classes. I would argue that good science teaching for bilingual students requires bilingualism in two senses. We need classrooms in which students can use their first language, and we also need discussions, "science talks," that provide a space for the power and thinking that these Haitian students have shown us exists in their everyday language.

Unfortunately, the sort of curriculum these students experienced, one driven by student questions, including hands-on investigations, the use of written resources, and the sort of discussions Jean-Charles and Manuelle participated in, is in no way typical of our schools. We need to try different ways to organize the talk in our classrooms, to organize our curriculum. Our classrooms, particularly those for bilingual students or other students who aren't considered "advanced, " rarely make room for students' questions, for their way of constructing the topic, for their connections, for their jokes. And when we do make room, as I said at first, it is not always easy to hear the science and the seriousness in the rollicking talk that sometimes results. The discussion we just explored was in many ways a rollicking talk. All the thinking and the value that appears in that discussion when you do an analysis afterward was not obvious at the moment — it seemed mainly full of jokes and challenges. That it was allowed to go on was based on trust, the teacher's trust that the students were making sense and making progress. Sylvio, the teacher, trusted that this everyday language, this rollicking talk, and their first language, Haitian Creole, were more than adequate to the task of exploring metamorphosis; he trusted that jokes are part of thinking, that familiar talk in a Creole language has the capacity for subtlety, that his way was not the only way of constructing the topic, that his students were intelligent, had questions and serious intentions, and that they wanted to know.

As educators, we often feel we are being kind and compassionate when we say that children whose parents don't speak English, who were not able to be educated themselves, who work too hard to talk to their children about their homework or read storybooks to them, cannot do the same things in school that children with college-educated parents can. We know these poor children are intelligent, we say, but they haven't had certain advantages. How can we expect as much from them? I would like to suggest that one assumption we are making when we say this sort of thing is that the way these children speak in their homes, in their everyday language, does not contain the same capacity for deep thought, for refinement of ideas, for complex argument that we believe we hear in the speech of children of educated parents (Hudicourt-Barnes, 1999). We see bilingual children and poor children as cut off from important forms of expression and thought, from cultural traditions that the middle-class and English-speaking children gain by means of their language. On the contrary, we need to take seriously the power and complexity in the language children, and all of us, use every day. We know they consider problems of ethics on the playground. We need to recognize that in the science classroom as well their own questions and their familiar ways of discussing them contain invaluable intellectual resources.

Notes

1. The research on which this chapter is based was supported by funding from the Office of Educational Research and Improvement, U.S. Department of Education, under Cooperative Agreement No. R117G10022. The subsequent development of this chapter has been supported under the Educational Research and Development Centers Program, Cooperative Agreement R306A60001-96,

as administered by the Office of Educational Research and Improvement, U.S. Department of Education, and by the National Science Foundation, Grant No. ESI-9555712. The opinions and views expressed in this chapter do not necessarily represent the positions or policies of these agencies.

2. *Chèche Konnen,* which means "search for knowledge" in Haitian Creole, is a multiyear teachers' seminar in which researchers and teachers collaborate, both in doing science and in addressing issues of access to science learning for children in bilingual classes.

References

Ballenger, C. (1997). Social identities, moral narratives, scientific argumentation: Science talk in a bilingual classroom. *Language and Education, 11,* 1 –14.

Ballenger, C. (1999). *Teaching other people's children: Literacy and learning in a bilingual classroom.* New York: Teachers College Press.

Freire, P. (1970). *The pedagogy of the oppressed.* New York: Continuum.

Gallas, K. (1995). *Talking their way into science: Hearing children's questions and theories, responding with curricula.* New York: Teachers College Press.

Halliday, M. A. K., & Martin, J. R. (1993). *Writing science: Literacy and discursive power.* Pittsburgh: University of Pittsburgh Press.

Heath, S. B. (1983). *Ways with words.* New York: Cambridge University Press.

Hudicourt-Barnes, J. (1999). Our kids can't. *Hands On, 22,* 1, 4–7.

O'Loughlin, M. (1992). Rethinking science education: Beyond Piagetian constructivism toward a sociocultural model of teaching and learning. *Journal of Research in Science Teaching, 29,* 791–820.

Rosebery, A., Warren, B., & Conant, F. (1992). Appropriating scientific discourse: Findings from language minority clasrooms. *Journal of the Learning Sciences, 2,* 61 –94.

Snow, C., & Ninio, A. (1986). The contracts of literacy: What children learn from learning to read books. In W. Teale & E. Sulzby (Eds.), *Emergent literacy: Writing and reading* (pp. 116–138). Norwood, NJ: Ablex.

Teale, W. H., & Sulzby, E. (Eds.). (1986). *Emergent literacy: Writing and reading.* Norwood, NJ: Ablex.

Warren, B., & Rosebery, A. (1995). Equity in the future tense: Redefining relationships among teachers, students, and science in linguistic minority classrooms. In W. Secada, E. Fennema, & L. Adajian (Eds.), *New directions for equity in mathematics education* (pp. 298–328). New York: Cambridge University Press.

Warren, B., & Rosebery, A. (1996). "This question is just too, too easy!": Perspectives from the classroom on accountability in science. In L. Schauble & R. Glaser (Eds.), *Innovations in learning: New environments for education* (pp. 97–125). Hillsdale, NJ: Erlbaum.

Warren, B., Rosebery, A., & Conant, F. (1994). Discourse and social practice: Learning science in language minority classrooms. In D. Spencer (Ed.), *Adult biliteracy in the United States* (pp. 191–210). McHenry, IL: Center for Applied Linguistics and Delta Systems.

Appendix

Manuelle: Mesye Hyppolite kòman fè lè moun manje, yo si tèlman gwo, ou pa konn wè moun nan, yo pa janm transfòme, po yo pa sòti.
Manuelle: Mr. Hyppolite, how come when people eat they are so fat, you don't see the person, they never transform, their skin doesn't come off?

Yon elèv: Mhm po moun konn sòti.
A student: Uh hunh, people's skin does come off.

Yon lòt elèv: Ou wè lè yo dekale a Manuelle.
Another student: You've seen when they peel, Medette.

Sylvio: Non e pa sa l di tande kesyon n nan pou wè.
Sylvio: No, that's not what she said, listen to the question to see.

Manuelle: Men yo pa transfòme.
Manuelle: But they don't tranform.

Yon elèv: Oh ya yo pa transfòme, ou ka wè bagay la y ap chanje po, bagay sa yo.
A student: Oh yeah, they don't transform, you can see the thing they are changing, skin, those things.

Manuelle: Eske ou ka wè po sa a sòti.
Manuelle: Can you see this skin come off?

Sylvio: Repete kesyon an pou n tande byen.
Sylvio: Repeat the question so we can hear it well.

Manuelle: Kouman fè lè moun manje yo manje, yo manje, yo manje yo pa janm vin tounen tankou lè pupa manje l vin tounen yon beetle.
Manuelle: How come when people eat and eat and eat they never become like when the pupa eats and turns into a beetle?

Marie: Manuelle e pa tout bèt yo ki fè sa.
Marie: Manuelle, it's not all animals that do that.

(tout moun tonbe pale ansanm)
(everyone starts talking at once)

Sylvio: Ti moun e pou youn alafwa; youn alafwa Marie sa ou panse?
Sylvio: Kids, one at a time, one at a time. Marie, what do you think?

Marie: M panse lè rad la sou ou a po ou tou chanje.
Marie: I think when the clothing is on you your skin changes.

Junior: Ou pa wè sa.
Junior: You haven't seen that.

Sylvio: Oke[inaud] sa ou panse de sa?
Sylvio: OK, what do you think about that?

Elèv la: Reprann kesyon an pou mwen ankò.
Student: Repeat the question for me again.

Yon elèv: Ou paka reponn ni.
A student: You can't answer it.

Fabiola: M panse ke nou se moun bondye te kreye nou konsa, nou paka chanje po.
Fabiola: I think that we people, God created us like this, we can't change skin.

Sylvio: Raoul.

Raoul: Lè ou jwe basketball lè ou al benyen lè ou gade ou wè yon pakèt kras k ap sòti sou ou. Sa vle di se po ou li ye.
Raoul: When you play basketball [and] you go to bathe when you look you see a lot of dirt come off you. That means it's your skin.

Sylvio: Kras se po ou.
Sylvio: Dirt is your skin.

(tout moun welele ansanm)
(everyone cries out together)

Sylvio: Tande sa Marie di a.
Sylvio: Listen to what Marie said.

Marianne: Mesye Hyppolite e pa tout moun ki jwe; gen moun ki rete konsa y ap mache nan lari a konsa e pa . . .
Marie Bernard: Mr. Hyppolite, not everyone plays; there are people that stay like this, they walk in the street like this and don't —

Junior: Po ou gen lè pou l chanje mesye Hyppolite paske m te gade sa nan yon TVnèg lan te di chak konbyen fwa po ou chanje; li chanje nan rad ou, lè ou wè rad ou sal pa anndan e po ou li ye, epi tou lè w ap benyen tou po ou chanje.
Junior: There are times for your skin to change, Mr. Hyppolite, because I was watching on TV a guy said every so often your skin changes; it changes in your clothes, when you see your clothes are dirty inside it's your skin, and also when you bathe your whole skin changes.

Manuelle: M te di sa wi pa gen moun ki dakò avè m.
Manuelle: I said that, there aren't people who agree with me.

(tout moun pale ansanm)
(everyone speaks at once)

Stefan [deliberately]: Men sa m t ap di bèt avèk moun pa menm bagay.
Stefan [deliberately]: Here's what I was saying: animals and people aren't the same thing.

Sylvio: Jean-Charles ou gen kesyon, ou gen yon kòmantè?
Sylvio: Jean-Charles, you have a question or comment?

Jean-Charles: Manuelle se tankou, po ou chanje wi se tankou lav la lè l te anndan ze a, kòm si la a lè ou te anndan vant manman ou. Se tankou lè ou te ti bebe, kou ou fèt lè ou te ti bebe ou pat gen cheve menm epi e pa chanje ou chanje la a e pa ou gen cheve.
Jean-Charles: Manuelle, it's like your skin does change, it's like the [larva] when it was in the egg, like when you were in your mother's belly. It's like when you were a little baby. When you were born, when you were a little baby, you didn't have any hair, and now you've changed, don't you have hair?

Manuelle: E pa tout moun ki fèt san cheve . . .
Manuelle: Not everyone is born without hair . . .

Joanne: Ou grandi e pa chanje ou chanje.
Joanne: You grow, you don't change.

Sylvio: Oke kite Manuelle fin pale.
Sylvio: OK, let Manuelle finish speaking.

Joanne: Mesye Hyppolite ou chanje, lè ou grandi e pa menm, lè Manuelle grandi e pa menm jan l ap sanble.
Marie Jo: Mr. Hyppolite, you change, when you change it's not the same, when Manuelle grows up she won't look the same way.

Sylvio: Oke ya Manuelle kontinye.
Sylvio: OK, Manuelle continue.

Manuelle: Eske lè po a wetire konsa, vloop vloop
Manuelle: Does the skin comes off like that, *vloop vloop*?

Families and Communities Learning Together: Becoming Literate, Confronting Prejudice

JIM CUMMINS AND DENNIS SAYERS

I n this chapter, we provide three portraits of learning partnerships between students, parents, and teachers, who, though located in different parts of the globe, have used Internet technology to help build literacy and confront prejudice. The distances that separated them were not only geographic; language and cultural differences had to be bridged as well.

Our portraits begin with a project between bilingual classes in the United States and Spanish-speaking students in Puerto Rico. Participating students focused on sharing and comparing proverbs collected with the assistance of families and elders, thus linking bilingual literacy learning while validating community knowledge. We then consider a parent-child collaboration between communities in California, Colorado, and Puerto Rico that led to heightened awareness of the value of becoming and staying bilingual, while building children's and parents' literacy in their own languages. Finally, we examine an exchange between two elementary school bilingual education classes, one in San Francisco, the other in Brooklyn, New York, that transform a project on recognizing family ancestors into an opportunity for undermining racist attitudes.

De Orilla a Orilla is an international teacher-researcher project that, through systematic research, has documented promising practices for intercultural learning over global learning networks. Since 1985, Orillas has served as an international clearinghouse for establishing long-distance team-teaching partnerships between pairs or groups of teachers separated by distance, forming "sister" or "partner" classes. Orillas team-teaching partnerships are multilingual (in English, French, Haitian, Japanese, Portuguese, and Spanish) and multinational (with schools in Puerto Rico, Quebec, and the United States, but also in English-speaking Canada, Costa Rica, France, Japan, and Mexico).

Teachers in Orillas can participate by engaging in at least one of three different types of activities: 1) the exchange of cultural packages through the postal service to help the participating classes get to know one another; 2) partner-class projects involving joint investigations resulting in a single product based on contributions by both classes; or 3) group projects involving many teachers and their classes, which usually result in an Orillas-wide publication.

The collaborating teachers make use of e-mail and computer-based conferencing to plan and implement comparative learning projects between their distant partner classes. Such parallel projects include dual community surveys, joint math and science investigations, twinned geography projects, and comparative oral history and folklore studies. Teachers in Orillas often publish their students' collaborative work electronically over the Internet.

Research on Orillas has focused on those networking activities that effect social change, validating community traditions (such as oral history and folklore) in the schools, antiracist education, and linguistic human rights, while allowing teachers to explore the classroom practicalities of teaching based on collaborative critical inquiry. Robert DeVillar and Chris Faltis, in *Computers and Cultural Diversity,* judged Orillas "certainly one of the more, if not the most, innovative and pedagogically complete computer-supported writing projects involving students across distances" (1991, p. 116). In our view, Orillas remains, after more than a decade, a leading global learning network working to expand the theoretical and practical boundaries of multilingual and intercultural learning.

Orillas began with learning exchanges between bilingual classes in the United States and Spanish-speaking classes in Puerto Rico, and over the years the network has continued to explore the potential of global learning activities to foster the academic and social development of the children of immigrant families whose native language is not the language of the wider society. Global learning networks hold special promise for students in bilingual education programs. First, they provide an intellectually and emotionally stimulating context within which students' fledgling literacy skills can be developed in their native language. Indeed, in many cases documented by Orillas's teacher-researchers, students develop native language literacy through contact with distant "classmates" from the country of their parents' origin.

Second, global learning exchanges create a rich dynamic that encourages students in bilingual education classrooms to display, share, and compare their differing linguistic and cultural knowledge. Students in bilingual education classes, as any bilingual teacher will attest to, can range from recent arrivals to students who were born in their host country, from students with strong oral and at times highly developed literacy skills in their native language (owing to schooling in their country of origin) to those who feel ill at ease with their academic skills in the language of the home. Global learning networks can permit all these students to enter into productive communication of a highly interdependent nature. For example, in the context of a learning exchange between students in Puerto Rico and a bilingual classroom with many Puerto Rican students in New England, the most recent arrivals to the United States, while novices in terms of English-language skills and their knowledge of U.S. society, can act as linguistic and cultural "experts" with deep, fresh knowledge of the language, norms, and values of the partner class in Puerto Rico. Their expertise on and knowledge of the Puerto Rican culture can be interpreted by the bilingual students in the classroom and made available to other classmates whose English dominance would otherwise prevent them from fully experiencing the learning exchange. Global learning networks can thereby create a context that can challenge and begin to equalize the low status in which minority language students are too often held.

The potential of global learning networks is illustrated in the three portraits that follow, based on the writings of Enid Figueroa, Kristin Brown, and Dennis Sayers of the Orillas teacher-researcher network (Brown, 1993; Sayers & Brown, 1994). The first portrait describes a group project in which many Orillas teachers participated. Group projects are designed to take advantage of the rich possibilities for intercultural learning provided by an international network. A community is created of teachers interested in a single theme dealing with an issue of global interest, such as the environment, human rights, or the loss of oral traditions. Group projects are particularly suited for themes that benefit from multiple perspectives on a single issue or in which collective effort can create impressive bodies of information that students can analyze later for patterns and regional differences.

Portrait One

La Escuela Abelardo Díaz Morales and the Orillas International Proverbs Project: Using Telecommunications to Conduct Folklore Investigations

In 1989, Orillas announced a group project to collect and analyze proverbs. It is important to note that the categories proposed were simply suggestions, based on the previous experiences of successful team-teaching partnerships. In all Orillas projects, teachers are invited to design and shape the activities according to their local needs. Here we provide a close-up of one particular class in Puerto Rico and then describe different ways in which other teachers have adapted the project to their own curriculum.

La Escuela Abelardo Díaz Morales, named after the distinguished Puerto Rican educator, is an elementary school in Caguas, Puerto Rico. Its students are proud of their computer lab, the walls of which never fail to catch the eye of the visitor. On these bulletin board walls are photographs of students and their teachers, flags of Mexico and California, illustrated maps, richly colored student artwork, a collection of Yaqui legends from the Southwest, and several issues of the student-produced newsletter, *Cemí*. The bulletin boards trace the history of this school's participation in Project Orillas.

Each year since 1986, the computer writing teacher, Rosa Hernández, has engaged in a long-distance team-teaching exchange with a teacher in another part of the world, using a classroom computer, a modem, and a computer network. Networking also has made it possible for Ms. Hernández and her students to stay in touch with the wider group of Orillas teachers and to participate in a variety of Orillas group projects, including a survey of endangered species, an in-

ANNOUNCING

ORILLAS INTERNATIONAL PROVERBS PROJECT

from Kristin Brown, Dennis Sayers, and Enid Figueroa
Orillas Co-Directors

Orillas is sponsoring a multilingual proverbs contest. We invite your students to participate in one or more of the following categories:

BEST DRAWING: Illustrating one of the following proverbs: "Those who live in glass houses should not throw stones" or "It takes all kinds to make the world go around."

BEST ORIGINAL FABLE: Students pick a proverb, write an original story illustrating that proverb, then give the proverb at the end of the story as the "punch line."

GREATEST NUMBER OF "ANIMAL" PROVERBS SUBMITTED BY A SINGLE CLASS: Example: "A barking dog never bites." Helpful hint: Ask the parents and relatives of your students to help out!

GREATEST NUMBER OF CONTRADICTORY PROVERBS SUBMITTED BY A SINGLE CLASS: Example: "There's no place like home" contradicts "The grass is greener on the other side of the fence."

BEST ORIGINAL ESSAY ON "WHAT'S WRONG WITH THIS PROVERB": Pick a proverb you don't agree with and write an essay explaining what is wrong with the views it projects. Not all proverbs are wise; some of them say terrible things about others. For example, the sexist proverb "A woman's place is in the home" suggests that women should only do housework. Other proverbs are racist, ageist, or ridicule people with handicaps.

The contest is open to students of all grades and speakers of all languages. By identifying proverbs whose social, moral, or political views are obsolete, by searching for modern examples to illustrate noble or wise proverbs, and by exploring under what circumstances seemingly contradictory proverbs are true, we can all help define the "collective wisdom" of the twentieth century, and beyond.

At the end of the semester each participating class will receive a booklet containing selected student essays, photocopies of the drawings, and a list of all the proverbs collected.

ternational human rights project, and several intergenerational folk-lore investigations, such as the proverbs project originally presented to Orillas teachers in the project announcement on the opposite page.

Over the next few weeks, Ms. Hernández's class, like many others throughout the Orillas network, gathered proverbs, focusing espe-cially on ones containing animals. The list grew as students collected proverbs from parents, older brothers and sisters, grandparents living at home, neighbors, and other nearby relatives. During the school's spring break, the week of Semana Santa (the Holy Week preceding Easter), when families travel to other parts of the island to visit friends and relatives, the list grew most dramatically. Just before the vacation, Ms. Hernández printed out for each student a copy of the animal prov-erbs collected up to that point. When the students returned to school the following week, their lists were well worn and much longer. *"Nearly a hundred animal proverbs!"* they exclaimed when they had fin-ished adding the new proverbs to the old.

The class discovered that the task of categorizing the proverbs they gathered by theme was not as easy as it first appeared. The stu-dents debated the meanings of the proverbs and eliminated duplicates while making note of the frequency of use of each proverb. They iden-tified different versions and regional variations, and compared notes with their classmates about the contexts in which their parents and grandparents actually used the proverbs. As they continued to gather and analyze proverbs, they stayed in touch with other classes on the network.

In other classes, teachers and students had integrated the project into their own curriculum in a variety of ways. In Watsonville, Califor-nia, for example, the proverbs project was used to build parent in-volvement in the school's bilingual program. A migrant farmer-parent at Watsonville and his kindergarten child wrote the following critique of a proverb:

> **Vale más un pájaro en mano que ver cien volando**
> *No estamos de acuerdo con este refrán porque las personas no nos debemos conformar con lo que tenemos sino luchar y esforzarnos para vivir mejor cada día —Por los padres de Angélica Pérez García, Kinder-garten, Watsonville, California*

> [**A bird in the hand is worth two in the bush**
> We don't agree with this proverb because people shouldn't be satisfied with what we have but instead should struggle and

make an effort to make each day better —by the parents of Angélica Pérez García, Kindergarten, Watsonville, California]

In a bilingual fifth/sixth-grade class in Connecticut, students worked on a unit on fables, first reading fables in Spanish and English written by Samaniego, Aesop, and La Fontaine, then writing their own fables that illustrated some proverbs that the class in Puerto Rico had collected. In this class, students chose proverbs that reflected their own experiences. Here is one story or fable they wrote illustrating a proverb and tying it to academic learning:

El mismo perro pero con diferente collar

Había una vez una maestra llamada Sra. Caraballo. Le estaba enseñando a sus estudiantes de tercer grado como multiplicar. Ella les enseñaba todo lo necesario a sus alumnos

"Bueno estudiantes," dijo la Sra. Caraballo. "¿Cuánto es 2 x 3?" Sólo una estudiante levantó su mano y dijo, "Seis." Todos los estudiantes entendieron eso, menos Pedro.

"Maestra," dijo Pedro, "Yo no sé como hacer eso."

"Bueno Pedro," dijo Sra. Caraballo amablemente. "Esto es como si tú dijeras 3 + 3, pero en otra forma. Como si dijera 3 + 3 + 3 que es lo mismo que 3 x 3, que es igual que 9, pero en otra forma."

"Ahora ya entiendo," dijo Pedro. "Es como mi abuelo me dijo del refrán — 'el mismo perro pero con diferente collar.'"

[The same dog but with a different collar

Once there was a teacher named Ms. Caraballo. She was teaching her third-grade students to multiply. She taught her students everything they needed to know.

"Okay, students," said Ms. Caraballo. "How much is 2 x 3?" Only one student raised her hand and said "six." All the students understood this, except Pedro.

"Teacher," said Pedro. "I don't know how to do that."

"Well, Pedro," said Ms. Caraballo in a friendly way, "it is like saying 3 + 3 but in a different form. Just as 3 + 3 + 3, 3 x 3, and 9 are all different ways of saying the same thing."

"Now I understand," said Pedro, "it's just like the proverb my grandfather taught me — 'The same dog but with a different collar.'"]

At another school, a sixth-grade class asked students at other grade levels to illustrate familiar proverbs. They then classified the drawings in terms of whether each illustration was based on a literal or figurative interpretation of the proverb. The teacher was excited to note that for the first time in all her years of trying to get her upper-elementary-level students to understand the textbook terms *literal and figurative speech,* her students had announced in class, "Now we understand, Sra. Druet, it's like the way you can be talking about the horse's mouth and really it has nothing to do with a horse."

In other classes, this folklore project evolved into a lesson on sophisticated editorial writing. Proverbs are controversial by nature. They cannot be separated from the inequities of power relationships within the social fabric from which they have developed and in which they inextricably exist. In several classes, students wrote about proverbs they could not agree with. In the following examples, students from New York draw on their own experiences as they critique proverbs that they feel are unfair. The least favorite proverb among students in the United States was "A woman's place is in the home." A New York student explains:

El lugar de la mujer es en el hogar

Yo, Martha Prudente, no estoy de acuerdo en que la mujer esté en el hogar. Eso era el pensamiento de los tiempos antigüos. Así era como mis padres pensaban pero yo no, porque soy rebelde. Sí, yo voy a tener un hogar pero si quiero trabajar, voy a trabajar. Y pienso ser enfermera antes de casarme y después yo sigo trabajando en mi carrera.

[A woman's place is in the home

I, Martha Prudente, do not agree that a woman's place is in the home. This kind of thinking is old-fashioned. This is how my parents thought, but not me because I am a rebel. Yes, I will have a home, but if I want to work I will work. I hope to be a nurse before I get married and afterward continue working in my career.]

Cervantes once referred to proverbs as "short sentences drawn from long experience." The Orillas International Proverbs Project (see p. 117) just described stems from a longstanding and continuing interest on the part of Orillas teachers in exploring folklore in networked classrooms. In this project, telecommunications made it possible for bilingual students from diverse regions to collaborate rapidly in a wide-ranging investigation of proverbs. Moreover, the students created materials that classroom teachers everywhere were able to use to stimulate reading and writing skills, often across two languages. Folklore collections of all kinds can be instrumental in building bridges between schools and families and within the wider community of speakers of a particular language — both among the diaspora of local immigrant communities, and their cultures of origin around the world. They also can bring cross-cultural awareness and language skills to students who otherwise would never have access to people from distant lands and other worldviews. Once again, students from every background stand to benefit from participation in global learning networks.

The second portrait illustrates a team-teaching partnership among just three schools. It is particularly interesting because of the wide range of ages, languages, and literacy skills of the participants. While most Orillas partnerships take place between school-age children, this example describes the experiences of a group that included both parents and children.

Portrait Two

The Sherman School After-School Computer Course for Parents and Their Children

Sherman Elementary is located in Barrio Sherman in San Diego, California, in a neighborhood principally composed of Latino, African American, Cambodian, and European American communities. During the 1989–1990 school year, ethnic- and linguistic-minority parents and their children from this school participated in an Orillas telecommunications exchange with other groups of parents and children from Denver, Colorado, and from Caguas, Puerto Rico. At the start of the school year, Sherman School planned an after-school computer course for both parents and their children. All parents, regardless of their linguistic or academic backgrounds, would be welcome; indeed both the teacher of this literacy class, Lourdes Bourás, and the school contact person, Laura Parks-Sierra, had worked extensively with students in the Orillas project in previous years and had discovered the effectiveness both of using computers for a variety of communication activities and of having students work in teams.

The design of the parent-child literacy course would be similar to the approach already used in the Orillas network: local partners would work on the computer, learning to use it both as a writing tool (word processing) and as a communication tool (telecommunications). Next, the many local partners who made up the Sherman School literacy course would form another kind of partnership with distant partner classes, using e-mail. Finally, what they wrote eventually would be published locally in a newsletter distributed in the community. The only difference between previous Orillas projects and this literacy course would be that this time the local partnerships would be made up of a parent or caretaker and his or her child.

The "computer" course was announced at school to all second-through sixth-grade students. On the first night of the class, dozens of parents appeared. Several confided that they were tired after long days at work and of caring for their families. They might not have left the house, they admitted, except for the insistence of their children for whom computer time is a favorite activity. However, by the end of the evening many commented that they were intrigued with the prospect of learning how to use a computer with their children, and particularly the idea of communicating with other parents and children in far-off places.

At the outset there were some difficulties just in learning to use word processing and other software programs. Explanations to the group seemed labored: The teacher was fluent in Spanish and in English, but English speakers initially expressed some impatience at having to wait for the lessons to continue during what seemed like lengthy translations; they complained of time "wasted" or "taken" from more important, computer-related tasks. Moreover, Ms. Bourás reported that, during initial computer projects, whoever was at the keyboard assumed control, creating barriers for others to join in as full participants.

Yet once communications from the distant parent groups began to arrive, some interesting changes seemed to take place in parents' and students' attitudes, both toward engaging in computer-based collaborations and toward language use. The group, faced with the task of representing and describing San Diego in response to the initial questions from the distant groups, became more cohesive.

To help introduce themselves to their partner groups in Colorado and Puerto Rico, the Sherman School parents and children decided to make and send a "culture package" that featured a book to which everyone could contribute, regardless of their level of literacy in their mother tongue or in English. For example, the Cambodian family in which parents could not speak, read, or write English brought in the most pictures, hand-drawn sketches, and magazine articles. Together, parents and children elaborated a clear picture of the book they wanted to send; the parents and children worked in teams to create the different sections and then shared their writing and the pictures they had gathered with the rest of the group. As the parents learned to help one another, they could draw on the model of how their children had helped them all along, especially in terms of computer skills and English literacy. All the text had been typed in and printed out using computers. The parent-and-child-authored book had become a "seamless" group product where the individuality usually expressed in the concept of "sole authorship" had become unimportant.

Moreover, the Spanish speakers' status changed when most of the messages began arriving over the computer in Spanish. As the group logged on to the electronic mail system to read messages from Colorado and Puerto Rico, parents and children pulled their chairs as close as possible to the computer to read the text. Suddenly, proficiency in Spanish became highly prized as messages that everyone was so interested in reading scrolled by in Spanish. English speakers now saw the importance of devoting time to translation, even insisting that translation be done carefully to ensure that everyone understood the incoming messages. English-speaking parents who previously had worked on their own sought seats next to Spanish speakers, and were active in ensuring that the teacher had translated every detail (at times, double-checking with their local bilingual and bicultural "expert"). In Ms. Parks-Sierra's words, "These discussions really seemed to bring the group together."

Thus the concept of teamwork was expanding. To be sure, all teams did not function identically. Some parents and their children "shared" equally all stages of writing (prewriting, drafting, and revising and editing) and translating (from their home language to English and back). Other teams divided the writing task in a variety of effective ways, with some parents playing the key role of topic "definers" in the home language while their children, who sat at the keyboard, acted as English language interpreters and "refiners." One child described this relationship to his intergenerational coauthors:

Dear parents and children,

Our names are Keovong, Maria and Eam. I am Keovong the one that is typing because I am good at typing. I was born in Philippines and my parents are from Cambodia. My mom come to

computer class. My mom is writing in Cambodian and someone
will translate it in English or Spanish. My dad used to come with
me to the computer. Many of the people had died in Cambodia.
My land has been taken by the bad people. But now I am far away
from my home land and I am safe in San Diego.

    Your new Friend,

    Keovong Sar

This was just the first stage in what might be termed a "nested sequence of intergenerational collaborations," where children and parents interacted and later communicated their new understandings to
other parents and children. Next, there would be closer collaboration
between different linguistic groups, as parents and children translated
for one another and began to share their differing cultural and linguistic skills.

Unlike previous courses for parents sponsored by the Sherman
School, the high attendance in the parent-child computer course justi-
fied continuing it for the entire academic year. Parents and children
attributed the course's popularity, in large part, to the communications with the faraway parent groups and the parents' continuing interest in what the distant partner classes would write. By the end of the
year, the Sherman School parents and children had created numerous
collaborative publications. We list those publications, along with key
excerpts, below:

- A bilingual booklet of parent-teacher conference guidelines distributed to all of Sherman School's parents and teachers:

  Tu participación es importante: ¿Qué es una conferencia familiar? Una
  conferencia familiar es cuando nos reunimos con los maestros de
  nuestros hijos para hablar sobre su aprovechamiento escolar y su com-
  portamiento en la escuela. Es el momento de aprender más acerca de
  nuestros hijos y sus maestros. [Let's Lead the Way: What is a Family
  Conference? A family conference is an update on your child's
  progress and to discuss their future goals. It is a network between
  teacher, student and parents.] (Sayers & Brown, 1994, p. 180)

- An international collection of articles on self-esteem and technology, for which the Sherman School computer class worked with
  university professors, psychologists, teachers, and other parents
  and children from North and South America:

I think that a computer is good for children as well as adults because it lets you put down your thoughts and feelings and express your opinions. . . . I think it's great that the children are learning about computers and how they work and how to use them and write their own stories and to read what they have written. I think it gives them a good feeling inside to know that they did it and that they are as important as we are. —Christyl McCorley (African American mother with two children in the computer class)

In response to the question, on learning by technology, it is my personal belief that it is a good way to prepare our children and ourselves to meet the future for it is changing daily. It is nothing to be afraid of, it is like turning on your television or dialing your phone. The difference is that here you are upon something new, and if you do not have familiarity with the equipment, it's natural to feel uneasy about technology. . . . In the case of computers, at first you may feel not capable to be able to manipulate its system. As you start playing the keyboard, you begin to get a much better feeling about what you are doing. It then becomes a challenge between you and the system, until you are able to master it. —Hector Reynoso (Mexican American parent)

- A community newspaper — the product of collaboration with teachers and administrators and children at Sherman School. (Original spelling and punctuation is retained in the following anonymous article written by mothers in the class about another mother.)

An Exemplary Mother

Eam is originally from Cambodia, she is medium high has a beautiful black hair and is always smiling. She started coming to the computer class almost from the beginning. She never missed a class and she always had a positive attitude toward everybody. Eam looks so young that you will never believe she is thirty-six years old. She was a mother of nine children, but three of them died in the war in Batanbag, in Cambodia.

Eam was 15 when she got married, even though this sounds too young, this is normal for Cambodians. . . . Eam didn't want to have children right away but contraceptive methods were not very advanced in Cambodia so she got pregnant right away. Her new family grew fast and she had to work harder and harder, since in Cambodia your children depend very much from the mother's care. It was fascinating talking with Eam and getting to know such a different culture, but what makes this story more fascinating is the fact that no matter where in the world we are or where do we come form the importance of being a caring and loving parent is always the key for our future generations. And Eam is one of these great mothers that has helped six children grow up with an incredible future in front of them.

As parents recognized the many resources and talents of their local and distant colleagues, they realized how much they could accomplish if they pooled their efforts in new ways. They gained greater confidence in their ability to publish newspapers and write books. They came to see that other parents would be interested in what they had to say and that together they had the potential to effect change in their local community through the sharing of their distant voices. And bilingual literacy skills emerged without having been explicitly "taught" in these intergenerational long-distance partnerships.

Portrait Three

Confronting Interethnic Prejudice in New York and San Francisco Schools

In this portrait, we examine the way teachers in inner-city schools have used global learning networks to bridge cultural distances and reduce interethnic prejudice. In doing so, these teachers revisited the contact theory advanced by social psychologist Gordon Allport in 1954, which argued that prejudice could be reduced through cooperative learning in which students of different racial backgrounds worked together interdependently to achieve common academic goals (Allport, 1954).

Sheridan Elementary is a recently integrated school located in a predominantly African American neighborhood in San Francisco. In response to a court-mandated desegregation order, immigrant students from the primarily Latino Mission District have been bused to Sheridan in recent years. As in many other inner-city schools, teachers face the challenge of educating an increasingly diverse student population while counteracting the negative effects of prejudice between the different ethnic groups at their school.

The social distance between the African American and Latino students is exacerbated at Sheridan Elementary because the school is under construction, with portable classrooms nearly filling the playground. Students have little chance to meet even during recess. The Latino students are not only isolated but fearful, conscious of the resentment their presence causes in the community and in the schools. Juan Carlos Cuellar, a bilingual resource specialist for the school district, points out that strained relations in the desegregated schools reflect tensions in the broader society: "U.S.-born minority students such as African Americans, Chicanos, Asian Americans and Native Americans have been hardened by their own difficult experiences in the dominant U.S. culture. They see themselves as pitted against the new arrivals, and are not very welcoming of the new immigrants" (J. C. Cuellar, personal communication, 1995). Tracy Miller, a teacher at Sheridan Elementary, reports overhearing on the playground such negative comments from African American children as "You can't sit here because you're Latina," and Latinos reacting with "You can't play because the black might rub off on me." Ms. Miller feels these prejudices stem from attitudes learned at home and are worsened through nonproductive interactions during school hours (T. Miller, personal communication, 1995).

In the fall of 1993, Cuellar and Kristin Brown, Orillas codirector and a telecomputing consultant for California school districts, met to explore the role that telecommunications might play in addressing the academic and social problems faced by students in San Francisco's newly desegregated schools. Previous research conducted in Orillas classrooms had shown that carefully planned projects conducted over global learning networks could lead to the reduction of negative attitudes toward recently arrived Puerto Rican students among U.S.-born Latinos (Sayers, 1994).

In creating partnerships for the San Francisco teachers, Brown and Cuellar would carefully select distant bilingual classes that included Latino students from the Caribbean who are themselves of African descent. As they recall their first conversation:

> Since the partner classes in New York or Puerto Rico would include Spanish-speaking Latino students of African descent, we would be linking San Francisco's Latino students with faraway colleagues who in many ways were like them — students who spoke the same mother tongue and shared the experience of learning English as a second language — but whose physical attributes and pride in their African heritage more closely resem-

bled their African American schoolmates. In this way we hoped to provide a bridge between the African Americans and the Latinos who saw one another every day at school but whose interactions were distorted by fears and deep-seated prejudice. (J. C. Cuellar, personal communication, 1995)

As a result of this initial strategy session, Cuellar and Brown set to work recruiting teachers who would be interested in participating in year-long Orillas team-teaching exchanges designed to confront prejudice between groups in their schools.

At Sheridan Elementary, Tracy Miller's third/fourth-grade bilingual class was paired with Anne-Marie Riveaux's third-grade bilingual class at P.S. 19 in Brooklyn, New York. The teachers would stay in touch using a variety of technologies, including computers and e-mail, fax, telephones, videotapes, audiotapes, and photos. Ms. Miller's class was composed entirely of Latino students. As the students explained to the partner class in an introductory note,

> Nosotros somos de varios países de América Latina, México, Nicaragua, El Salvador y Guatemala. Todos nosotros somos bilingües. Hablamos inglés y español. [We're from various countries in Latin America. . . . All of us are bilingual. We speak English and Spanish.]

Ms. Riveaux's class in New York, composed predominantly of African Caribbean students, replied that (like the students in San Francisco) they also spoke Spanish and some English but that "most of our students are from the Dominican Republic, with Puerto Rico, Colombia, Ecuador, and Venezuela represented in the class as well." Ms. Riveaux described her own Caribbean roots, explaining that although she grew up in New York, her mother is from Puerto Rico and her father came from Trinidad. Both classes were eager to get to know the students in the other class. Their teachers hoped that by getting to know their distant counterparts, students in both classes would get to know themselves and their classmates better.

Both teachers felt that a video exchange could accomplish several goals. Videos would allow students to introduce themselves while providing an informal setting within which students could begin drawing comparisons between Latin American and Caribbean cultural traditions. The two teachers came to an agreement. In Ms. Miller's class, students would create a video about indigenous celebrations of El Día de Los Muertos (the Day of the Dead); in Ms. Riveaux's class, students would produce a video about traditional games passed down through oral traditions within their families and communities.

It was at the end of October 1993 when Tracy Miller's class began planning the video they would send to Ms. Riveaux's class. On everyone's mind were the upcoming cultural activities they had planned for the Day of the Dead on November 2. Not surprisingly, then, they selected this topic as the theme of their video. Because the Latino students in Ms. Miller's class realized that the students in Ms. Riveaux's class might not know about the Day of the Dead, they composed an explanation to read at the beginning of their video.

> *En California las comunidades latino-americanas celebran el Día de los Muertos haciendo altares en las galerías de los centros culturales. Además se organiza una procesión dentro de la comunidad en la noche. Para los altares los niños cortan papel picado y hacen figuras de papel picado. También hacen máscaras de "papier-mâché." En los altares ponen comida y lo que le gusta al muerto en el altar. Se hace una variedad de artes dramáticas y visuales para festejar esta celebración.*
> [In California the Latin American communities celebrate the Day of the Dead by making altars in the galleries of cultural centers. In addition, processions are organized through the community at night. For the *altars*, children make designs and figures out of cut tissue paper. We also make masks of "papier-mâché." Food and whatever the dead would like is placed on the altar. The festivities include a variety of dramatic and visual art for this celebration.]

In the class, students began discussing what else they might show their new friends in New York. As Ms. Miller recalls, their ideas poured forth: "We could teach them the '*Naranja Dulce*' [sweet orange] song, we'll show them the masks we're going to make, we can tell them about the field trip we have planned to visit the Mission Cultural Center, we'll tell them about the altar we're making in our class and the people in our families who we are remembering."

Activities in the classroom took on a new level of excitement as the students planned how they would sequence the video for their partner class. They would begin it with a dance behind masks and then later reveal who they were. This way the other class would also have a chance to learn about Mexican masks. As they would later explain in their video:

> We make masks by cutting strips of plaster material that people use to make casts for broken bones. We put Vaseline all over the

face so it doesn't stick to the skin. Then we wet the material and put it on the face and leave the strips on about ten minutes. It feels cold and scary. Later we paint the masks.

Next the students created a brightly colored altar in the corner of their classroom, covering cardboard boxes with fuchsia and blue fadeless paper and cut tissue-paper designs and then balancing skeleton puppets on top made from cut paper and brads. On the front of the altar they prominently displayed one of the well-known Day of the Dead prints by Guadalupe Posada, a Mexican artist from the early twentieth century. The print the students chose to display was of La Catrina, the prototype of an aristocrat — a fancy lady with feathers and flowers in her hat — "a fancy dead lady" the students liked to point out, adding, "because everybody dies."

This flurry of activity and excitement caught the attention of other teachers and students at Sheridan, who asked if they could stop by the room to see the altar, which was becoming more elaborately decorated each day as students brought in artifacts, photos, and other items by which to remember the dead in their families. In the teachers' lounge, Ms. Miller discussed the video exchange with Ms. Hornsby, an African American teacher of a second-grade class composed predominantly of African American students, with a few Chinese and Filipino students and one Native American child. These teachers were good friends and were both interested in improving race relations at the school. Both saw an opportunity for bringing their classes together and expanding the original scope of the project in order to get the African American students into direct, productive contact with the Latino students. They saw the powerful potential of global learning networks to act as a catalyst for change at the local level.

And so Ms. Miller's class (Room 17) formally invited the students from Ms. Hornsby's second-grade class (Room 7) to see their altar. They also invited Ms. Hornsby's class on the day they had set aside to film the video for the partner class in New York. While Mr. Cuellar set up the video camera, the students of Room 17 proudly taught the students from Room 7 the song "Naranja dulce, Limón Silvestre," a traditional Day of the Dead song. They wrote the words on the board so the two classes could sing it together on the video. All the students wanted the video to come out well and so were constantly whispering instructions to Mr. Cuellar about how to arrange the room to get the best takes.

As Mr. Cuellar started taping, Tracy Miller began by explaining the altar to their distant audience in New York City, providing her introduction in English so Ms. Hornsby's class would understand, but also taking advantage of the "teachable moment" to have all the students pronounce key words in Spanish, such as *ofrenda* and *pan de muerto* (meaning "offering" and "bread of the dead").

> *Ms. Miller:* Greetings to our friends at P.S. 19 in New York. We are very excited. We are here today with Ms. Hornsby's class to talk to you about our altar. A lot of people call this *ofrenda*. In many countries in Latin America and in Mexico this is a national holiday, and people don't have to go to school or work because on this day they visit the cemeteries and they decorate the graves with skeletons and candles and bread of the dead, or *pan de muerto*, which is supposed to look like a mummy. The reason they put food on the altar is because people in the land of the dead are going to come back and visit us and so we need to have some food for them to eat because they are going to be very hungry and very thirsty. We have on our altar also a glass of water. My students have brought things to the altar remembering the people they knew who have died.

At this point Ms. Miller picked up one of the items on the altar and signaled to a young girl from Mexico in front of her. Coralia jumped up. Ms. Miller continued, "For example, Coralia has brought a little house she made of cardboard and a little figure of a chicken. Coralia will tell you about it."

> *Coralia* (in Spanish*): Porque a mi abuelo le gustaba pintar* houses *y a mi abuela le gustaba dar de comer a las gallinas.*

(Ms. Miller motions to Mario, a bilingual student in the class who translates)

> "Her grandfather liked to paint houses and her grandmother liked to feed chickens."

Ms. Miller continues. "Lydia will tell you why she brought a cup." She motions to Lydia, who explains, "*Yo traje esta taza porque a mi tia le gustaba tomar mucho café y por eso le traje la taza para que la recuerde.*" Mario translates: "Her aunt really loved to drink coffee and so to remember her aunt she put a coffee cup on the altar."

"Now Jesse will explain what he brought," Ms. Miller says as the tape continues.

Jesse: I brought this because I have a photo of my grandfather that died. Here is his picture. That's him. He died because he had a heart attack. Tomorrow I'm going to bring a little plastic horse for the altar because he liked to ride a horse.

Ms. Miller: José will go next.

José: El nombre de mi tío es Juanito. Mi tío murió cuando yo tenía dos años y él vivía sólo en una casa de piedra y mi abuelita le llevaba de comer a la casa de tío Juanito.

Mario: The name of my uncle is Juanito. My uncle died when I was two years old and he lived alone in a stone house and my grandmother brought food to the house of my uncle Juanito.

Ms. Miller: Jessica will tell how they celebrate in Guatemala.

Jessica: In Guatemala they celebrate the Day of the Dead with food, water and flowers and they go to Chichicastenango where the Indians are. They go to church with their friends and relatives, and they go to the cemetery where the old people died, and after that they go to church and put food and water.

Everyone notices that this time it is not one of Ms. Miller's students who has her hand raised to speak but a student from Ms. Hornsby's class. Ms. Miller calls on Winnie. Winnie begins shyly, "We have the same thing but it's not the same." Ms. Miller realizes she hasn't introduced Winnie as she had each of the others who have spoken in front of the video camera. So she says, "Winnie Young will tell us how they remember the dead in her homeland, China."

Winnie: We got two ways in our family. One is to go to the cemetery to put some food and flowers. Another way we celebrate is in the house. At home the people who died, we put their picture on the top of the wall and we put the food and flowers and something else by this. The other day when we celebrate we put some paper things in the fire so that they burn.

After Winnie breaks the ice, an African American boy from Room 7 raises his hand. Ms. Miller calls on him and he says his uncle has died. After Ms. Miller introduces him, Renell continues:

What we do is call all our family up and send them invitations to come over to the city of San Francisco. They come on Friday and first when they come we do fun things together but on Saturday morning about 11 we go to the graveyard and give my uncle flowers and after that we stare at the grave and then we just leave and go and have a barbecue and we usually just get together, like eat and other good things. I like remembering my uncle and another thing. . . . Some people don't like to remember in my family because they think it's tragic but it's a good thing to remember your family because they'll always be dead. Except for the spirit, he'll always be dead. It's a good thing to remember your family.

Everyone in the classes at Sheridan was eager to know if Ms. Riveaux's class in New York would like their video. Soon a package arrived in the mail from New York. Inside they found a note in which the partner class said they were excited to receive the video. It had inspired Anne-Marie Riveaux's third graders to create a class altar and discuss the universal theme of life and death. Tracy Miller's class was excited to learn that the package also included a video. The students in Ms. Riveaux's class had taped students playing games they had learned from their families and parents. Ms. Miller's students watched animatedly and eagerly, making comments about each game as they took delight in seeing the games that they were familiar with, games like the ones they had played in Mexico before they arrived in the United States.

The partner teachers (now expanded to include Ms. Riveaux in New York and Ms. Miller and Ms. Hornsby in San Francisco) decided that their next joint project would be to make a book of games collected from the families in all three classes. Ms. Riveaux wrote:

When I first introduced the idea to my students they were so excited at the thought we were going to be playing games. Little did they know that by playing games we were going to be learning so much. When I mentioned it to the parents on open school night, they showed much enthusiasm also. The children went home and worked with parents on writing up their reports. When they brought them in, the children came in front of the classroom and told us about their game: how to play it, their experience working with a relative on the project, and memories of when they played the game in their homeland. (J. C. Cuellar, personal communication, 1995)

Ms. Riveaux faced a difficult situation at the beginning of the year: students were being moved in and out of her class so frequently that they felt rejected and had lost any sense of community. She shared with the other teachers the value of the games project, describing it as a "great community-building activity with my class."

For the teachers at Sheridan, the most attractive aspect of the games project was the opportunity it provided for drawing parents' traditional knowledge into their curriculum. Ms. Hornsby was already doing a thematic unit on families and ancestors; what better way to complement her unit than to ask children, equipped with tape recorders, to interview their parents about the games they had played as children, folk games passed down through countless generations? And since folk games were universal while remaining culture-specific, what more powerful way to help their students discover a common humanity across cultural differences?

The hardest part at both schools was finding a place to teach one another the folk games they were collecting. New York City public schools often lack even asphalt playgrounds, and Ms. Riveaux's was no exception. Sheridan Elementary was "under construction" that year. As it turned out, the common area at both schools was the cafeteria before or after lunch. The teachers at Sheridan rearranged their schedules so that both their recreation periods fell in the morning when the cafeteria was free. They were careful to assign their students to small groups, consisting of some African American and some Latino students. In these small groups, the students would teach each other folk games, with the "expert" bilingual students doing the translating — causing their status to soar among their peers.

Ms. Hornsby's class began by showing Ms. Miller's students how to play Mancala, a game from Africa. Then Ms. Miller's class showed Ms. Hornsby's students how to play *Haciendo Cuadritos,* a pencil-and-paper strategy game. Day after day, the students moved from cross-cultural marbles, to jacks, tops, and hopscotch, all simple, enjoyable games. Here is what the students wrote about what it meant to them to share their games:

> *Nos gusta aprender las costumbres de otros estudiantes. Por eso, la unidad Juegos Tradicionales es perfecta para nuestra clase. Compartimos juegos de Nicaragua, El Salvador y Guatemala con el salón 7 mientras que ellos nos enseñan juegos originando de África.* [We like to learn the customs of other students. For this reason, the unit

on "folk games" is perfect for out class. We share games from Nicaragua, El Salvador, and Guatemala with Room 7 while they teach us games originating in Africa.]

Reflecting the bilingual character of their learning context, one student wrote in *both* languages:

> *Hemos aprendido que muchos de los juegos tienen algo en común. De hecho, todos nosotros tenemos algo en común y todos nosotros podemos ser amigos. Después de participar en este programa, Mario Riva expresó lo que aprendió así: "In this world there is a friend for everyone!"* [We have learned that many of the games have something in common. In fact, we all have something in common and we all can be friends. After participating in this project, Mario Riva expressed what he had learned in this way: "In this world there is a friend for everyone!"]

And the African American students in Room 7 also knew they were doing something important while enjoying the pleasure of sharing folk games. They wrote:

> We began our games unit to help us with social studies, multiculturalism, and conflict resolution. By sharing games with one another, we have learned that we all have something in common — we like to have fun together! We have all made new friends through sharing the games our parents played as children. This is a project we'd like to continue.

But their teachers knew the real question was, Would their newfound friendships, based on short-term intercultural sharing, actually last longer than the school year? There were some signs that it did. A year later, Ms. Hornsby and Ms. Miller continued to collaborate. Indeed, Ms. Miller had two African American girls in her bilingual class (Ms. Hornsby's former pupils) since their parents *demanded* that their children be given the opportunity to learn Spanish by studying with Spanish-speaking students. Last reports were that the two girls were learning Spanish as a second language, and according to Ms. Miller, "They love it and think it's great." And for the first time at Sheridan Elementary, Latina girls joined the Girl Scout troop, originally organized by African American and European American mothers. Who were the new recruits? *Every single girl* in Ms. Miller's bilingual class during the games project. Perhaps Tracy Miller deserves the last word on the potential of global learning networks for reducing prejudice:

We still need to do so much more, to integrate the classes themselves, to have after-school programs where all students play and work together. It's a very slow process, but there was real understanding, and one thing leads to another. Some schools don't do anything. But this was a good starting point.

Conclusion

Our three portraits have illustrated learning exchanges between differing groups of learners: Bilingual classes in the United States learning with Spanish-speaking students in Puerto Rico; parent-child collaborations in California, Colorado, and Puerto Rico; and bilingual classrooms in elementary schools on the Atlantic and Pacific coasts sharing children's games. Yet these differing collaborations have several common threads.

Overcoming the initial barrier of geographic distances with the aid of technology tools led to what we have come to call "engaged distancing," a process of perspective taking in which the open and honest disclosure of local realities are shared and compared, leading to critical insight and potentially, as we saw most clearly in the San Francisco–Brooklyn exchange, some initial efforts toward confronting prejudice and changing perceived injustices. Moreover, these types of learning exchanges can work powerfully to establish a productive change in classroom dynamics across language and cultural differences, as seen in the portrait on children's games and the example on intergenerational exchanges between California, Colorado, and Puerto Rico, where bilingualism came to be valued as an essential tool for sharing cultural knowledge. Finally, the proverbs exchange illustrated the potential of global learning projects to involve often-devalued oral cultural traditions in the process of literacy learning. This is especially important as bilingual students seek meaningful ways to engage in the struggle to keep their linguistic and cultural knowledge from receding into another kind of distance, that of a fading memory.

References

Allport, G. (1954). *The nature of prejudice*. Cambridge, MA: Addison-Wesley.
Brown, K. (1993). Balancing the tools of technology with our own humanity: The use of technology in building partnerships and communities. In A. F. Ada & J.

Tinajero (Eds.), *The power of two languages: Literacy and biliteracy for Spanish-speakers* (pp. 178–198). New York: Macmillan.

DeVillar, R. A., & Faltis, C. J. (1991). *Computers and cultural diversity: Restructuring for school success.* Albany: State University of New York Press.

Sayers, D. (1994). Bilingual team-teaching partnerships over long distances: A technology-mediated context for intra-group language attitude change. In C. Faltis, R. DeVillar, & J. Cummins (Eds.), *Cultural diversity in schools: From rhetoric to practice* (pp. 299-331). Albany: State University of New York Press.

Sayers, D., & Brown, K. (1994). Putting a human face on educational technology: Intergenerational bilingual literacy through parent-child partnerships in long-distance networks. In D. Spener (Ed.), *Adult biliteracy in the United States* (pp. 171–189). Washington, DC: Center for Applied Linguistics and Delta Systems.

Teachers' Judgments Do Count: Assessing Bilingual Students

EVANGELINE HARRIS STEFANAKIS

My interest in classroom assessment stems from my experience as a bilingual researcher, teacher, and special educator. For twenty years in public and private classrooms in the United States and overseas, I struggled with the standardized instruments used to assess children from diverse language and cultural backgrounds. These tests, or evaluations, normed on native English speakers, were the only tools available to assess and place bilingual children in regular or special educational settings. I faced the inherent contradiction of using linguistically and culturally biased tests to evaluate the abilities of bilingual students. Like many educators, I needed expertise in using assessment tools that would better reflect my students' academic skills.

I recall a child named Arnet, a sixth grader who arrived in my classroom from Israel, dazed and nonverbal. Despite my serious efforts to engage her in classroom activities, she remained unresponsive for seven months. She spoke no English, but her parents insisted that she was an excellent student in her native language. The school psychologist, speech therapist, counselors, and administrators evaluated her with their tests, and she was diagnosed as "in serious need of special educational and psychological services." One day, as I started to read the fairy tale *Cinderella* to the class, Arnet motioned to me that she wanted the book. I handed it to her, and she stood up in front of the class and articulately read the entire story in English. I was shocked that we could have labeled her as limited in potential, which was due to our limited methods of *evaluating her abilities.*

Despite the rising number of bilingual students in U.S. classrooms, few educators are trained to make sense of the language and learning differences of children in their classes. Consequently, bilingual students are frequently misdiagnosed and misplaced, often into special education programs.

So what can educators do to better understand and assess bilingual children? First, I believe the educational community has to clarify two terms — *evaluation* and *assessment* — which are not equivalent terms. *To evaluate* is "to ascertain or fix the value or worth of something according to a predetermined set of criteria." *To assess*, on the other hand, which is from the Latin *assidere*, means "to sit beside" in order to gather information. I define *assessment* specifically as an interactive process of "sitting beside the learner" to gather authentic and meaningful data for improving student learning, instructional practice, and educational options in the classroom. While evaluation is based only on interpreting students' products, assessment is based on gathering information on the teaching and learning process, learning products, and the interaction between teacher and learner.

Whose judgment counts when it comes to assessing bilingual children? I believe that teachers' judgments should count because they are the assessors who know their students and sit beside them daily. To better understand the nature of educational assessment, therefore, we should look carefully at the interactions between teachers and learners as they sit beside one another. "Whose judgment counts?" is the question posed to me by the first teacher I studied, who said that her expertise is in understanding what bilingual children *can* do:

> *Whose judgment counts* when it comes to assessing bilingual children in schools? It is usually the school psychologist. Their expertise in assessment — that is, *in giving tests* — is seen as the judgment that counts.
>
> If you really want to learn about assessing bilingual children, ask the classroom teachers who have years of strategies behind them to use. After about three weeks in my classroom, I can usually tell what a child needs and how best to teach them, even if they speak little English. (Narrative summary, 1994)

In this chapter, I offer a set of recommendations for the assessment of bilingual children, which are based on what I learned from reviewing recent literature and from studying expert teachers.[1] I begin by outlining the complexities of assessing bilingual children as documented in the bilingual research literature. To address the limitations of formal assessment methods, I present my sociocultural framework for classroom assessment, which addresses the call by researchers for a more comprehensive approach to the issue. To conclude, I summarize successful classroom assessment strategies used by a group of highly skilled urban teachers with over twenty years of expertise.[2] My summary of best assessment practices based on teachers' successful strategies capture the intricacies of daily classroom assessment and provides real-life examples for other teachers whose goal is to understand the learning abilities, rather than the disabilities, of bilingual children.

The Changing Context: Challenges of Assessing Bilingual Learners

There are several reasons why an understanding of effective assessment of bilingual children is timely and vital to both researchers and practitioners. First, changing demographics in the United States suggest that most educators will soon be required to know how to effectively assess and teach bilingual children in their classrooms. Second, early in their educational careers, linguistic-minority children are often misplaced in special education classrooms, which seriously affects their opportunity to learn. Current research indicates that teachers often misidentify bilingual children as language or learning disabled, when in reality they are simply limited in English proficiency:

> Minority over-representation in special education continues. . . . Once a referral is made, the likelihood of testing is high. Once testing takes place, strong gravitational forces toward special education placement are in motion. The referral to assessment to placement rate oscillates between 75 and 90 percent. Once a bilingual child is referred for testing, that same child is placed in special education about 85 percent of the time. Once a child is placed in special education, despite a mistaken assessment, it takes them on average six years to get out. (Fedoruk, 1989, p. 41)

Further, many bilingual researchers believe that the misplacement of bilingual children into special education continues because school leaders and teachers are not knowledgeable about how to assess these children (Baca & Almanza, 1991; Hamayan & Damico, 1991), and thus refer them for testing by "experts." This dangerous practice of testing to find a disability must stop, and can only be addressed by better informing practitioners about alternative assessment practices and a different framework for the process.

By understanding more about the complexities of assessment, school leaders and teachers, as the primary agents of change, can stop inappropriate referrals and placements of bilingual students into special education. Simultaneously, both the research and practitioner communities must focus attention on documenting best practices in assessment for bilingual students. As Ambert (1991) suggests,

> The research and practitioner communities are confused and this is affecting bilingual children. Information for researchers, educators, and parents is needed on the best assessment practices for bilingual children . . . practices that give teachers and students actual feedback on teaching and learning. (p. 358)

Understanding the Complexity of Assessing Bilingual Children

Assessing a linguistically and culturally different child's language and learning abilities is a complex task. I refer to an image of assessment, proposed by Chapman (1988), to examine how the field of education has dealt with the multiple questions related to assessing bilingual children. Sixty years ago, Chapman, in a biography of Lewis Terman, father of the intelligence testing movement, portrayed the assessment process using the image of a powerful assessor (an adult representing education) looking at the population of young and diverse learners through a magnifying glass (of intelligence tests) to determine their educational pathways (see illustration, p. 143).

What the assessor sees while looking carefully at an individual child is affected by many components of the assessment process. In the foreground, we see "the new sorting method," in which an educational assessor uses intelligence tests to examine the individual child through a magnifying glass. This examination is based on a set of educational theories, as depicted by the books in the illustration: a scientific method of investigation, a psychology of individuality, and mental forces. This image of individualized assessment is juxtaposed with

the old method, depicted on the left side of the illustration, in which education applies guesswork or rules to sort groups of children into classes of A's, B's, or C's.

This 1922 image from *Schools as Sorters*[3] (Chapman, 1988) reminds us that we are still facing the same dilemma as in Chapman's time — how to sort students according to their language and learning abilities. We see that assessment was historically considered a complex process of sorting individuals into groups using either a scientific method or some form of guesswork. Chapman's image captures the dilemma of educational assessment, which was trying to rely either on a scientific or formal approach, or on a less scientific or informal approach.

The process of assessing bilingual children is much more complex. It raises important questions about a practitioner's knowledge, skills, and attitudes. *The background of the assessor,* for example, strongly affects the image of the student that person sees. Does this individual speak another language? Has this person known a non-native English speaker or lived outside the United States?

Further, *the relationship of the assessor to the learner* affects what that person sees. Is the assessor a stranger to the child, perhaps a psychologist or an educational specialist trained to study individual behavior? Or is the assessor a classroom teacher familiar with studying individuals as part of a group, and someone who is familiar with the child and the child's capabilities?

Each assessor uses a different lens, a different kind of expertise, to view the learning abilities of a bilingual child. Their expertise determines

(a) the format — how they approach the assessment process;
(b) the tools they use — formal tests or informal assessments;
(c) the time spent — how long they spend with the child;
(d) the setting — where they assess the child (classroom, office, playground).

Finally, my practice has taught me that *the context* of assessment is a key element in understanding what any child knows, especially a bilingual child. The closer and more frequently assessors look, the clearer they can see the language and learning abilities of a bilingual child. Classroom teachers collect many "episodes of learning" (Wolf, 1989) in daily observations, providing a much fuller picture of the child's strengths and weaknesses. Through this lens, they can develop their own assessment of that child's knowledge of language and literacy.

Part I: What Research Suggests about Assessing Bilingual Children

The complexity of the assessment process warrants a careful look at what the research recommends regarding how to best assess bilingual students. In this section, I summarize the educational research from 1987 to 1996,[4] and suggest that assessment practice is evolving from a standardized product format to a more complex problem-solving process. I use the term *formal assessment* to define standardized, normed evaluation, and *informal assessment* to define nonstandardized assessment tools, including observations, interviews, checklists, and surveys. *Classroom assessment* refers to a form of informal assessment carried out by teachers during daily instruction. It involves a variety of interactive strategies, including observations, interviews, and collecting student work, often in portfolios. Recent bilingual research suggests that, because bilingualism is a complex cognitive asset, the assessment designed to describe it should *also* be complex. Therefore, there are no simple answers for how best to assess bilingual students, but there are recommendations for conducting a variety of formal and informal assessments (Alvarez, 1991; Ambert, 1991; Hakuta & Garcia, 1989; Hernandez, 1994; Rhodes, 1993; Snow, 1992).

Formal Assessment

Educational assessment of bilingual children, including their language proficiency and cognitive learning, is a controversial topic in the research literature. Formal assessment — that is, standardized normed evaluation — presupposes that the child must meet an expected norm of educational performance; if he or she does not, then remediation is needed. The process is taken as a socially and politically neutral process, when in reality it is not. Language, culture, and social-class biases enter the process at various points (see Cummins, 1989; Damico et al., 1992; Dolson, 1994; Duran & Szyanski, 1994).

Recent literature suggests that formal assessment tools and procedures for evaluating language proficiency and cognitive abilities as a single measure lack specific aspects of validity and reliability for bilingual students (Alvarez, 1991; Ambert 1991; Baca & Almanza, 1991; Damico et al., 1992; Dolson, 1994; Duran, 1991; Hernandez, 1994; LaCelle-Peterson & Rivera, 1994).

Some tests that are translated from English into the child's native language have the technical aspects of valid instruments but are not open-ended enough to capture the complexity of a bilingual child's language and learning strengths (Baca & Clark, 1992; Padilla et al., 1988). For example, a child may be able to translate the name of an animal, but they may not have any personal experience with this animal to draw on to answer a test question correctly. Other areas of concern to watch for in standardized tests or tests in translation are 1) bias in test data interpretation; 2) construct validity (how they were put together) of tests in translations; 3) cultural bias of test items and vocabulary used; and 4) the child's previous experience in test taking.

Educators and psychologists need to examine carefully the validity of tools they use, even those that are translated from English into the child's native language. Educators should ask the following validity questions:

- How and when was the test normed?
- Were bilingual students included in the norming population?
- How were items and test questions developed, and by whom?
- In which language were the tests created, and how were they translated?
- How difficult is the vocabulary used in giving directions and in administration?

Current research (Dolson, 1994; Figueroa, 1989; Ortiz, 1990; Wilkinson & Holzman, 1988) warns against using a single standardized instrument for decisionmaking with bilingual students. Assessment of these students should focus on the assessment process (how a child learns, under what conditions, and with what materials), rather than on the single-session assessment products (individual test results and grade equivalent scores).

A body of research seriously questions the validity and reliability of bilingual students' test performance, noting that it is affected by issues related to language and culture, including test format, timing, reasoning strategies, language proficiency, and vocabulary. Other factors are the setting for the test taking and the child's relationship to the test giver (Gonzalez, Bauerle, & Felix-Holt, 1996; Gonzalez, 1998).

Furthermore, the capabilities of bilingual students can best be understood through examining evidence of performance in their first *and* in their second language. These issues require careful attention from those responsible for evaluating bilingual students and interpreting test results. To guard against discriminatory practices, decisionmaking related to bilingual students should be made through a variety of formal and informal assessments in both the native language (L1) and English (L2).

Researchers such as Dolson (1994), Gonzalez (Gonzalez, Bauerle, & Felix-Holt, 1996; Gonzalez, 1998), and Snow (1992) call for a comprehensive process for the assessment of bilingual children, including a sociocultural approach. Baca describes the shift in bilingual assess-

CRITICAL EDUCATIONAL PRACTICES TO CONSIDER WHEN USING
FORMAL ASSESSMENTS

Research shows that

1. performance on timed tests may be invalid because bilingual
   students *take more time* to complete tasks in their second language;
2. a systematic, sequential testing approach may be unfamiliar and
   of questionable validity because bilingual students *may use a
   different reasoning strategy* stemming from their native language;
3. *evaluation of native language proficiency* (using both formal and
   informal assessments) *must precede* any assessment of learning
   potential.

ment from creating tests in translation in the 1980s to needing to redefine the testing process as an assessment process:

> I thought that if we could fix the assessment issues of reliability
> and validity, then we could provide non-discriminatory assess-
> ment. . . . But now I realize that 25 percent of the bias is in the in-
> struments, and 75 percent of the bias is in the humans and the
> process of assessment. (L. M. Baca, personal communication, 1994)

In summary, bilingual students have more language and cultural
abilities to assess, not one language to *score!*

Informal Assessment

Research suggests that informal, classroom-based assessment of bilingual children is preferred over formal assessment as a way to deal with
the complexity and multiple perspectives of bilingual learners
(Alvarez, 1991; Ambert, 1991; Damico, 1991; DeLeon, cited in Damico
et al., 1992). Informal assessments, including formats for observation,
interviews, checklists, and surveys, are recommended to gather information about both the language skills and the cognitive abilities of bilingual students. Checklists for assessing language, literacy, numeracy,
problem solving, and learning style are available in the research of
Airasian (1991), Anthony et al. (1991), and Teirney, Carter, and Desai
(1991). A summary of the informal assessment recommendations for
what to observe and who to interview are presented below.

SUMMARY OF THE RESEARCH ON INFORMAL ASSESSMENT

Observe

- native-language use
- second-language use
- peer interactions
- parent interactions
- teacher interactions

Interview and Survey

- parents
- caretakers
- family members
- peers
- teachers
- school staff

Informal assessments are designed to gather specific information in two ways — by watching a child (observations), and by talking to the child and the family (interviews) — which provides a better understanding of the social and cultural factors that affect a student's language and learning.

Classroom Assessment

Researchers agree that to understand and assess adequately bilingual students' language and learning capabilities, it is critical to see both the process and the products of their work. This suggests that classroom assessment, an unrecognized and unexplored area of study, is of vital importance. Further, teachers' classroom assessments should often be considered in the educational assessment of bilingual children because teachers see how a child learns every day, and they know what a child can produce under varied conditions and in response to varied classroom activities.

Reflecting a sociocultural approach to assessment, Alvarez (1991) refers to these classroom evaluations as "assessment embedded in instruction" (p. 284), which are a set of strategies directly linked to daily instruction that focus on the setting (ecological assessment), the pedagogy (curriculum-based assessment), and the process of teacher-student interaction (portfolio assessment).[5]

Overall, recent research points to a changing picture of assessment for bilingual children. In the United States, the literature suggests a move toward informal assessment (Genesse & Hamayan, 1994; Hernandez, 1994; Wiggins, 1989; Wolf, 1989). The trend is to create assessment tools that more accurately reflect learning *in context,* and to

CLASSROOM ASSESSMENT RESEARCH SUGGESTIONS

Use curriculum-based assessments to

1. observe the student, the classroom environment, teaching format, and peer interactions;
2. document and keep track of achievement levels in content areas using classroom materials and student work;
3. observe student responses to what is known, what needs to be taught, and the pace of instruction;
4. keep track of student performance using samples of student work and portfolios.

gather information from specialists, teachers, and family members (Baca & Clark, 1992; Damico et al., 1992; DeLeon, 1990; Dolson, 1994; Wilkinson, 1992). Whether labeled "authentic" or "alternative" assessment, the goal is to gather information from a variety of sources while *sitting beside the learner.*

In conclusion, based on my research review, I recommend using a wider lens for looking at assessment practices with bilingual children. This means combining formal and informal assessments to assess language proficiency and cognitive abilities, both in test situations and in the context of daily learning. Therefore, informal assessments such as observations, interviews, and portfolios of student work should be combined with information from standardized test results. Further, I recommend combining formal, informal, and classroom assessment to balance the needs of system-level compliance (formal) with child-centered assessment (informal and classroom) (Dolson, 1994; Harris Stefanakis, 1991).

Recommendations and Conclusions

A Sociocultural Framework and Approach to Redefine the Purposes of Assessment

The traditional psychometric model of formal assessment used to evaluate all children consists of standardized instruments and techniques to diagnose language and learning problems. These psychometric tools assume that any deficit is in the child. This model is in contrast to a sociocultural approach, which assumes that every child presents an example of difference and complexity, and that understanding the difference — not the deficit — is the role of educational assessment.

Based on my review of the research, I argue that understanding the nature of educational assessment involves looking carefully at the interaction between teacher and learner. This suggests redefining the purposes, the formats, and the process of assessment for diverse language learners. To redefine classroom assessment, I use a sociocultural framework to describe the complexity of assessing second-language proficiency and cognitive learning, taking into consideration the cultural, linguistic, social, and political factors involved. A sociocultural approach to assessment addresses the need for understanding the context, the linguistic and cultural backgrounds of the teacher and the learning, the relationships, and the setting, as well as the process and products of a bilingual learner.

A sociocultural perspective assumes that children learn language in real-life situations that depend on social interactions, and that bilingual children display a different knowledge and use of language that depends on the social context. The sociocultural perspective makes three assumptions:

1. Bilingualism is a potential cognitive asset that can enhance learning (Hakuta & Garcia, 1989).
2. Sociocultural factors can affect learning, and context is the key to understanding language output (Cummins, 1986, 1989; Snow, 1992).
3. Language proficiency and related learning abilities should be assessed in context and over time (Baca & Almanza, 1991; Damico, 1991; DeLeon, 1990; Dolson, 1994).

Studying classroom assessment has taught me that teachers' judgments *do* count and *should* count when it comes to understanding the complexities of young bilingual children and applying successful strategies to deal with this complexity.[6] My research, which studied skilled teachers, confirms that Marshall's (1992) definition corresponds to best practices for teachers' classroom assessment:

> Assessment [for these teachers] . . . is a process that facilitates appropriate instructional decisions by providing information on two fundamental questions:

- How are *we* (teacher and learner) doing, and
- How can *we* do better? (p. 3)

These two questions assume that the teacher *and* learner are equally vital in assessing the learning process. Thus, classroom assessment becomes an interactive process in which teachers "sit beside" children to assess and to teach them. If such an idea holds, then classroom assessment becomes a model that realigns the power relationship between the potentially dominant teacher and dominated child. If the interaction between teacher and learner equalizes the power relationships, then both what teachers do and what students do during learning activities must be looked at simultaneously, and not in isolation. Examining these political aspects of classroom assessment suggests seeing the teacher and the learner as collaborators in learning.

My research on the assessment practices of skilled teachers reveals that such teachers use a sociocultural assessment framework; that is, they consider the linguistic, cultural, social, and political factors related to the bilingual child and to his or her learning environment. As shown in the diagram below, best-practice teachers assess themselves and their learning environment first, before they focus on understanding the individual child as a learner.

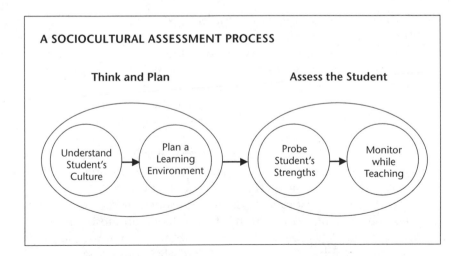

A SOCIOCULTURAL ASSESSMENT PROCESS

Think and Plan   **Assess the Student**

Understand Student's Culture → Plan a Learning Environment → Probe Student's Strengths → Monitor while Teaching

For example, Betty, an elementary school teacher, described her sociocultural assessment process, explaining how two of her students from very different home cultures adapted to the culture of the school:[7]

Understanding the Child's Culture and Language

I had two children arrive in September . . . very different cases. One was a child from Ethiopia named Heaven, who I later found out was raised in a refugee camp. She came to this country in March with no English. The other, Vivi, came from Scandinavia; her parents were visiting scholars at MIT.

Every day almost, I would talk to one of the parents at the end of the day to let them know what happened. I would describe to them what I observed their child do and ask them to tell me what they learned at home. This worked with Vivi, but for Heaven I had to do research about her previous world through contacting Catholic Charities.

Creating a Language-Learning Environment

I knew nothing about either language. We, for each of them, created an environment for learning language, and tried to do activities that did not totally depend on language. If we were doing songs, I would make sure they had visual cues or physical movements. If our talk were about a topic, I would have a picture or a sample object to show what we were learning about.

Probing for the Child's Strengths/Monitoring while Teaching

For activities I would make sure that I and one of the adults in the classroom were close by, making sure that these two students could get as much out of our work as they could. We would be noting their struggles and their breakthroughs in learning new skills. I often ask such a child to bring me their favorite book, as what they choose and how they share it tell me a lot about what they care about and what I can encourage.

What worked with Heaven was getting books from different countries to share in class. I remember that when I brought in books from Africa, I heard Heaven say her first words, "Africa, Africa." When she first came to us, she was squatting on a stool in the cafeteria and eating with her hands, living on mostly bread and ketchup. We heard that she was very hungry and we had to help her to learn to do everything differently in our school.

How do skilled teachers develop their own sociocultural framework for assessing their bilingual students? What strategies do they use first to assess these students and then to assess them in the context of their classrooms? My research suggest that classroom assessment can become a sociocultural process when teachers

1. first prepare to "do better" at assessing bilingual students by understanding their cultures and creating a culturally sensitive learning environment;
2. then assess the child by probing for individual learning strengths;
3. then verify their understanding of that student by monitoring their daily interactions within the classroom.

How does this sociocultural process unfold in a teacher's daily classroom practices? The first step is a preparation stage for teachers, a self-assessment in which they think about issues of language and culture related to a student, and then plan a classroom environment that supports second-language learners, interactions, and opportunities to monitor individuals carefully.

The next step involves *doing* the assessment of a bilingual student. This, in effect, determines how teachers link assessment to instruction for these students. Skilled teachers indicated that they informally assess bilingual students using a variety of strategies to gather observations and samples of student work, as detailed below.

Although there were variations in skilled teachers' individual practices, their process for gathering information, which includes ob-

TEACHERS' SELF-ASSESSMENT: THINK AND PLAN TO ASSESS	
Understand issues of language and culture: "Learn about who they are"	*Create an environment for learning language: "Provide a setting for cross-cultural learning"*
• Show you accept and value a bilingual learner	• Organize the physical environment for interactions
• Research student's cultural and linguistic background	• Use symbols to translate classroom expectations
• Acknowledge cultural issues in child-rearing	• Provide routines in schedules
• Recognize the cultural transition process and offer support	• Build assessments into the curriculum

FOCUS ON THE CHILD: ASSESS THE CHILD

Probe individual with informal assessment strategies: "Discover student's strengths"	*Monitor the individual while assessing and teaching: "Note their struggles and breakthroughs"*
• Observing social interactions	• Observing student's language and literacy over time
• Questioning students while learning	• Analyzing student's learning process
• Interviewing students	• Reflecting on student's work using observations and portfolios
• Developing a portfolio of student work	• Creating a mental file on each child

BASIC PREMISES OF CLASSROOM ASSESSMENT

1. Each classroom has a culture, and other children, acting as "cultural brokers," can communicate that culture to help a new bilingual child adjust.
2. Understanding the differences between a bilingual child's home culture and school culture is vital to any assessment process, which begins with ongoing dialogue between parents and teachers.
3. Bilingual children have more, not less, going on cognitively, yet accessing what they know may take time, interpretation, and translation on the part of teachers and parents.

serving, recording, questioning, interviewing, and collecting student work, was strikingly similar.

These teachers also recognized that each bilingual student's learning process involves complex issues of language and culture, which require a more extensive classroom assessment process. Best-practice teachers follow a sociocultural framework for assessment that looks first at social interactions, then at issues of culture and language, and then learning skills.

TEACHERS' SOCIOCULTURAL ASSESSMENT FRAMEWORK

Teacher Assessment Focus	Considerations	Strategies
Social interaction	Pairs and large group	• Observations during day • Paired reading • Whole-group literacy activities
Cultural issues	Parents, language models,family, social class, culture	• Observations • Work samples • Journal writing • Writing workshop • Parent conferences
Language and literacy	Fluency, comprehension, decoding, word attack skills	• Observations • Paired reading • Taped oral reading • Whole-group reading • Journals and other writing

CURRICULUM–BASED ASSESSMENTS

Assessment Strategies	Classroom Activities
Kid watching Learning about children by watching	Observing daily interactions Recording using checklists Anecdotal notes during literacy activities Writing workshop
Keeping track Collecting descriptive data on individual children	Questioning students about their work Collecting journal pages Literacy-based activity record sheets Taped oral reading samples Interviewing students and parents Conferencing with students and parents around portfolios
Documenting Observing and collecting evidence of children's learning	Teacher narrative summaries Student portfolios of sample work Tape recordings of oral reading Binder on each student with samples of journal pages Literacy record sheets Bimonthly self-portraits Quarterly summary profiles

Applying a sociocultural assessment means using informal and classroom strategies to observe, keep track, and document a student's learning in context and over time. My research found that best-practice teachers use a collection of curriculum-based assessments (Wilkinson, 1992), which are built into the course of their daily instruction. These teachers combine strategies of kid watching, keeping track, and documenting to assess bilingual children as part of their classroom programs. Best-practice teachers combine these strategies to collect data on each student's progress.

According to best-practice teachers, sociocultural assessment practices should include teachers' looking first at their own teaching and then at the products and the process of a bilingual student's learning. Experienced teachers use various formal and informal assessments to look closely at what individual bilingual children know and can do. These experienced teachers consider:

1. social and cultural factors — who a child is and how they learn;
2. political factors — how a child reacts in an environment/setting;
3. linguistic factors — how a child uses native and second languages;
4. academic/educational factors — how a child performs a given task.

Overall, my sociocultural assessment framework suggests that educators not only look at what is "wrong" with the child, but also what is "wrong" with the learning environment (the school, the classroom, or the curriculum).

Conclusions and Implications

My review of the literature and my research with teachers uncovers the political, social, cultural, and linguistic nature of teachers' classroom assessment practices. The key to improving assessment practice for bilingual students, according to skilled teachers, lies in realigning the power relations in the interpersonal interactions of school communities and recognizing the vital role of trained teachers as skilled assessors of the children they teach.

This improvement begins with professional development for teachers, as they have the critical power to hone their daily assessment practice by examining both the process and products of their students' work. Simply stated, teachers can be trained to do better at assessing bilingual students for instructional purposes. What might this training include? First, teachers can learn a sociocultural approach to classroom assessments that considers the intricate political, social, cultural, and linguistic factors that affect bilingual learners. Second, teachers need to consider who this child is as a learner, and how this child learns in a given environment.

Policymakers and administrators also need to apply research recommendations when designing and delivering comprehensive assessment systems in order to avoid discriminatory practices that rely on single measures, or solely on standardized tests, to make decisions about bilingual students. System-level assessments for students with diverse cultural and linguistic backgrounds should include formal, informal, and classroom assessments to address the complexities of evaluating both language proficiency and cognitive achievement.

Finally, all educators need to remember that the process of assessing and teaching bilingual students is ongoing and requires strategies of observing, keeping track, and documenting student learning in portfolios. Best-practice teachers are collaborators in their students' learning. They consider and gather evidence of both the process and products of their individual students using formal and informal assessments. As practitioners, they demonstrate how carefully they scrutinize their own assessment process by first thinking about what *they do* as teachers, and then carefully designing what they do to assess bilingual students. Most important, skilled teachers' assessment practices involve a series of social and cultural interactions, demonstrating to the educational community a sociocultural framework for the assessment process. These strategies and the framework show us that teachers' judgments *do* count when it comes to truly understanding first who a child is, and then how that child learns.

Notes

1. These recommendations are based on my book, *Whose Judgment Counts? Assessing Bilingual Children, K–3* (Stefanakis, 1998).
2. The Appendix of *Whose Judgment Counts? Case Studies of Teachers' Classroom Assessment of Linguistic Minority Children* (Stefanakis, 1995) presents the methodology for using a vignette interview with classroom observation and naturalistic interviews to study these teachers, all of whom worked in the Cambridge (MA) Public Schools.
3. The work of Virginia Gonzalez et al. (1996) discusses the diminished responses of linguistic-minority students when they are assessed by outside authorities.
4. This review culls from the literature on bilingual education, early childhood education, and educational assessment from 1989 to 1996.

5. For a more complete review of the classroom-assessment literature, see Stefanakis, 1998, pp. 15–18.
6. This section is based on my research with experienced classroom teachers in the Cambridge Public Schools who worked to develop best-practice standards in assessing bilingual children (see Stefanakis, 1995, 1998).
7. All names used are pseudonyms.

References

Airasian, P. (1991) *Classroom assessment.* New York: McGraw-Hill.

Alvarez, M. D. (1991). Psychoeducational assessment of linguistic minority children: Current perspectives and future trends. In A. N. Ambert (Ed.), *Bilingual education and English as a second language: A research handbook, 1988–90* (pp. 233–248). New York: Garland.

Ambert, A. N. (1991). *Bilingual education and English as a second language: A research handbook, 1988–90.* Garland Publishing Inc.

Anthony, J., Johnson, T., Mickelson, N., & Preece, A. (1991). *Evaluating literacy.* Portsmouth, NH: Heinemann.

Baca, L. M., & Almanza, E. (1991). *Language minority students with disabilities.* Reston, VA: Council for Exceptional Children.

Baca, L. M., & Clark, C. (1992, November 14). *EXITO: A dynamic team assessment approach for culturally diverse students.* Paper presented at the Council of Exceptional Children Conference, Minneapolis.

Chapman, P. (1988). *Schools as sorters: Lewis M. Terman, applied psychology and the intelligence testing movement, 1890–1930.* New York: New York University.

Cummins, J. (1986). Empowering minority students: A framework for intervention. *Harvard Education Review, 56,* 18–36.

Cummins, J. (1989). A theoretical framework for bilingual special education. *Exceptional Children, 65,* 111–119.

Damico, J. S. (1991). Descriptive assessment of communicative ability in limited English proficient children. In E. V. Hamayan & J. S. Damico (Eds.), *Limiting bias in the assessment of bilingual students* (p. 96). Austin, TX: Pro-Ed.

Damico, J. S., Cheng, L., DeLeon, J., Ferrer, J., & Westernoff, F. (1992, November 14). *Descriptive assessments in the schools: Meeting new challenges with new solutions.* Paper presented at the Council for Exceptional Conference, Minneapolis.

DeLeon, J. (1990). A model for advocacy-oriented assessment process in the psychoeducational evaluation of culturally and linguistically different students [Special Issue]. *Journal of Educational Issues of Language Minority Students, 7,* 53–67.

Dolson, D. (1994). *Assessing students in bilingual contexts: Provisional guidelines.* Sacramento: California State Department of Education.

Duran, E. (1991). *Functional language instruction for linguistically different students with moderate to severe disabilities.* Reston, VA: ERIC Clearinghouse on the Handicapped and Gifted Children.

Duran, R., & Szyanski, M. (1994*). Improving language arts assessment of linguistic minority students in cooperative learning settings.* Los Angeles: National Center for Research on Evaluation, Standards and Student Testing.

Fedoruk, G. (1989). Kindergarten screening for first-grade learning problems: The conceptual inadequacy of a child-deficit model. *Childhood Education, 66,* 40–42.

Figueroa, R. (1989). Psychological testing of linguistic minority students: Knowledge gaps and regulations. *Exceptional Children, 56,* 145–152.

Genesse, F., & Hamayan, E. (1994). Classroom based assessment. In F. Genesse (Ed.*), Education and second language children: The whole child, the whole curriculum, the whole community* (p. 54). New York: Cambridge University Press.

Gonzalez, V. (1998). *Assessment and instruction of linguistically diverse students with or at risk of learning problems: From research to practice.* Boston: Allyn & Bacon.

Gonzalez, V., Bauerle, P., & Felix-Holt, M. (1996). Theoretical and practical implications of assessment cognitive and language development in bilingual children with qualitative methods. *Bilingual Research Journal, 20,* 93–131.

Hakuta, K., & Garcia, E. (1989). Bilingualism and education. *American Psychologist, 44,* 374–379.

Hamayan, E., & Damico, J. S. (1991). Developing and using a second language. In E. V. Hamayan & J. S. Damico (Eds.), *Limiting bias in the assessment of bilingual students* (pp. 35–75). Austin, TX: Pro-Ed.

Hernandez, R. (1994). Reducing bias in assessment of culturally and linguistically diverse populations. *Journal of Issues on Language Minority Students, 14,* 260–300.

LaCelle Peterson, M., & Rivera, M. (1994). Is it read for all kids: A framework for equitable assessment policies for English language learners. *Harvard Educational Review, 64,* 555–575.

Marshall, S. (1992). Managing the culture: The key to effective change. *School Organization, 13,* 255–268.

Ortiz, A. A. (1990). Using school based problem solving teams for prereferral intervention. *Bilingual Special Education Perspective, 10,* 1–5.

Padilla, A. M., Valadez, C., & Chang, M. (1988). Young children's oral language proficiency and reading ability in Spanish and English. *CLEAR Technical Report.* Berkeley, CA: University Center for Language Education and Research.

Rhodes, N. (1993). *Literacy assessment: A handbook of instruments.* Portsmouth, NH: Heinemann.

Snow, C. E. (1992). Perspectives on second language development: Implications for bilingual education. *Educational Researcher, 21*(2), 16–20.

Stefanakis, E. (1991). Early childhood education: The effects of language on learning. In N. Ambert (Ed.), *Bilingual education and English as a second language: A research handbook, 1988–90.* New York: Garland.

Stefanakis, E. (1995). *Whose judgment counts? Case studies of primary teachers' classroom assessment of young linguistic minority students.* Unpublished doctoral thesis, Harvard University Graduate School of Education.

Stefanakis, E. (1998). *Whose judgment counts? Assessing bilingual children, K–3.* Portsmouth, NH: Heinemann Boynton.

Tierney, R., Carter, M., & Desai, L. *Portfolio assessment in the reading-writing classroom.* Norwood, MA: Christopher Gordon.

Wiggins, G. (1989). Teaching to the (authentic) test. *Educational Leadership, 46*(7), 41–47.

Wilkinson, C. (1992, November 14). *Curriculum based assessment.* Paper presented at the Council for Exceptional Children Conference, Minneapolis.

Wilkinson, C., & Holzman, W. (1988, April). *Relationships among language proficiency, language test of administration, and special education eligibility for bilingual Hispanic students with suspected learning disabilities.* Paper presented at the annual conference of the American Educational Research Association, New Orleans.

Wolf, D. P. (1989). Portfolio assessment: Sampling student work. *Educational Leadership, 46*(7), 35–39.

PART THREE

Transforming Bilingualism

Toward a New Paradigm
of Bilingualism

Though there are countless examples of pedagogical excellence in bilingual classrooms, too many language-minority students continue to lose their native language, receive low-quality education, and underachieve academically. The current monolingual/monocultural paradigm that defines the bilingualism of language-minority students as "problematic," "deficient," and "a sign of inferior intellectual abilities" is undermining efforts to improve bilingual programs. In order to realize the promise of bilingualism and bilingual education, a paradigmatic shift is necessary in our classrooms, schools, and society. As part of a larger project to transform our multilingual society into a linguistic democracy, we as a nation must resolve that language-minority students deserve *and* have a right to develop their native language and English, and we must mobilize resources to nurture their bilingualism in our schools. In the third and final part of *Lifting Every Voice*, three Latina teacher educator/researchers, Lilia Bartolomé, Sonia Nieto, and Maria Brisk, and one Cape Verdean ESL teacher and community activist, Ambrizeth Lima, discuss specific supports necessary to realize the promise of bilingualism.

One important way to support and improve bilingual education would be a reconceptualization of comprehensive teacher preparation. In her essay, Lilia Bartolomé envisions a teacher preparation program that would offer abundant opportunities for teachers to reflect upon their values, beliefs, and ideology, and to gain political clarity — that is, to understand the close connection between the larger political, economic, and social systems that subordinate some groups and the academic failure of these groups in schools and classrooms. Bartolomé suggests that current and future bilingual teachers be supported with an education that equips them both with the instructional and theoretical tools that they need to respond to their students' academic strengths and needs, and the political clarity necessary to transform rather than reinforce inequitable group relations in the society. Her vision is that such teacher preparation programs will graduate teachers who do not unconsciously reproduce the existing inequities of U.S. society in their classrooms through, for example, setting low academic expectations for language-minority students.

Sonia Nieto continues the discussion of the important role that colleges and teacher preparation programs can play in improving bilingual education. Nieto emphasizes the responsibility of teacher education programs in preparing all teachers — not only bilingual teachers — for working with language-minority students. While it is important that teacher education programs address effective instructional strategies in multilingual classrooms and varied approaches to first- and second-language development, Nieto argues that it is also crucial that the political and ideological underpinnings of each approach become the subject of study.

In order to better prepare teachers to work with bilingual student populations, Nieto suggests three essentials for teacher education programs. Her first essential is that every teacher preparation program engage in institutional self-inquiry and reflection regarding fundamental questions such as how the program defines the academic and linguistic goals of education. A second essential emphasizes reexamination of the program's curriculum — including content, readings, and assignments — to better represent and reflect linguistic diversity issues. A third essential involves encouraging teachers to become advocates for their students and not only to teach, but also to learn from, their students. Nieto's third essential also calls for a reorganization of teacher preparation programs to create frequent opportunities for prospective teachers to reflect on their cultural and ethnic identities and their privileges of class and color.

Another factor that can either support or undermine bilingual programs is the quality of the public schools in which they are housed. Drawing from her field-based experience and research, Maria Brisk observes that good bilingual programs are housed in high-quality public schools. Efforts to improve bilingual program quality must therefore be thought of as an integral part of school reform efforts. Brisk notes that, in addition to the school quality factor, effective bilingual programs share other common characteristics. These characteristics include a strong commitment on the part of the school administration to the program; academic goals that are clearly communicated to the entire school community, including staff, parents, and students; a respectful and collaborative relationship between parents and school personnel; and social and academic integration of the bilingual program into the larger school. Experiences of schools that have identified these characteristics as important, not only for bilingual students but for all students, show that in time and with hard work, high-quality bilingual programs are attainable.

Unfortunately, most bilingual programs are isolated and devalued within schools. In the final essay of this volume, Ambrizeth Lima discusses specific strategies that interrupt and begin to remove the stigma and hostility that bilingual students and teachers encounter in schools. She proposes three necessary areas of advocacy to build support for bilingual education — within the classroom, within the school, and beyond the school. Lima first describes strategies that she uses in her classroom, such as educating her students about their civil rights and encouraging them to be good advocates for themselves and the program by participating in schoolwide decisionmaking bodies and by sharing their culture with the larger school population. Second, she argues that bilingual teachers themselves need to be more actively involved in decisionmaking bodies within the school, in educating mainstream teachers about bilingualism and bilingual programs, and in organizing active support among their colleagues. Finally, advocacy must continue beyond the school, as teachers problematize demeaning labels such as "compensatory program" and "limited English proficiency," educate the public about bilingualism and bilingual education through the media and presentations at professional conferences, and participate actively in their union and in local elections.

Democratizing Bilingualism: The Role of Critical Teacher Education

LILIA I. BARTOLOMÉ

Much of the discussion about the preparation of bilingual teachers focuses on the best strategies to address the academic and linguistic development of linguistic-minority students. While this focus is necessary, it often prevents our addressing the important role of political and ideological clarity in teachers' thinking and teaching. In this chapter, I argue that teachers need to gain greater political and ideological clarity in order to increase the chances of academic success for their linguistic-minority students and subordinated minority students.[1] I believe that teacher education programs that enable prospective teachers, first, to recognize the existence of the political dimensions of education, and second, to increase their ideological clarity will produce the type of intellectual practitioners we urgently need to teach in today's increasingly culturally and socially diverse urban schools. I believe that uncritical prospective teachers often end up blindly following lockstep methodologies and promulgating unexamined beliefs and attitudes that can compound the difficulties faced by linguistic-minority children in school.

It is important to understand that, while issues such as teaching strategies and techniques are important, focusing only on technical issues often distracts teachers from the very real ideological and political dimensions of linguistic-minority education. I define *political clarity* as the process by which individuals achieve a deepening awareness of the sociopolitical and economic realities that shape their lives and their capacity to transform them. It also refers to the process by which individuals come to better understand possible linkages between macro-level political, economic, and social variables and subordinated groups' academic performance in the micro-level classroom. Thus, it invariably requires educators to struggle to link sociocultural structures and schooling.[2] A related concept, *ideology*, refers to the framework of thought that is used by members of a society to justify or rationalize an existing social (dis)order. Thus, *ideological clarity* refers to the process by which individuals struggle to identify both the dominant society's explanations for the existing societal socioeconomic and political hierarchy, as well as their own explanation of the social order and any resulting inequalities. Ideological clarity requires that teachers' individual explanations be compared and contrasted with those propagated by the dominant society. It is to be hoped that the juxtaposing of ideologies forces teachers to better understand if, when, and how their belief systems uncritically reflect those of the dominant society and support unfair and inequitable conditions.

Teachers and prospective teachers working on improving their political and ideological clarity recognize that teaching is not a politically or ideologically neutral undertaking. They understand that educational institutions are socializing institutions that often mirror the greater society's culture, values, and norms. Schools reflect both the positive and negative aspects of a society. Thus, the unequal power relations among various social and cultural groups at the societal level are usually reproduced at the school and classroom level, unless concerted efforts are made to prevent their reproduction. Teachers working toward political and ideological clarity understand that they can either maintain the status quo, or they can work to transform the sociocultural reality at the classroom and school level so that the culture at this micro-level does not reflect macro-level inequalities, such as asymmetrical power relations that relegate certain cultural groups to a subordinate status.

It is important to reiterate that, while I strongly agree that bilingual teachers must be well versed in language acquisition theory and practice, classroom management and organization, and a variety of instructional approaches, it is important to understand that, in addition to having these technical skills, we must also be ready to struggle with the greater political and ideological challenges that we face in our attempts to work with subordinated linguistic-minority populations. In fact, the present assault on bilingual education illustrates that key objections to it do not necessarily reflect technical or instructional concerns but are, rather, highly political and ideological in nature. Opponents of bilingual education do not generally question specific instructional practices used in such programs (for example, reading and math instructional techniques). However, they vociferously oppose linguistic-minority students being taught in any language other than English. The opposition is not solely pedagogical in that opponents truly believe that linguistic-minority students will actually achieve higher academically if taught in English only. In fact, I argue that their so-called concern for linguistic-minority academic achievement is not an authentic concern in these debates. Rather, the key concern with using native language instruction grows out of the misperception by the mainstream[3] that using languages other than English (especially Spanish[4]) in school incorrectly accords those languages equal status in relation to English, thus shifting the historically superordinate status of English to one of equality with other "foreign" languages.[5] In addition, despite the fact that many bilingual teachers are White, middle-class females, mainstream (mis)perceptions are that bilingual teachers are primarily non-White "ethnics" self-interested in promulgating their various native languages.[6] This (mis)belief also serves to further the mainstream's perceptions that bilingual education threatens to disrupt the existing social order by eventually toppling White English speakers' "rightful" positions of superiority.

Teachers and prospective teachers need to develop the necessary political and ideological clarity to understand these attacks on bilingual education. Thus, in addition to teaching theory and teaching methods, teacher educators have the responsibility to provide prospective teachers with learning opportunities to better understand the political dimensions of education in general, and in particular those present in linguistic-minority education. In the following sections of this chapter I will expand on my argument in the following fashion. First, I discuss the historical negation of the politics and ideology of teaching in teacher preparation programs. Second, I discuss select research on effective teachers and show how the research, despite not explicitly naming teacher political and ideological clarity, in fact suggests that teachers who possess this type of understanding are more likely to successfully counter dominant culture assimilationist and deficit ideologies and better serve their linguistic-minority students. Third, I conclude by offering general recommendations for improving teacher preparation programs to better prepare teachers (both English monolingual and bilingual) to deal with issues of politics, ideology, and ethics in order to more effectively and successfully work with subordinated linguistic-minority students.

The Need to "Name" and Interrogate Assimilationist and Deficit Ideologies in Teacher Education

The issue of teacher ideology and the role that it may play in teachers' thinking and behavior in education in general and in linguistic-minority education in particular has usually been ignored or negated in most teacher education programs, as well as in much of the teacher education literature. Historically, we have tended to treat the preparation of teachers as a chiefly technical issue.[7] Giroux and McLaren point out that

> as far back as 1890, Horace Willard cogently argued that in contrast to members of other professions, teachers lived "lives of mechanical routine, and were subjected to a machine of supervision, organization, classification, grading, percentages." Forty years later Henry W. Holmes, dean of Harvard University's new Graduate School of Education, echoed these sentiments in his criticism of the National Survey of the Education of Teachers in 1930. According to Holmes, the survey failed to support teachers as independent critical thinkers. Instead, it endorsed a view of the teacher as a "routine worker under the expert direction of principal, supervisors, and superintendents."[8]

Although there have been experimental teacher education programs in the past to develop teachers as critically minded intellectuals or "transformative intellectuals," the dominant tradition has tended to equate teacher preparation with training and the imparting of technical skills in classroom instruction, classroom management, and curriculum. The role and effects of the teacher's political and ideological orientation have not been sufficiently acknowledged as relevant to the task of teacher preparation.

For example, when reviewing the 1998 American Educational Research Association (AERA) conference program, I was struck by the

variety of conference presentations dedicated to discussing teacher beliefs, predispositions, unconscious perceptions, assumptions, and
their "thoughts" about culturally diverse student populations — culturally diverse, of course, being a euphemism for non-White and non-
middle-class students.[10] Even though AERA seemed to have made
great strides to move beyond views of teacher education as a chiefly
technical endeavor, even progressive educators remained somewhat
trapped by a euphemistic discourse that fails to interrogate the role of
ideology in the creation of inequities and other forms of discrimination along the lines of gender, class, ethnicity, language, and culture.

Educators need to "name" ideology for what it is. Although there
have been, and continue to be, efforts to examine teacher beliefs and
attitudes, as illustrated in the AERA conference program example,
there have been few systematic attempts to examine the political and
ideological dimensions of teacher "beliefs," "assumptions," "unconscious perceptions," and how these worldviews are part of a particular
ideological orientation. Indeed, teachers' beliefs and attitudes have
been treated as apolitical, overly psychologized constructs that "simply" reflect personality types, individual values, and predispositions
that have little to do with the existing larger political, social, and economic order. Teachers' conscious and unconscious beliefs and attitudes regarding the legitimacy of the greater social order and of the resulting unequal power relations among various cultural groups at the
school and classroom levels, by and large, have historically not been
acknowledged as significant to improving the educational process and
outcome of linguistic-minority education.

However, even without utilizing the term *ideology*, the literature
suggests that prospective teachers tend to uncritically and, often, unconsciously hold beliefs and attitudes about the existing social order
that reflect the dominant ideology. Unfortunately, this reproduction
of thinking often translates into teachers' uncritical acceptance of
assimilationist and deficit-based views of linguistic-minority students.
I believe that the assimilationist and deficit ideologies held by most
White teachers and many non-White teachers have had and continue
to have detrimental consequences for the education of non-White and
linguistic-minority students.

Assimilationist ideology, as used here, is treated as synonymous
with the concept "Anglo conformity model," which refers to the belief
that immigrants and subordinated indigenous groups should be

brought to conform to the practices of the dominant Anglo-Saxon culture. Implicit in this model is the belief that the socioeconomic hierarchy resulting from this system is an appropriate and fair one that need not be questioned by educators. Educators operating under this ideology argue that this socioeconomic hierarchy is based on merit; that non-White and linguistic-minority students who want to achieve simply need to learn English and adopt the mainstream culture. Yet, we have only to look at African Americans and Native Americans, rendered English-dominant by the forced loss of their native languages, to understand that English language proficiency in and of itself does not guarantee first-class citizenship.

The combination of an assimilationist belief system with a deficit ideology proves to be an especially deadly one because it rationalizes disrespecting linguistic-minority students' native language and primary culture, misteaching them dominant culture and English, and then blaming their academic difficulties on the students' "pathological deficiencies." The deficit ideological model has a long history in U.S. education, as discussed in the education literature. Richard Valencia traces its evolution over three centuries: also known in the literature as the social pathology model or the cultural deprivation model, the deficit approach explains disproportionate academic problems among low-status students as largely being due to pathologies or deficits in their sociocultural background (e.g., cognitive and linguistic deficiencies, low self-esteem, poor motivation).[11] Barbara Flores documents the effect this deficit ideology has had on the schools' past and current perceptions of Latino students.[12] Her historical overview chronicles descriptions used to refer to Latino students over the last century. The terms range from *mentally retarded, linguistically handicapped, culturally and linguistically deprived,* and *semilingual,* to the current deficit euphemism for Latino and other subordinated students: the *at-risk* student.

The elements of both harmful assimilationist and deficit ideologies are inadvertently captured in a research project that set out to describe teachers' beliefs regarding how to best educate linguistic-minority students.[13] Although the intended focus of the study was to examine teachers' beliefs about specific instructional theories and practices, she describes a school situation in which the mainstream teachers in a sample are waging an "ideological war" against their bilingual counterparts. Mainstream teachers resorted to disrespectful and backhanded attacks on Latina teachers when voicing their opposition to bilingual education. The mainstream teachers did not present their opposition in terms of pedagogical theory, but instead attacked the Latina teachers' English-language proficiency as faulty. Furthermore, they criticized the Latina teachers' Spanish-language proficiency despite the fact that they did not comprehend or speak Spanish! Although the monolingual teachers claimed that their anti-bilingual education stance reflected their concern for the academic well-being of linguistic-minority children, they offered little in the way of concrete suggestions for modifying or improving instruction to ensure the academic success of these children. Despite their ignorance about the instructional theories or issues concerning linguistic-minority students, the teachers were not at all apologetic or embarrassed about their lack of knowledge. Instead, they focused on maintaining business as usual, which translated into an English-only, sink-or-swim approach. Despite the exploratory nature of this research and the small sample size, it captures the very real power struggles to maintain hegemony of English and the dominant social order in school settings. One can only imagine the ill treatment that linguistic-minority students receive in a setting such as this one, where even the adults are viewed and spoken about with such contempt.

Another relevant study focused on the effects of Mexican American students' speech style and skin color on bilingual teacher candidates' and teachers' perceptions of them.[14] This study also inadvertently captured the presence of teachers' assimilationist and deficit views of non-White and nonstandard-language-speaking students. The study indicated that both sets of educators, most of whom were Latinas themselves, rated students more favorably on social and academic scales when they spoke standard Spanish rather than a nonstandard variety. In addition, the teachers rated lighter-skinned students higher than their darker-skinned counterparts. Finally, both groups of educators rated the males more favorably than the female students. Although this is an attitudinal study, one can certainly imagine possible adverse and hurtful instructional practices growing out of this ideological stance.

This exploratory study powerfully captures how minority teachers, members of subordinated groups themselves, often also subscribe to assimilationist and deficit ideologies. In this case, the educators' ideological stance clearly reflected an uncritical acceptance of a social order in which the light-skinned, the male, and the standard language speakers are viewed (and possibly treated) as more intelligent and socially competent. Given this ideological reality, simply providing linguistic-minority students with teachers who are from their ethnic group and who speak their native languages does not guarantee that the teachers will not subscribe to assimilationist ideologies and deficit views of their students.

The two research studies discussed indicate the need to further investigate and address the ideological and political dimensions of education in teacher preparation programs. Though no research has definitively linked teachers' ideological stance with particular instructional practices, I believe that a teacher's ideological stance is often reflected in the way s/he interacts with and treats students in the classroom. There is an urgent need for additional research that identifies teachers' ideologies and explores the possible harmful effects of such uncritical and narrow ideological belief systems.[15] Too often, prospective and practicing teachers come out of (pre-service) teacher education programs having unconsciously absorbed assimilationist and deficit views of non-Whites and the low-income students. This ideological stance often constitutes the foundation on which future (in-service) teacher training is built. Teachers are not forced to reflect critically on their ideological orientation, and thus "bring with them, unintentional or otherwise, racist and xenophobic views with the potential to corrupt teacher-student interactions and academic instruction."[16] The restricted perspectives from which some teachers view their students is a product of their own personal theories, internalized beliefs, and values that reflect their own formative and restricted life and cultural experiences and influences. However, they do not recognize that these beliefs and attitudes reflect a dominant ideology, but instead view them as "natural," "objective," and "common sense" — in other words, *the norm*.[17] One's ideology serves as a lens that filters new information or knowledge. Conventional teacher education programs for both bilingual and monolingual teachers fail to acknowledge the existence of this ideology and treat pre-service teachers as blank slates who simply need to learn the latest in teaching and discipline techniques to function effectively in the classroom.

The dramatic increase in low-income, non-White, and linguistic-minority students in U.S. public schools signals the urgent need to understand and challenge the ideological orientations of prospective teachers in teacher education programs. One current challenge is to adequately prepare the overwhelmingly White, female, and middle-class pre-service teacher population to work with subordinated student groups that are quickly becoming the majority in many of the largest urban public schools in the country.[18] While the nation's school population is made up of approximately 40 percent minority children, nearly 90 percent of teachers are White.[19] In addition, social-class differences between teacher and student continue to widen. For example, 44 percent of African American children and 36 percent of Latino children live in poverty, yet more teachers come from White lower-middle and middle-class homes and have been reared in rural and suburban communities.[20] There are also significant differences in teacher-student language backgrounds. The majority of teachers are English monolingual, while there are approximately 5 to 7.5 million non-native English students in the public schools.[21] Even in bilingual education, the majority of teachers are White, which points to the common misperception that non-White teachers fill the majority of bilingual teacher slots. In California, for example, only 15 percent of bilingual teacher positions are held by Latinos.[22] In addition, while Hispanic students constitute two-thirds of non-native English students, only 15 percent of bilingual teachers are Hispanic.[23]

Given these changing student demographics, it becomes evident that *all* teachers, not just bilingual teachers, are responsible for preparing linguistic-minority children. And, given the social class, cultural, and language differences between teachers and students, it becomes especially urgent that teachers critically understand their ideological orientations with respect to cultural and class differences and begin to comprehend that teaching is not a politically or ideologically neutral undertaking.

Although the need to help teachers and prospective teachers name and interrogate their ideological stance is urgent, it is not an easy task. The reality that educators unknowingly accept and support the status quo even when it can potentially harm their students is unfortunate, but it is not surprising, given, as Bourdieu states, that

> teachers are the products of a system whose aim is to transmit an aristocratic culture, and are likely to adopt its values with greater ardor in proportion to the degree to which they owe it their own academic and social success. How indeed could they avoid un-

consciously bringing into play the values of the milieu from which they come, or to which they wish to belong, when teaching and assessing their pupils? Thus, in higher education, the working or lower middle class student will be judged according to the scale of values of the educated classes which many teachers owe to their social origin and which they willingly adopt. [24]

Current research on prospective teachers' beliefs, attitudes, and preferences suggests that teachers prefer to teach students who are like themselves in communities that are familiar to them. Most pre-service teachers very clearly state that they do not want to teach in inner-city schools or work with minority or linguistic-minority students.[25]

Approaches for preparing prospective teachers to deal with increasing cultural and linguistic diversity in schools can, with few exceptions, be described as fragmented additions to the existing teacher preparation curriculum. While most teacher education programs have begun to acknowledge issues of cultural and linguistic diversity, they usually do so by requiring only one or two courses in multicultural education or electives that discuss cultural, ethnic, or gender issues.[26] Few programs have seriously attempted to infuse or permeate the existing teacher education curriculum with key concepts that require prospective teachers to critically examine and interrogate their ideological orientations as part of their learning process.[27] Critics of such fragmented multicultural education claim that it fails to address seriously issues of structural and ideological inequality or to challenge prospective teachers' ethnocentric and culturally parochial ideologies. Because of these limited and superficial attempts to prepare teachers for meeting the needs of children from subordinated groups, there is little opportunity for them to begin to develop political and ideological clarity.

On the other hand, I would argue that the restricted perspectives from which some teachers view their linguistic-minority students are not fixed and irreversible. Teachers' actions and beliefs that eventually contradict the dominant norms serve as evidence that the individual is a creator as well as a recipient of values, and many members of the dominant culture, as well as subordinated cultures, are open to recognizing the political dimensions of teaching, questioning the status quo, and working toward creating more just and democratic educational conditions for all students.[28] I propose a radical transformation in teacher preparation that prioritizes teachers' political and ideological clarity.

In fact, I believe that much can be learned from effective teachers of linguistic-minority students and applied to our thinking about the types of concepts and learning experiences prospective teachers should encounter in teacher preparation programs. Current studies that identify the characteristics of exemplary bilingual teachers suggest that successful teachers share an anti-assimilationist and anti-deficit ideological orientation.[29] In other words, the teachers in these studies question, in one form or another, the correctness or fairness of the existing social order and actively work to prevent its reproduction at the school and classroom levels. Ideas for improving the preparation of teachers can be drawn from these exemplary teachers' ideological orientations and resulting practices.

Research on Effective Teachers of Linguistic-Minority Students: Politically and Ideologically Clear Student Advocates

A study by Eugene Garcia provides an example of effective bilingual teachers' thinking and practice around the issue of subordinated students' education. Although Garcia discusses these teacher attributes as apolitical constructs, I believe that some of these "attributes" contain elements of teachers' political and ideological clarity. It is evident from Garcia's description of the three teachers that they go beyond the technical aspects of their job when they explain that "part of their job . . . is to provide the kind of cultural and linguistic validation that is missing in Field Town [the local community], a community known for deprecating the Latino [Mexican American] culture and the Spanish language."[30] Teachers in this study appear to question the fairness of the existing social order in the larger community and take a clear stand to prevent its reproduction in their classrooms. Even though they recognize the subordinate status accorded to Latinos in the greater society and in the immediate community, they firmly and unequivocally reject feeling sorry for or treating the students in a condescending manner. All the teachers reported a conscious rejection of the *pobrecito* (poor little one) syndrome and the belief that schools can do little to teach children from low socioeconomic backgrounds. Their unwavering support of their children and their idealistic but realistic hopes in the educational process is illustrated in the following teacher's comments:

No "pobrecito" syndrome here. I want all my students to learn and I know they can learn even though they may come from poor families and live under "tough" conditions. I can have them do their homework here and I can even get them a tutor — an older student — if they need it. I understand that their parents may not be able to help them at home. That's no excuse for them not learning.[31]

In addition, all of the teachers explained the importance of establishing strong and caring relationships between the teacher and students, as well as among the students themselves. In my opinion, their argument for creating caring and family-like classroom environments appears to be informed not simply by an apolitical "touchy-feely" approach, but by a political understanding that working-class Mexican American students (similar to other subordinated student groups) usually experience less-than-caring teachers and school personnel in schools. It appears to me that they see their job as requiring that, in addition to imparting academic content, they also create classroom conditions where the children are not viewed through deficit lenses and expected to survive English-only assimilationist education. Although Garcia does not distinguish between those teachers who are caring and loving human beings and those teachers who are caring and loving human beings *driven by a political and ideological quest for greater social justice,* the work of Tamara Beauboeuf clearly and explicitly explains this important distinction.[32]

In her research, Beauboeuf interviews six effective African American women teachers regarding their beliefs, attitudes, and actual instructional practices. Her teachers resembled the teachers Garcia describes in his research. Beauboeuf describes the teachers as similarly caring and committed to incorporating their students' life experiences and cultures into the curriculum, yet *consciously dedicated* to preventing unequal power relations from being reproduced in their classrooms (my emphasis). Beauboeuf reports that the teachers she studied have come to see education for social justice through maternal, *political,* and moral lenses (my emphasis). She describes their teaching as "politicized mothering" and explains her renaming of "culturally relevant teaching" to "politically relevant teaching" precisely because of the significant role the teachers' political and ideological clarity plays in their attempts to transform their classrooms and schools into more just and democratic institutions for *all* students. Beauboeuf explains her decision to use the term *politicized mothering:*

Offering the renaming of [culturally relevant teaching to] "politically relevant teaching" was my attempt to focus on schools as political institutions that can legitimize inequality but that can also promote justice. This renaming also urges us to recognize teachers as political beings who have the power and responsibility to be advocates for students and agents for social change rather than defenders of the status quo.[33]

Similarly, my research with Maria Balderrama (in progress), which examines the ideological beliefs of effective White teachers of linguistic-minority students, suggests that these White teachers, for a variety of reasons, have developed an understanding that education is a political act that can either support the status quo or challenge it.

Despite the teachers' differing explanations for the existing social order, they all question the validity of a meritocratic explanation for it. As a result of their questioning, these high school teachers work hard to protect and shelter their students from the hardships present in their personal lives and from possible discrimination and ill treatment encountered outside of school. These White teachers do not accept a deficit view of linguistic-minority students or take an assimilationist stance in educating them. In fact, they promote native language instruction so that students "can learn academic subject matter appropriate to their grade level and to maintain positive self-esteem and cultural pride." In addition, instead of subscribing to an assimilationist orientation, the majority of these teachers voiced their belief that cultures in contact (such as Mexican Americans and Anglo Americans in contact in the Southwest) should transform and inform the other, with each cultural group taking the "best" from the other culture and discarding the "worst" from their respective cultures.

Given their own life experiences as "cultural border crossers," these teachers reported having experienced, first hand, the arbitrariness and unfairness of being accorded subordinate or low status at some point in their lives. For example, one of the teachers in the sample grew up a lower-middle-class girl in an affluent community, and early on she experienced and resisted low-status treatment. Given her life experiences as a young girl, she recognized the myth of an "equal playing field" and discovered ways of circumventing the inequalities. Now this teacher works hard at imparting academic skills while struggling to equalize her students' educational playing field.

This teacher, along with most of her colleagues, clearly articulated her strategies for creating a more equal playing field and *comfort zone* for all students at her school.[34] These teachers mentioned activities such as fundraising to give their working-class students experiences similar to those of more affluent students, bringing in consultants and other experts to educate the teaching staff about various linguistic-minority educational issues, and spending extra time and personal income to improve students' educational learning experiences. They also mentioned the importance of consistently treating the students with authentic respect and care regardless of their academic standing. They all spoke of creating a comfort zone for their students — students who, in their opinion, have historically not been made to feel welcome or comfortable by schoolteachers, counselors, or administrators.

It is evident that the effective teachers of linguistic-minority students discussed above understand that teaching is not an apolitical undertaking. Although the teachers may vary in their levels of political and ideological clarity, they nevertheless appear clear that linguistic-minority students often, through no fault of their own, are viewed and treated as being of low status in the greater society and in school settings. These teachers appear to question dominant-culture explanations of the existing social order. They reject deficit and assimilationist ideologies, they are well versed in current instructional theory and practices, especially in relation to second-language learners, and they courageously and aggressively work to create structures at the classroom and school level that authentically respect and legitimize working-class children from a variety of ethnic groups. Their clarity and ethics make them unconditional advocates, or cultural brokers, for their students — all in order to "equalize the unequal playing field."

Developing Political and Ideological Clarity in Teachers: Recommendations

I would like to close this chapter by sharing my general recommendations regarding the types of knowledge areas that prospective teachers need to acquire in order to become more effective teachers of subordinated minority students. The literature on effective teachers of linguistic-minority students, though limited, points out that we must go beyond simplistic and unidimensional recommendations for creating more effective teacher preparation programs. My recommendations reflect the ideological stance and practices of the effective teachers discussed in the previous section.

It is clear from the literature and my own research that effective teachers of linguistic-minority students have acquired some degree of political and ideological clarity, possess a great deal of courage, see themselves in solidarity with their subordinated students as well as their communities, and possess an unwavering sense of ethics. What is not clear is how these teachers acquired such an understanding and commitment to linguistic-minority education. While it may be true that these individuals may have gained this clarity not in teacher education programs but through their individual life experiences, it is my belief that efforts can be made in teacher education programs to better understand and teach to prospective teachers the significance of political and ideological clarity, courage, solidarity, and ethics related to working effectively with subordinated populations.

Although there are numerous teacher preparation programs that provide particular learning experiences with the potential to help prospective teachers increase their political and ideological clarity, as well as confront issues of courage, solidarity, and ethics, few programs are structured to ensure that these key areas of knowledge are present across the course of study. For example, many teacher education programs require that their students visit, observe, and student teach in culturally diverse and low-socioeconomic communities. In addition, a number of programs present their students with opportunities to study abroad in order to develop bilingual and bicultural competencies. Despite good intentions, students are generally left to their own devices in terms of "making sense" of these cross-cultural and cross-socioeconomic class experiences. Often, students who participate in these cross-cultural and cross-socioeconomic status experiences become unconscious voyeurs who view their new situations through never-acknowledged assimilationist and deficit ideological lenses.

The unanticipated end result is that students often emerge from these experiences ever more bound to their unquestioned ethnocentric ideologies. I recall working with a group of prospective bilingual teachers who had spent a year abroad in Mexico City and had returned to the United States to complete required course work. These students, the majority of whom were White and middle class, were well-intentioned individuals who returned from Mexico City expressing disillusionment with aspects of Mexican culture. They shared having witnessed blatant acts of sexism, classism, and racism (against indigenous Mexicans by light-skinned Mexicans). Without a theoretical framework for interpreting their experiences, the students unconsciously fell back on ethnocentric ideological frameworks. Many of the students expressed relief at being back in the United States because they believed that sexism, racism, and classism were less of an issue in the United States than in Mexico. Had the students' perceptions been left unexamined, the students could have come away with an incomplete analysis and understanding of their experience abroad. The goal of the Mexico teacher education program included producing teachers who would emerge bilingual, bicultural, and sensitive to cultural differences. Yet, merely providing students with cultural opportunities and not providing some type of critical framework for perceiving and interpreting new experience neutralized the teacher education program's good intentions.

My response was to encourage the students to examine the hurtful and dehumanizing experiences they had lived through in Mexico. I explained that as outsiders they had been in a unique situation to clearly perceive the dominant social order and its manifestations of unequal treatment. I urged them to remember how painful and humiliating it feels to be accorded low-status positions and then be treated accordingly. I challenged them to decide whether or not they could make the commitment as teachers to work against these oppressive and undemocratic tendencies present across societies. I also urged them to consider whether their opinion that racism, sexism, and classism are less important issues in the United States would be confirmed by the poor, by people of color, and by women of color in this society. We discussed their perceptions of differential status given their location as White, middle-class people.

My point in discussing this incident in what I consider to be a good teacher preparation program is to illustrate that there are a number of teacher education programs that already offer valuable courses of study and educational experiences to their students, but which lack a clear and coherent mission for ensuring that students consistently reflect upon and question their ideological orientations vis-à-vis non-White and non-middle-class students.

What is needed in many teacher preparation programs is commitment, on the part of administrators and educators, to weave key concepts such as political and ideological clarity, courage, solidarity, and ethics throughout the existing curriculum in order to better prepare prospective teachers to become effective teachers of all students and, in particular, of subordinated minority students.

Prospective and current teachers must begin to develop the ideological and political clarity that will guide them in denouncing a discriminatory school and social context so as to protect and advocate for their students. In addition, this clarity will also serve to help them move beyond the present and announce a utopian future in which social justice and a humanizing pedagogy are always present in our classrooms.

According to Paulo Freire, beyond technical skills, teachers should also be equipped with a full understanding of what it means to have courage — to denounce the present inequities that directly cripple certain populations of students — and effectively create psychologically harmless educational contexts.[35] He challenges us to become courageous in our commitment to defend subordinated student populations, even when it is easier not to take a stand.

In addition to ideological and political clarity and courage, prospective teachers must see themselves in solidarity with their students and their students' communities. They must understand the meaning and risk of solidarity so as to protect the dignity of their students. Again, actions of solidarity require politically and ideologically clear and courageous individuals, as demonstrated by many of the effective teachers discussed in the previous section.

Finally, schools of education should also create spaces where the development of an ethical posture informs not only the technical acquisition of skills, but also one's position vis-à-vis the human suffering that certain populations of students face in their community and in their school. All too often, in our quest to become "culturally relativistic," we fail to discuss the ethical and moral dimensions of our work as educators. Regardless of the diversity of cultural opinions found in any school of education, concepts such as equality, democracy, fairness, and justice need to serve as ever-present anchors across the teacher education curriculum to remind prospective teachers that teaching is ultimately a moral and ethical undertaking. Such an undertaking requires a high level of commitment and political clarity. In addition to the mastery of the content of one's field of specialization, political and ideological clarity becomes a decisive factor in effective teaching and learning. As one cannot be a successful teacher without a rigorous content preparation, one cannot be effective pedagogically without the political and ideological clarity that forces one to ask the a priori political question: What content, against what, for whom, and against whom? Thus, the role of a teacher can never be reduced to a facile and mechanistic transmission of selective content. The role of a teacher is invariably political, as eloquently argued by Paulo Freire:

> My very presence in the school as a teacher is intrinsically a political presence, something that students cannot possibly ignore. In this sense, I ought to transmit to the students my capacity to analyze, to compare, to evaluate, to decide, to opt, to break with. My capacity to be just, to practice justice, and to have a political presence. And as a presence, I cannot sin by omission. I am, by definition, a subject "destined" to choose. To have options. I honor truth. And all that means being ethical. It may help me or hinder me as a teacher, to know that I cannot escape the attention and evaluation of the students. Even so, it ought to make me aware of the care I need to take in carrying out my teaching activity. If I have made a choice for open-minded, democratic practice, then obviously this excludes reactionary, authoritarian, elitist attitudes and actions. Under no circumstances, therefore, may I discriminate against students. In addition, the perception the student has of my teaching is not exclusively the result of how I act but also of how the student understands my action.[36]

Notes

1. *Subordinated* refers to cultural groups that are politically, socially, and economically subordinate in the greater society. While individual members of these groups may not consider themselves subordinate in any manner to the White "mainstream," they nevertheless are members of a greater collective that historically has been perceived and treated as subordinate and inferior by the dominant society.
2. For a more detailed discussion of the concept *political clarity*, please see L. I. Bartolomé, "Beyond the Methods Fetish: Toward a Humanizing Pedagogy," *Harvard Educational Review, 64* (1994), 173–194.
3. *Mainstream* refers to the U.S. macro-culture that has its roots in Western European traditions. More specifically, the major influence on the United States, particularly on its institutions, has been the culture and traditions of White Anglo-Saxon Protestants (WASPs). Although the mainstream group is no longer composed solely of WASPs, members of the middle class have adopted traditionally WASP bodies of knowledge, language use, values, norms, and beliefs.
4. According to Rosaura Sanchez, over seventeen million people in the United States speak Spanish as a first language. See R. Sanchez, "Mapping the Spanish Language along a Multiethnic and Multilingual Border," in *The Latino Studies Reader: Culture, Economy, and Society,* ed. A. Darder and R. D. Torres (Malden, MA: Blackwell, 1998). The United States is the sixth-largest Spanish-speaking country in the world. See N. F. Conklin and M. A. Lourie, *A Host of Tongues: Language Communities in the United States* (New York: Free Press, 1983).

5. I placed quotation marks around the word "foreign" because many of the languages perceived as foreign are actually indigenous to geographic areas now part of the United States; for example, the numerous Native American languages, Spanish in the Southwest, and French in the Southeast.

6. Sanchez reports that although Latino children constitute 32 percent of students in the United States (of whom approximately two-thirds are limited English proficient), only 10 percent of bilingual teachers are Latino. See Sanchez, "Mapping the Spanish Language."

7. The term *technical* refers to the positivist tradition in education that presents teaching as a precise and scientific undertaking and teachers as technicians responsible for carrying out (preselected) instructional programs and strategies.

8. H. Giroux and P. McLaren, "'Politics of Teacher Education," *Harvard Educational Review, 56* (1986), 214.

9. Henry Giroux and Peter McLaren define a "transformative intellectual" as "one who exercises forms of intellectual and pedagogical practice which attempt to insert teaching and learning directly into the political sphere by arguing that schooling represents both a struggle for meaning and a struggle over power relations. We are also referring to one whose intellectual practices are necessarily grounded in forms of moral and ethical discourse exhibiting a preferential concern for the suffering and struggles of the disadvantaged and oppressed." See Giroux and McLaren, "Politics of Teacher Education," p. 215.

10. Taken from the 1998 American Educational Research Association Annual Meeting Program (pp. 162, 239, 257); the event was held April 13–17 in San Diego.

11. R. Valencia, *Minority Academic Underachievement: Conceptual and Theoretical Considerations for Understanding the Achievement Problems of Chicano Students,* Paper presented to the Chicano Faculty Seminar, Stanford University, November 2, 1985, p. 3.

12. B. Flores, *Language Interference or Influence: Toward a Theory for Hispanic Bilingualism,* Unpublished doctoral dissertation, University of Arizona at Tucson, 1982; B. Flores, *Interrogating the Genesis of the Deficit View of Latino Children in the Educational Literature During the Twentieth Century,* Paper presented at the American Educational Research Association Annual Meeting, Atlanta, April 1993.

13. E. Howard, *Teachers' Beliefs about Effective Educational Practices for Language-Minority Students: A Case Study,* Qualifying paper, Harvard Graduate School of Education, 1997.

14. G. Bloom, *The Effects of Speech Style and Skin Color on Bilingual Teaching Candidates' and Bilingual Teachers' Attitudes towards Mexican American Pupils,* Unpublished doctoral dissertation, Stanford University, 1990.

15. For examples of past studies that examined the relationships between teachers' biased beliefs and their classroom practice, see J. Brophy and T. Good, *Teacher-student relationships* (New York: Holt, Rinehart, & Winston, 1974); and J. Brophy and T. Good, "Teacher Behavior and Student Achievement," in *Handbook of Research on Teaching,* 3rd ed., ed. M. Wittrock (New York: Macmillan, 1987), pp. 328–375.

16. R. Gonzalves, *Resistance in the Multicultural Education Classroom,* Unpublished manuscript, 1996.

17. Gonzalves, *Resistance in the Multicultural Education Classroom.*

18. M. L. Gomez, "Teacher Education Reform and Prospective Teachers' Perspectives on Teaching "Other People's" Children," *Teaching and Teacher Education, 10* (1994), 319–334.

19. National Center for Education Statistics, *American Education at a Glance* (Washington, DC: Office of Education Research and Improvement, 1992).

20. N. Zimpher, "The RATE Project: A Profile of Teacher Education Students," *Journal of Teacher Education, 40,* No. 6 (1989), 27–30.

21. B. McLeod, "Introduction," in B. McLeod (Ed.), *Language and Learning: Educating Linguistically Diverse Students* (Albany: State University of New York, 1994), p. xiv.

22. See Sanchez, "Mapping the Spanish Language."

23. S. Nieto, *Affirming Diversity: The Sociopolitical Context of Multicultural Education* (New York: Longman, 1992).

24. P. Bourdieu, "The School as a Conservative Force: Schools and Cultural Inequities, in *Knowledge and Values in Social and Educational Research,* ed. E. Bredo and W. Fernberg (Philadelphia: Temple University Press, 1982), p. 399.

25. American Association of Colleges of Teacher Education, AACTE/Metropolitan Life Survey on Teacher Education Students (Washington, DC: Author, 1990); M. L. Gomez, "Teacher Education Reform"; K. Zeichner and K. Hoeft, "Teacher Socialization for Cultural Diversity," in *Handbook of Research in Teacher Education,* ed. J. Sikula, T. Buttery, and E. Guyton (New York: Macmillan Library Reference USA, 1996), pp. 525–547.

26. K. A. Davis, "Multicultural Classrooms and Cultural Commnities of Teachers," *Teaching and Teacher Education,* 11 (1995), 553–563.

27. C. E. Sleeter and C. A. Grant, "An Analysis of Multicultural Education in the United States," *Harvard Educational Review, 57* (1987), 421–444; Zeichner and Hoeft, "Teacher Socialization for Cultural Diversity."

28. E. Garcia, "Effective Instruction for Language Minority Students: The Teacher," *Boston University Journal of Education, 173,* (1991), 130–141; R. T. Jimenez, R. Gersten, and A. Rivera, "Conversations with a Chicana Teacher: Supporting Students' Transition from Native to English Language Instruction," *Elementary School Journal, 96* (1996), 333–341; R. Rueda and H. Garcia, "Teachers' Perspectives on Literacy, Assessment, and Instruction with Language-Minority Students: A Comparative Study," *Elementary School Journal, 96* (1996), 311–332.

29. Garcia, "Effective Instruction for Language Minority Students."

30. Garcia, "Effective Instruction for Language Minority Students," p. 139.

31. Garcia, "Effective Instruction for Language Minority Students," p. 139.

32. T. Beaubouef, *Politicized Mothering among African-American Women Teachers: A Qualitative Inquiry,* Unpublished doctoral dissertation, Harvard Graduate School of Education, 1997.

33. Beaubouef, *Politicized Mothering,* p. 169.

34. *Comfort zone* denotes an emic term developed and used by the teachers in this study. Although I prefer the term *safety zone* because of the apolitical counseling and psychological connotations attached to *comfort zone*, I use the term preferred by the teachers.

35. P. Freire, *Pedagogy of Freedom: Ethics, Democracy, and Civic Courage* (Lanham, MD: Rowman & Littlefield, 1998).

36. Freire, *Pedagogy of Freedom,* p. 90.

Bringing Bilingual Education out of the Basement, and Other Imperatives for Teacher Education

SONIA NIETO

S chools and colleges of education by and large have failed to adequately prepare future and practicing teachers to teach language-minority students. Those teacher education programs that offer specializations in bilingual education and/or ESL, and even more so those that combine these strands, are well equipped to prepare teachers to face the challenges of the growing language-minority student population in our nation. But programs without such strands are frequently guided by the assumption that the job of schools of education is to train teachers to work in "regular" — that is, monolingual English — classrooms. They give little consideration to the fact that *all* classrooms in the future will have students whose first language is not English, even if they do not currently serve such students.

The number and variety of language-minority students have escalated tremendously in the past several years. For example, according to a 1996 report (Macías & Kelly, 1996), there were 3,184,696 students classified as having limited proficiency in English, almost a 5 percent increase in just one year. The same report indicated that students of limited English proficiency represent 7.3 percent of all public school students, and that far fewer than 50 percent of these students were enrolled in federal or state programs in bilingual education. As a result, over half of all students whose native language is other than English spend most or part of their day in monolingual English classrooms. This situation is reason enough to propose that all teachers, not only bilingual teachers, need to be prepared to work with language-minority students.

In this chapter, I suggest that, although schools and colleges of education need to teach specific skills and strategies for working with language-minority students, it is even more essential that teacher education programs help teachers to develop positive attitudes and beliefs toward these students. After all, questions of language are *pedagogical* as well as *ideological*. Ideologies reflect a deeply ingrained system of beliefs, and they generally include a political program for action. In terms of linguistic differences, ideologies reflect positive or negative values concerning specific languages and the people who speak them. In addition, ideologies either uphold or challenge established authority and existing policies. In the case of language diversity, ideologies can either engage human efforts behind pluralism and social equality, or they can support the status quo.

What is the responsibility of schools and colleges of education to prepare teachers to work with students who speak native languages other than English? What should *all* teachers know about language-minority students, and what kinds of skills do teachers need to be effective with these students? In the case of bilingual and ESL teachers, what distinct competencies do they need to develop? In what follows, I will review the kinds of knowledge that schools and colleges of education need to develop in all their teacher candidates, whether these future teachers expect to work in bilingual settings or not. I will also mention a number of explicit areas of study that bilingual and ESL teachers need. But I will focus my attention on the values, beliefs, and attitudes that I believe should be at the core of teacher education programs. I will propose three imperatives for teacher education programs as they prepare teachers for the new generation of Americans, many of whom are language-minority students. Specifically, I will suggest that teacher education programs need to

1. take a stand on language diversity;
2. bring bilingual education out of the basement;
3. promote teaching as a lifelong journey of transformation.

What Should Teachers Know?

Students who are speakers of languages other than English are in classrooms in all communities throughout the United States, ~om the most urban to the most rural and from the ethnically diverse to the seemingly homogeneous (Macías & Kelly, 1996). Yet most teacher education programs continue to behave as if language-minority students were found only in ESL or bilingual classrooms. As a result, teachers who have taken traditional courses in pedagogy and curriculum or who have had typical practicum experiences in English monolingual settings will not be prepared to teach the growing number of language-minority students who will end up in their classrooms. Even when language-minority students are primarily in ESL or bilingual settings, presuming that these students are the sole responsibility of ESL and bilingual teachers strengthens the perception that these youngsters should be in separate classrooms, halls, and even schools rather than integrated with their peers whenever pedagogically possible.

Because language-minority students are often physically isolated from their English-speaking peers, this separation adds to their alienation. The same is true of bilingual teachers, who in most schools are both physically and emotionally separated from other teachers. Bilingual teachers report feeling estranged, dismissed, or simply ignored by their peers and supervisors (Montero-Sieburth & Pérez, 1987). Consequently, the relationships among bilingual and "mainstream" teachers, and among students in bilingual and English-monolingual classrooms, are regularly fraught with misunderstanding. The emotional and physical separation experienced by bilingual and nonbilingual teachers does not lend itself to developing collegial relationships or opportunities to work collaboratively.

What might allow collaborative relationships between bilingual and nonbilingual teachers? One way to promote opportunities for them to work together is to start off all teachers with common knowledge concerning language diversity. All teachers, not only bilingual and ESL teachers, need to develop the following kinds of knowledge:

- familiarity with first- and second-language acquisition
- awareness of the sociocultural and sociopolitical context of education for language-minority students

- awareness of the history of immigration in the United States, with particular attention to language policies and practices throughout that history
- knowledge of the history and experiences of specific groups of people, especially those who are residents of the city, town, and state where they will be teaching
- ability to adapt curriculum for students whose first language is other than English
- competence in pedagogical approaches suitable for culturally and linguistically heterogeneous classrooms
- experience with teachers of diverse backgrounds and the ability to develop collaborative relationships with colleagues that promote the learning of language-minority students
- ability to communicate effectively with parents of diverse language, culture, and social-class backgrounds

In addition to these skills, all teacher candidates, regardless of the setting in which they will be working, should be strongly encouraged to learn a second language, particularly a language spoken by a substantial number of students in the community in which they teach or intend to teach. No matter how empathic teachers may be of the ordeal that students go through to learn English, nothing can bring it home in quite the same way as going through the process themselves. Bill Dunn, a doctoral student of mine who "came out of the closet" as a Spanish speaker a number of years ago, wrote eloquently about this experience in a journal he kept (Nieto, 1999). Bill teaches in a town with a student body that is about 75 percent Puerto Rican, and after twenty years in the system, he realized that he understood a good deal of Spanish. He decided to learn Spanish more systematically through activities such as taking a Spanish class at a community center, sitting in on bilingual classes in his school, and watching Spanish-language television shows. Although Bill had been a wonderful teacher before learning Spanish, the experience of placing himself in the vulnerable position of learner taught him many things: a heightened respect for students who were learning English; a clearer understanding of why his Spanish-speaking students, even those who were fluent in English, made particular mistakes in grammar and spelling; and a renewed admiration for the bilingual teachers in his school.

The skills and knowledge listed above are a common starting point for all teachers, but for those who are preparing to become bilingual and/or ESL teachers, the knowledge base needs to be expanded to include:

- fluency in at least one language in addition to English
- knowledge of the conceptual and theoretical basis for bilingual education
- knowledge of specific pedagogical strategies that promote language development
- ability to serve as cultural mediators between students and the school
- knowledge of various strategies for assessing students' language proficiency and academic progress

This list is not meant to be exhaustive, but rather to suggest that there are numerous specific strategies and approaches that teachers of language-minority backgrounds need to learn. But in spite of the importance of knowing particular strategies and approaches, I believe that the focus of teacher educators has to be elsewhere. Although bilingual education is about language and pedagogy, it is equally about power and ideology. That is, questions of *which* language to use, *when* and *how* to use it, and *why* it should be used are above all ideological questions. In the final analysis, native-language education brings up questions of whose language has legitimacy and power, and of how far our society is willing to allow differences to exist and even flourish. These questions go to the heart of what our schools are for, and what we value as a society. Consequently, I suggest that besides pedagogy and curriculum, schools and colleges of education need to help teachers develop critical perspectives about education. This means that the *values, beliefs,* and *attitudes* that underscore particular approaches also need to become the subject matter of their study and analysis.

The Ideological Underpinnings of Bilingual Education

As we have previously discussed, ideology is a systematic set of principles usually linked with political action that either upholds or challenges the status quo. A generation ago, Paulo Freire's (1970) assertion that education is always political was greeted with denial or skepticism in many quarters in our society. The claim that education is political — that is, that it is fundamentally concerned with issues of power and dominance — flies in the face of education as understood in the United States, where we have always asserted that education is universal, equal, and fair. But the ideological basis of education is exposed through such blatant practices as vastly differentiated funding for rich and poor school districts (Kozol, 1991), and the detrimental effects of ability tracking and other sorting practices on students of diverse socioeconomic, racial, ethnic, and linguistic backgrounds (Oakes, 1985; Spring, 1989). The political nature of education has also been evident in the case of bilingual education, which has been under attack since its very inception (Nieto, 1992). Scholars of bilingual education have always known that it is political, and some books on the subject discuss openly its political nature and include reference to it in their titles (Arias & Casanova, 1993; Crawford, 1992).

But what does it mean to say that bilingual education is political? For one thing, it means that every discussion of bilingual education is based on a philosophical orientation concerning language diversity in our society and on the official status that languages other than English are to be given. It also means that all educational decisions about bilingual education — when and how to use which language, the nature of the program, who should teach in such programs, and the educational expectations of students who speak languages other than English — reflect a particular worldview. Prospective teachers need to understand that the mere existence of bilingual education affronts one of the most cherished ideals of our public schools, that is, the assimilation of students of nondominant backgrounds into the cultural mainstream. And because bilingual education challenges the assimilationist agenda of our schools and society, I believe that the greatest fear among its opponents is that *bilingual education might in fact work*. If this were not the case, why is there so much opposition to it?

Prospective teachers need to know that bilingual education developed in the 1960s as a result of the civil rights era; that linguistic democracy has been as crucial a civil rights issue for language-minority communities as desegregation has been for African American communities; and that language is a central value and birthright that many families treasure and seek to maintain. Prospective teachers also need to understand that the families of language-minority students want their children to become fluent speakers of English because they know that this knowledge will provide their children with their greatest opportunity for academic and economic success. Many of these families insist, however, that their children also maintain and use their first language.

The curriculum, as well as the quality and quantity of materials, available to students in bilingual programs, and decisions about when to move students from bilingual to nonbilingual classes are all political, and not merely pedagogical, decisions. Language-minority students in the United States are overwhelmingly poor and powerless, and their dominated status is related in no small way to how they are perceived and to the nature of the education they receive. For instance, because bilingual education is ordinarily a program for economically disadvantaged and oppressed communities, city and state boards of education are often unenthusiastic about spending money on a program they perceive as too expensive and "wasteful." But in middle-class neighborhoods, the costs associated with teaching children a second language are rarely challenged.

Imperatives for Teacher Education

If indeed all teachers will at some time or another be faced with teaching students whose first language is other than English, what is the responsibility of teacher educators and teacher preparation programs? Let me suggest three imperatives for teacher education: first, teacher educators and teacher preparation programs need to take a stand concerning the education of language-minority students; second, they need to bring bilingual education out of the basement, both literally and figuratively; and third, they need to prepare future teachers to think of teaching as a lifelong journey of transformation. I will comment briefly on the first two, and more thoroughly on the third of these imperatives.

Take a Stand on Language Diversity

Schools and colleges of education need to decide what they stand for concerning education in general, as well as in the specific case of language diversity and language-minority students. They can begin this process by asking a number of key questions, the answers to which they may assume are shared, but which very often are not:

• *What is the purpose of education? What are schools for?*
Other than to prepare lofty mission statements that have little to do with their day-to-day practice, it is rare for faculties of education to get together to discuss the very purposes of education: Is the purpose of schools to fit students into society? Is it to prepare students for specific jobs? Or is it to prepare students to become productive and critical citizens of a democratic society? Must schools replicate societal inequities? Should they seek to prepare a few good managers and many compliant workers? Or is the role of schools to prepare students for the challenges of a pluralistic and rapidly changing society? Answers to these questions can determine the scope and quality of a teacher preparation program curriculum and the field experiences provided to students. If, for example, the faculty determines that the primary objective of education is to prepare students for our rapidly changing and pluralistic society, then attention to language diversity becomes a key component in their course offerings.

• *What do we do about language diversity?*
The issue of difference lies at the heart of the way that U.S. schools have defined their responsibility to educate young people. From the time that compulsory schooling in the United States began, the ideals of equality and fairness have struggled with the ideals of pluralism and diversity (Dewey, 1916; Spring, 1997; Weinberg, 1977). That is, the balance between *unum* and *pluribus* has always been contested. Many times, the zeal to assimilate and homogenize all students to one norm has won out; rarely has diversity been highlighted as a value in its own right.

In the case of language diversity, Luis Moll (1992) has pointed out the singular focus on the English language taken by many educators and society at large, suggesting that

> the obsession of speaking English reigns supreme — as if the children were somehow incapable of learning that language well, or as if the parents and teachers were unaware of the importance of English in U.S. society — and usually at the expense of other educational or academic matters. (pp. 20–21)

Historically, answers to the question of what to do about language diversity have ranged from grudging acceptance, to outlawing the use of languages other than English in instruction, to brutal policies, especially those directed at Mexican Americans and American Indians, that enforced the use of the English language at the exclusion of other languages (Crawford, 1992; Deyhle & Swisher, 1997; Donato, 1997). How schools of education answer these questions can help them either to focus on assimilation as a goal, or to think of ways to use language diversity as a resource.

Bring Bilingual Education out of the Basement

The basement is a fitting metaphor for the status of bilingual education, both in elementary and secondary schools and in schools and colleges of education. Basements are dark, dank places where people store what they do not want to display in their homes. Bilingual programs are frequently found in basements next to the boiler room, in supply closets, or in trailers or hallways isolated from the rest of the school. Their very physical placement is a giveaway to their low status in schools and among the general public. But language-minority students will not disappear simply because they are hidden from sight. If it is true that the number of language-minority students will increase over the coming years, then all teachers need to learn how to best teach them. Further, all schools and colleges of education, no matter how remote they may be from the urban areas where most language-minority students live, have to prepare teachers who will specialize in teaching these students, because no geographic area will remain a monolingual enclave of English for long.

In schools and in teacher preparation programs, bilingual education needs to be moved out of the basement and onto the first floor. Figuratively speaking, at the university level, this means giving bilingual education and language diversity issues a place of prominence in the teacher education curriculum. Although there is a need to continue to offer specialized courses for bilingual and ESL teachers who will spend the bulk of their time with language-minority students, as a profession we can no longer afford to teach about bilingual education only to prospective bilingual teachers. Rather, all courses should be infused with content relating to language diversity, from those in secondary science methods to those in reading. Courses in educational foundations, history, and policy matters also should include reference to bilingual education. Pre-practicum and practicum placements, other field experiences, course assignments, and course readings also need to reflect support for language diversity. In addition, schools of education might rethink their requirements for admission, giving priority to those candidates who are fluent in at least one language other than English. In sum, language and language diversity issues would become part of the *normal experience* for all prospective teachers. In this way, it becomes clear that the responsibility for teaching language-minority students belongs to all teachers.

An approach that gives language diversity a high status in teacher preparation programs will invariably mean that teacher educators will face a good deal of resistance from some prospective teachers. It is by now a truism that most prospective teachers are White, middle-class, monolingual English-speaking women with little experience with people different from themselves, and that most of them believe — or at least hope — they will teach in largely White, middle-class communities (Aaronsohn, Carter, & Howell, 1995). Having to take courses that focus on students whom they may not want to teach, and that give weight to issues that they may want to dismiss, will certainly cause some tension. In fact, teaching courses that focus on diversity in any way usually results in conflict, and there is ample demonstration of this fact in the literature (Chávez Chávez & O'Donnell, 1998). But infusing the curriculum with content in language diversity may also result in expanding the vision and therefore enriching the perspectives of prospective teachers. In turn, their success and effectiveness with language-minority students may also be positively affected.

As is the case with teachers, most teacher educators are also White, middle-class, monolingual English speakers, and many have had little experience or training in language diversity issues. This means that teacher educators must themselves rethink how their courses need to be changed to reflect language diversity, and they need to be given the support and time to do so. Likewise, if we are serious about giving language diversity a positive status in the general teacher education program, we must recognize that the current teacher education faculty needs to be diversified. Consequently, another implication of bringing bilingual education out of the basement is that schools of education will have to recruit a more diverse faculty with specific training and experience in bilingual education, second-language acquisition, and the education of language-minority students.

Recruiting a diverse faculty does not in and of itself guarantee that the result will be a faculty that is more diverse in ideological perspective. For example, not all Latinos/as are supporters of bilingual education, nor should they be recruited for this reason. However, recruiting a faculty that is diverse in training and expertise, as well as in background and experience, will probably ensure a broader diversity of perspectives than is currently the case.

Promote Teaching as a Lifelong Journey of Transformation

Teacher educators have the lofty but frightening responsibility to prepare future teachers and other educational leaders. In terms of diversity, I believe that our major responsibility is twofold: to help teachers and prospective teachers affirm the linguistic, cultural, and experiential diversity of their students while at the same time opening up new vistas, opportunities, and challenges that expand their worlds. But because teaching is above all a matter of forming caring and supportive relationships, the process of affirming the diversity of students begins as a journey of the teachers. A journey always presupposes that the traveler will change along the way, and teaching is no exception. However, if we expect teachers to begin their own journey of transformation, teacher educators must be willing to join them because until we take stock of ourselves, until we question and challenge our own biases and values, nothing will change for our students.

Affirming the diversity of students is not just an individual journey, however. It is equally a collective and institutional journey that happens outside individual classrooms and college courses. How do teachers prepare for the journey, and what is the role of teacher educators? Let me suggest several central points to keep in mind as teachers and faculty begin this journey (these are discussed in much greater detail in Nieto, 1999).

Teachers need to face and accept their own identities. As we have mentioned, most teachers in the United States are White, monolingual, middle-class females who are teaching a student body that is increasingly diverse in native language, race, ethnicity, and social class. Due to their own limited experiences with people of diverse backgrounds, including language-minority backgrounds, many teachers perceive of language diversity as a problem rather than an asset. This is probably due to the fact that they have internalized the message that their culture is the norm against which to measure all others. As a result, they seldom question their white-skin or English-language privilege (McIntosh, 1988). Schools and colleges of education need to provide prospective teachers with opportunities to reflect on all of these issues before teaching children from diverse backgrounds.

Because of the assimilationist nature of U.S. schooling, most people of European American background have accepted the "melting pot" as a true reflection of our society's experience with cultural pluralism. The immigration of Europeans is generally presented as the model by which all other groups should be measured, as if it represented the reality of others whose history, race, culture, and historical context differ greatly. Many teachers of European American descent, who are drawn primarily from working-class backgrounds, are quick to accept the myths about diversity, merit, success, and assimilation that they have learned along the way. In a compelling essay written over a quarter of a century ago, Mildred Dickeman (1973) explained how such myths operate:

> All mythologies serve to interpret reality in ways useful to the perpetuation of a society. In this case an ideology arose which interpreted the existence of ethnic diversity in America in ways supportive of the sociopolitical establishment. Probably the schools played an important role in the creation of this ideology. Certainly they came to serve as the major institutions for its propagation. (p. 8)

The myths to which Dickeman allude include the perception that people of nonmainstream backgrounds must completely "melt" in order to be successful; that individual effort is superior to community and collective identity and action; and that all it takes is hard work and perseverance to make it, with no attention paid to the structural barriers and institutional biases that get in the way of equality. If they believe these myths, it becomes easy for teachers to compare African American, Latino, American Indian, and Asian and Asian American students with the portrait of successful European immigrants they have accepted as the norm, and to blame students who do not achieve academically. Generally, the blame is couched in terms of the inferior culture or race of the students, or on passivity or lack of concern on the part of their parents.

One consequence of accepting these deficit views is that because only students of backgrounds visibly different from the mainstream are thought to have a culture, culture itself is defined as a problem. But teachers also have cultural identities, even though they have learned to forget or deny them. As cultural beings, they come into teaching with particular worldviews, values, and beliefs, and these influence all of their interactions with their students. For the most part, however, teachers of European American backgrounds are unaware that they even possess a culture, or that their culture influences them in any substantive way save for holiday celebrations or ethnic festivals they may still attend. All teachers of all backgrounds need to recognize, understand, and accept their own diversity and delve into their own identities before they can learn about and from their students. Specifically in the case of teachers of European American backgrounds, Dickeman suggests that they begin to uncover and recover their own histories:

> Coming as we do from a range of ethnic and cultural identities, and by the mere fact of recruitment primarily from the lower and lower middle classes, we have available to us, however forgotten, repressed or ignored, the experiences of self and family in the context of pressure for assimilation and upward mobility. . . . When teachers begin to recognize that their own ethnic heritages are valuable, that their own family histories are relevant to learning and teaching, the battle is half won. (p. 24)

Recovering their ethnic identities invariably leads European American teachers to a confrontation with their racial, linguistic, and social-class privilege (Howard, 1999; McIntosh, 1988), a painful but ultimately life-changing experience for many of them. For teacher preparation programs, this implies that opportunities and support need to be provided for teachers and prospective teachers to go through this process. These opportunities also need to be made available to teachers and future teachers from nondominant backgrounds. Although teacher educators often assume that prospective teachers of African American, Hispanic, and Asian American backgrounds are somehow automatically prepared to teach students of diverse backgrounds simply by virtue of their own backgrounds, this is not always true (Nieto, in press). That is, having an identity that differs from the mainstream — for example, being Chicana — does not necessarily guarantee sensitivity or knowledge about Vietnamese students. Likewise, being Chicana does not even mean that a teacher will be more knowledgeable about her Chicano students. Although it is generally true that teachers of nondominant backgrounds bring substantial skills, knowledge, and passion to their jobs, this is not always the case. Teacher preparation programs need to understand this, and they need to provide *all* prospective teachers, not just those of European American background, with the skills and attitudes to teach students of all backgrounds.

Teachers need to become learners and identify with their students. Without denying the need to teach students the cultural capital that they need to help them negotiate society, teachers also need to make a commitment to become *students of their students.* This implies at least two kinds of processes. First, teachers need to learn *about* their students, a change from the one-way learning that usually takes place in classrooms. For this to happen, teachers must become researchers of their students. Second, teachers need to create spaces in which they can learn *with* their students, and in which students are encouraged to learn about themselves and one another.

If we think of teaching and learning as reciprocal processes, as proposed by Paulo Freire (1970), then teachers need to become actively engaged in learning through their interactions with students. Developing a stance as learners is especially consequential if we think about the wide gulf that currently exists in the United States between the language backgrounds and other experiences of teachers and their students. Given this situation, the conventional approach has been to instruct students in the ways of White, middle-class, English-speaking America and, in the process, to rid them of as many of their differences as possible.

Learning about one's students is not simply a technical strategy, or a process of picking up a few cultural tidbits. It is impossible for teachers to become culturally or linguistically responsive simply by taking a course where these concerns are reduced to strategies. This does not mean that teaching is always an intuitive undertaking, although it certainly has this quality at times. But even more pivotal are the attitudes of teachers when they are in the position of learners. That is, teachers need to be open to their language-minority students' knowledge in order to find what can help them learn, and then change their teaching accordingly.

Defining the teacher as a learner is a radical departure from the prevailing notion of the educator as repository of all knowledge, a view that is firmly entrenched in society. Ira Shor (Shor & Freire, 1987) critiqued this conventional portrait of teachers vis-à-vis their students: "The students are not a flotilla of boats trying to reach the teacher who is finished and waiting on the shore. The teacher is also one of the boats" (p. 50). Yet in spite of how terrifying it may be for teachers to act as all-knowing sages, the conception of *teacher as knower* is a more familiar and, hence, less threatening one than *teacher as learner*. Once teachers admit that they do not know everything, they make themselves as vulnerable as their students. But it is precisely this attitude of learner on the part of teachers that is needed, first, to convey to linguistically diverse students that nobody is above learning; and second, to let students know that they also are knowers, and that what they know can be an important source of learning for others as well. It follows from this perspective that there needs to be a move away from the deficit model to a recognition of the cultural and linguistic knowledge and resources that students bring to their education. Teachers need to build on this knowledge as the foundation of their students' academic learning.

Teachers need to become multilingual and multicultural. Teachers can talk on and on about the value of cultural diversity, and about how beneficial it is to know a second language, but if they themselves do not attempt to learn another language, or if they remain monocultural in outlook, their words may sound hollow to their students. Even if their curriculum is outwardly supportive of students' linguistic and cultural diversity, if teachers do not demonstrate through their actions and behaviors that they truly value diversity, students can often tell.

Teachers who can call on their own identities of linguistic and cultural diversity usually have an easier time of identifying with their students of diverse backgrounds. But absent such connections with diversity, what is the responsibility of teacher preparation programs? I suggest that we need to find ways to engage future teachers in a process of becoming multicultural and multilingual, and I have already recommended a number of ways in which we can do so. I would just add that schools of education need to make their prospective teachers an offer they cannot refuse; that is, they need to make it worth their while to become multilingual and multicultural by having incentives that help future teachers view diversity as an asset. These incentives can include credit for learning another language; refusing to accept course work that does not reflect attention to diversity; and support for academic work that is tied to community service.

Becoming multilingual and multicultural is often an exhilarating experience, but it can also be uncomfortable and challenging because the process decenters students from their world. It necessarily means that students have to learn to step out of their comfortable perspectives and try to understand those of others. In the process, however, they usually gain far more than they give up: a broader view of reality, a more complex understanding of their students' lives, and a way to approach their students so that they can learn successfully.

Teachers need to learn to confront racism and other biases in schools. If teachers simply follow the decreed curriculum as handed down from the central office, and if they go along with standard practices such as rigid ability tracking or high-stakes testing that result in unjust outcomes, they are unlikely ever to question the fairness of these practices. But when they begin to engage in a personal transformation through such actions as described above — that is, when they become learners with, of, and for their students and forge a deep identification with them; when they build on students' talents and strengths; and when they welcome and include the perspectives and experiences of their students and families in the classroom — then they cannot avoid locking horns with some very unpleasant realities inherent in the schooling process, realities such as racism, sexism, heterosexism, classism, and other biases. For instance, teachers begin to discover the biased but unstated ideologies behind some of the practices that they had previously overlooked. As a result, teachers have no alternative but to begin to question the inequitable nature of such practices. They become, in a word, critical educators. In this respect, helping prospective teachers become critical is a fundamental role of teacher education programs, and it means challenging not only the policies and practices of schools but also those of the very teacher education programs they are in.

A critical stance challenges the structure of schools at the elementary and secondary school levels so that teachers begin to question, among other school realities, the following:

- seemingly natural and neutral practices such as asking parents to speak English at home with their children (in fact, teachers who are supportive of language diversity begin to ask their students' parents to do just the opposite: to speak their native language at home, and to promote literacy in all forms in their native language whenever possible);
- the lack of high-level courses in students' native languages (critical teachers begin to ask, for example, whether schools have parallel and equal courses in science, math, social studies, and other subject areas in students' native languages);
- counseling services that automatically relegate students of some language backgrounds to nonacademic choices (critical teachers become aware of both subtle and overt messages that students are incapable of doing high-level academic work because they are not yet proficient in English, as if English proficiency were the primary barometer of intelligence).

At the teacher education level, a critical stance means that faculty and prospective teachers begin to question the following:

- the isolation of bilingual education as a separate strand in the teacher education program, and the separation between bilingual education and ESL (as if this separation made sense in the real world where students are struggling to become bilingual and where bilingualism is, in all other settings except for school, a highly valued skill);
- screening practices that make it impossible for a more diverse student body to become teachers (these include an overemphasis on grades with little attention paid to skills they might already have in language ability and cultural awareness; during interviews, a rigid conception of how the "ideal teacher" behaves, without acknowledging how cultural and social-class differences might influence their responses; a bias against prospective teachers who have an accent; and so on);
- how faculty are recruited and hired, and how these practices might mitigate against the possibility of retaining a faculty that is diverse in language and culture (for example, by failing to include competencies in culture and language in the job descriptions for nonbilingual positions, even though such competencies could be highly effective in those positions).

Facing and challenging racism and other biases is both an inspiring and a frightening prospect. It means upsetting business as usual, and this can be difficult even for committed and critical teachers. It is especially difficult for young teachers, who recognize that they have little power or influence among more seasoned school staffs. As a result, they often either lose hope or become solitary missionaries, and neither of these postures can accomplish any appreciable changes.

Help future teachers learn to develop a community of critical friends. What I suggest instead is that we teach future teachers to become *critical colleagues,* that is, teachers who are capable of developing respectful but critical relationships with their peers. Working in isolation, no teacher can single-handedly effect the changes that are needed in an entire school, at least not in the long term. In fact, isolation builds walls, allowing teachers to focus on only their own students. In this way, it becomes far too easy to designate language-minority students as the responsibility of only the bilingual and ESL teachers. But developing a community of critical friends opens up teachers' classrooms — and their perspectives — so that they can acknowledge that the concerns of language-minority students are everyone's concerns, not just of one or two teachers in the school building.

Time and again, teachers in my classes have spoken about the need to develop a cadre of peers to help them and their school go through the process of transformation. But what is needed is not simply peers who support one another — essential as this may be — but also peers who debate, critique, and challenge one another to go beyond their current ideas and practices. This is especially useful in terms of bilingual education, a hotly contested issue seldom discussed in an in-depth way among teachers. Developing a community of critical friends is one way of facing difficult issues, and it is one more step in the journey of transformation.

Prospective teachers also need to build bridges to their students' families and to other members of the communities in which they work. Rather than viewing families and other community members as adversaries, prospective teachers need to develop skills in interacting effectively with them. Yet how many teachers have learned about these issues in their teacher education programs? Even in bilingual programs, where both parent involvement and communication with families are seen as central, there are few examples of actual exposure to these ideas. At the very least, teacher preparation programs need to provide courses, seminars, and practicum experiences so that prospective teachers learn to work with families.

In the end, teachers who work collaboratively with their peers and families in a spirit of solidarity will be better able to change schools to become more equitable and caring places for students of linguistically and culturally diverse backgrounds. Even personal transformation is best accomplished as a *collective* journey that leads to change in more than just one classroom. This means that prospective teachers need to learn to communicate and work with colleagues of varying perspectives; they need to learn to support and affirm one another, but also to question and confront one another to envision other possibilities.

That bilingual education works is a given in the chapters in this book. Rather than continue to endlessly debate its effectiveness, what are needed are strategies to improve it. What has *not* worked, on the other hand, are the approaches used by schools of education to prepare future teachers for the great diversity — linguistic, cultural, and socioeconomic, among others — that new teachers will face. These programs have a long way to go in preparing prospective teachers to respect and affirm the languages and identities of all the students who will inevitably be present in their classrooms in the coming years.

The three imperatives and numerous suggestions I have made in this chapter are only a beginning stage in the kinds of changes that are needed to help schools and universities shift from a focus on assimilation as their goal to an agenda of respect and affirmation for all students of all backgrounds. If teacher education faculties take these imperatives to heart, it means that they are willing to undergo a profound transformation in outlook, ideology, and curriculum. It also means that programs in general and faculty members in particular will welcome change, even though it may be a difficult prospect for many of us. But in the process of transformation, schools and colleges of education can become more hopeful places, because in the long run, we will be preparing better teachers for all students, including our bilingual and language-minority students. And the promise of social justice and equal educational opportunity for all students, an elusive dream in many places, will be closer to becoming a reality.

References

Aaronsohn, E., Carter, C. J., & Howell, M. (1995). Preparing monocultural teachers for a multicultural world: Attitudes toward inner-city schools. *Equity and Excellence in Education, 28,* 5–9.

Arias, M. B., & Casanova, U. (Eds.). (1993). *Bilingual education: Politics, practice, research.* Chicago: University of Chicago Press.

Chávez Chávez, R., & O'Donnell, J. (Eds.). (1998). *Speaking the unpleasant: The politics of non-engagement in the multicultural education terrain.* Albany: State University of New York Press.

Crawford, J. (1992). *Hold your tongue: Bilingualism and the politics of "English Only."* Reading, MA: Addison-Wesley.

Dewey, J. (1916). *Democracy and education.* New York: Free Press.

Deyhle, D., & Swisher, K. (1997). Research in American Indian and Alaska Native education: From assimilation to self-determination. In M. W. Apple (Ed.), *Review of research in education* (vol. 22, pp. 113–194). Washington, DC: American Educational Research Association.

Dickeman, M. (1973). Teaching cultural pluralism. In J. A. Banks (Ed.), *Teaching ethnic studies: Concepts and strategies* (pp. 4–25). Washington, DC: National Council for the Social Studies.

Donato, R. (1997). *The other struggle for equal schools: Mexican Americans during the civil rights era.* Albany: State University of New York Press.

Freire, P. (1970). *Pedagogy of the oppressed.* New York: Seabury Press.

Howard, G. (1999). *We can't teach what we don't know: White teachers, multiracial schools.* New York: Teachers College Press.

Kozol, J. (1991). *Savage inequalities; Children in America's schools.* New York: Crown.

Macías, R. F., & Kelly, C. (1996). *Summary report of the survey of the states' limited English proficient students and available educational programs and services 1994–1995.* Washington, DC: United States Department of Education, Office of Grants and Contracts Services, George Washington University.

McIntosh, P. (1988). *White privilege and male privilege: A personal account of coming to see correspondences through work in women's studies* (Working Paper No. 189). Wellesley, MA: Wellesley College Center for Research on Women.

Moll, L. D. (1992). Bilingual classroom studies and community analysis: Some recent trends. *Educational Researcher, 21*(2), 20–24.

Montero-Sieburth, M., & Pérez, M. (1987). *Echar pa'lante,* moving onward: The dilemmas and strategies of a bilingual education. *Anthropology and Education Quarterly,* 18, 180–189.

Nieto, S. (1992). We speak in many tongues: Language diversity and multicultural education. In C. Díaz (Ed.), *Multicultural education for the 21st century* (pp. 112–136). Washington, DC: National Education Association.

Nieto, S. (1999). *The light in their eyes: Creating multicultural classroom communities.* New York: Teachers College Press.

Nieto, S. (in press). Conflict and tension; growth and change: The politics of teaching multicultural education courses. In D. Macedo (Ed.), *Tongue-tying multiculturalism.* Boulder, CO: Roman & Littlefield.

Oakes, J. (1985). *Keeping track: How schools structure inequality.* New Haven, CT: Yale University Press.

Shor, I., & Freire, P. (1987). *A pedagogy for liberation: Dialogues on transforming education.* New York: Bergin & Garvey.

Spring, J. (1989). *The sorting machine revisited: National education policy since 1945.* New York: Longman.

Spring, J. (1997). *Deculturalization and the struggle for equality: A brief history of the education of dominated cultures in the United States* (2nd ed.). New York: McGraw-Hill.

Weinberg, M. (1977). *A chance to learn: A history of race and education in the U.S.* Cambridge, Eng.: Cambridge University Press.

Good Schools for Bilingual Students: Essential Conditions

MARIA ESTELA BRISK

wo major problems have plagued bilingual education in the United States: limiting the goal of language-minority students' education to learning English, and a focus on language and program models. English language development, however, is only one expected outcome of bilingual education; academic achievement is another. In some programs, further goals are bilingualism and sociocultural integration. The debate over the choice of language of instruction and the various models of bilingual education are most unproductive, as neither the particular language nor the program model determines bilingual program quality.

Effective bilingual programs share certain characteristics in their curriculum and instruction.[1] Most importantly, the success and stability of bilingual programs depend to a great extent on the quality of the schools in which they are housed (see Figure 1). Successful schools create a productive academic environment and promote an accepting community in which bilingual students can learn to embrace their new language and culture, while maintaining their respect for their own language and cultural identity. Such schools enjoy strong leadership; develop goals for all students collectively with staff and parents; welcome their students' languages, cultures, and families; and build a coherent community in which the bilingual program becomes an in-

FIGURE 1   QUALITY BILINGUAL EDUCATION PYRAMID

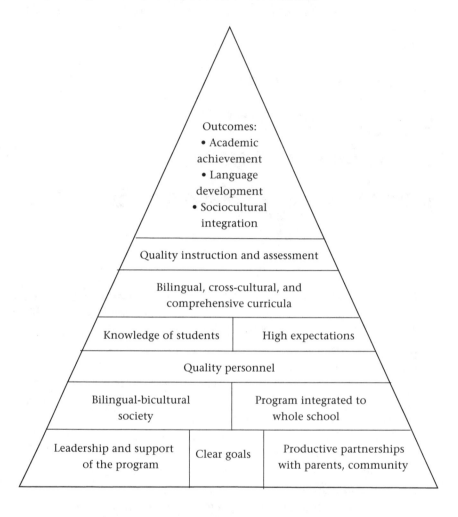

tegral part of the school. Graduates of bilingual programs attest to the importance of having well-prepared staff who know the students and have high expectations for them.

The ultimate desired outcomes of academic achievement, language development, and sociocultural integration require a comprehensive curriculum, as well as quality instruction and fair assessment. Curriculum and instruction must be bilingual and bicultural, regardless of the primary language of instruction. Much of the rhetoric about use of languages in education eludes the principal goal of schools, which is to develop knowledgeable, thoughtful, well-adjusted individuals. Use of children's home language and culture has a role in such development; knowledge of more than one language is also an educational asset. To achieve these goals it is important to focus on the quality of schools.

In order to provide good services for their bilingual populations, schools must

- provide leadership and support for the bilingual program;
- set clear goals;
- establish productive partnerships with bilingual students' parents and communities;
- incorporate the program into the school structure by creating a bilingual/bicultural society, and by integrating the bilingual program into the school community.

Strong and supportive leadership, clear goals, and productive communication with families are necessary to support personnel, curriculum, and good instruction in bilingual programs. A good bilingual/bicultural school benefits all students and staff because it prepares them for the world of the twenty-first century, where interaction among peoples of different cultures will become the norm.

Leadership

School leadership facilitates the work of bilingual instructional staff. It is not enough that principals tolerate the bilingual program; they must understand what works and take an active role in the education of bilingual students. According to Lucas (1993), they should

- become familiar with research and practices in bilingual education;
- include bilingual teachers in the development and implementation of educational goals;
- learn to work with personnel from various ethnic and cultural backgrounds;
- promote collaboration among bilingual and mainstream teachers;
- hire bilingual staff members from students' cultures;
- encourage participation of bilingual students' parents;

- support all staff's participation in professional development focused on bilingual students, and participate in such professional development as well;
- participate in curriculum development for bilingual students;
- work with the district level bilingual administrator.

The principal of a successful elementary school in Chicago with a high number of Spanish-speaking students embodies these qualities.[2] Having prepared herself by becoming familiar with the students' cultures and by learning Spanish, this principal turned the school into a model bilingual/bicultural society that welcomes all students and their families. Although the transitional bilingual program serves only 40 percent of the students, the principal made a concerted effort to hire bilingual personnel for the school in general. Music, gym, computer, and language arts teachers in the mainstream program are bilingual. They support bilingual students when they attend their classes and can communicate with the majority of parents who are Spanish speaking. This school is also a model of cooperative leadership. The principal exercises strong leadership but involves staff and parents in the decisionmaking process. Staff participates in school improvement and staff development committees. These committees review proposals with respect to curriculum, professional development, extracurricular activities, and so on. A Parent Advisory Council communicates directly with the school improvement committee. Thus the principal, staff, and parents work regularly toward common goals.

Leadership is also needed from the bilingual administrator at the district level. The district administrator or the bilingual program director plays a crucial role in supporting efforts of bilingual teachers and paraprofessional staff and advocating on behalf of bilingual students.

In particular, the bilingual program director has a key role in

- providing a network for bilingual staff;
- disseminating new instructional practice, materials, assessment, and so forth;
- assisting staff when school administration provides limited support.

Bilingual personnel are not always numerous in any given school. These teachers can feel isolated, and they may have few opportunities for professional growth in the bilingual field. The district administrator can supplement the needs of the bilingual program by convening special meetings for all bilingual teachers in the district to come together and share effective instructional practices. Another way that the district administrator can support staff is by organizing other professional development activities, such as relevant workshops by experts on theory and practice in bilingual education. Finally, the bilingual administrator can assist the program by writing grants to ensure additional financial support for bilingual books, resource materials, and so forth.

Goals

Strong leaders collaborate with staff and parents in developing goals for their school. Goals should be clear to staff, parents, and students in order to gain their support, measure progress, and facilitate academic attainment. A successful two-way bilingual program in Maine disseminates program goals and activities to teachers through professional development, to parents through a Parent Advisory Committee, and to the community in general by regularly producing news releases and newspaper articles.

Some bilingual programs have the goal that all students will develop oral and written ability in English. Others seek to develop another language in addition to English, and still others want to reverse the trend among language-minority students of losing their first language. When setting the language goals for a bilingual program, it is crucial to distinguish between attaining grade-appropriate fluency in the home language and using this native language to help with schooling and the development of English.

The *use* of the students' native language is an integral part of the *goal* of developing English. Contrary to conventional wisdom, schools that have been most successful in English language achievement have used students' native languages for an extended period of time (Green, 1998; Ramirez, 1992). Extended use of the native language strengthens students' linguistic and academic background and enhances their work in English.

Schools with the goal of bilingualism strive to develop proficiency in two languages for all students. Varied backgrounds and contextual differences make the task of achieving fluency in two languages difficult for these schools. In many of these programs, students' linguistic, educational, and socioeconomic backgrounds differ greatly. In a Spanish-English two-way bilingual program, for example, English-speaking students usually have a stronger educational background that facilitates literacy development in both their first language, English, and the second language, Spanish. However, these English-speaking students have greater needs in developing oral Spanish skills and have less support from the environment to learn Spanish. Spanish-speaking students in the program, on the other hand, usually have greater needs in literacy development in both their home and second language, and have strong support from the environment to develop English, their second language. The Oyster School in Washington, DC, stands between a Hispanic neighborhood and the area where diplomats live. The school draws students from both populations. The Oyster School is aware of the challenge of educating such different populations. Frequent reflection, efforts to improve, and consistency with its goals of educating all students and developing their dual-language ability have maintained the educational quality of this school over the years (Fern, 1995).

Parents must be clear as to whether or not the goal of their program is bilingualism. If the goal is bilingualism, the home language is taught to achieve mastery of it. When the goal is gaining English ability only, the home language is used to facilitate this process and there is no attempt to develop full and lasting proficiency in that language. Teachers must be clear that long-term and consistent use of both the home language and English increases the students' chances of English proficiency and academic achievement whether the ultimate goal is bilingualism or not. Clear understanding of the program goals and how to achieve them leads to honest relations with parents, consistent instruction, and coherent curricula.

In a two-way English/French program, for example, making the French-speaking community aware that the program had a goal of full bilingualism was considered essential for reversing the language shift among French-background students. It is often very hard to motivate students to regain a family language that they have lost. School alone cannot promote the acquisition or development of a minority language such as French in a predominantly English-speaking society, thus parents need to help the schools. Authentic use of language in contexts outside school greatly enhances student motivation to learn and the process of second-language learning (Graham & Brown, 1996).

Relationship with Parents and Community

Communication between school and home is essential to facilitate understanding of academic goals and easing cultural conflicts. Schools must understand the families' goals for their children, while families need to know the schools' educational agenda. Mutual understanding enhances collaboration. There are some ways in which the school and the family are each uniquely qualified to contribute to the children's education. Their work should complement each other. Cultural differences may cause tension among parents, students, and the school. Schools expect parents to understand the school's culture, and therefore regularly use the school's traditional means of communicating with families. It is only fair that schools make an effort to understand their families' cultures and seek effective ways to communicate with the communities of bilingual students as well. Schools and families that communicate well avoid disagreements that confuse students. Good school-parent communication contributes to the formation of bicultural individuals who can flourish in the new culture while they retain the ability to function in their own ethnic community (Kleinfeld, 1979).

Most parents are very interested in their children's education, but parents of some cultures do not always know how to demonstrate this interest to the school. Making sure that the children do their homework, that they are well behaved and clean, that they are interested in school, and that they are safe are factors that parents expect the school to view as parents playing their role in education (Hidalgo, Bright, Sui, Swap, & Epstein, 1995; Valdes, 1997). Teachers consider parent involvement to be attendance at school events, parent-teacher conferences, responding to school notices, and participation in classroom activities. Good communication, knowledge, and respect for each other's views are essential in the presence of such contrasting views. During parent-teacher conferences, one bilingual teacher always first reassured parents of their children's good behavior — most parents' top priority. Only then did she go into their academic performance — the teacher's top priority. Teachers who listen to parents are more likely to be listened to by parents.

Parents are more interested in participating in school when they are treated with respect and when they have opportunities to learn or to share their own knowledge. When trying to involve families, schools should not assume that home life is not teaching children anything. There is a need to investigate what parents are already doing so the school can complement and reinforce this teaching and learning. Asking parents to teach something to the students or participate actively in learning with their children stimulates parental interest in their children's education. The Funds of Knowledge Project (Moll, Amantin, Neff, & González, 1992) surveyed the community for the knowledge evident in their lives, incorporated it in the curriculum, and asked community members to participate in teaching. A successful project at an elementary school in Boston, which attempted to teach science in English and Spanish to English- and Spanish-speaking children, involved parents from both groups of students, thereby giving parents the opportunity to help and learn together with their children. A school can in turn suggest activities to be done at home that support what the school is doing.

Community organizations can also provide key support to schools when access to families is difficult or when there are language and cultural barriers. One project (Faltis, 1993) describes an English-speaking teacher who engaged community workers who spoke Spanish, Chinese, Korean, and Vietnamese to explain to parents how they might contribute to activities taking place at the school. Community workers also encouraged parents to form networks to support each other in understanding their relationship to the school. This teacher enjoyed high parental attendance at school events.

Another way to improve home-school relations is to promote school staff participation in community activities and encourage families to take advantage of school programs. School programs for adults bring parents to the schools for their own self-improvement. A successful middle school in Arizona offers evening courses taught by bilingual staff for students and for their parents in studio art, automotive maintenance, math enrichment, English, and citizenship. In turn, staff participation in community activities provides opportunities for casual interaction. The principal of a school with a large bilingual student population runs her errands in the neighborhood where she casually encounters children's parents. In this equalizing environment, parents comfortably interact with the school authority.

The Program's Place in School Structure

A school that addresses equally and fairly the needs of all students teaches students and staff to respect each other and to make the educational achievement of all students the main agenda of the school. Effective schools accept students' language and culture and teach them to add expertise in English and the American culture. This cross-cultural approach creates a safe school environment and fosters the formation of grounded individuals who can function in their own ethnic backgrounds while they smoothly and successfully interact in their new world.

Evidence of respect for the bilingual students' languages and cultures includes:

- treating knowledge of the native language as an advantage;
- allowing use of students' native language on an equal basis with English;
- making resources available in the bilingual students' languages;
- encouraging English-speaking personnel to learn and use other languages.

A school that creates such an accepting environment will be more successful in teaching students of other cultures to respect and appreciate English and the American culture.

A middle school in Arizona, in addition to promoting the school languages and cultures, offers a program called "Walk in an ESL student's shoes." In each class, bilingual teachers present 10-minute lessons on that subject in Spanish. After the lesson, the teacher and a counselor conduct a discussion with the classroom teacher and students on how it felt to attend a class in a second language and to have to participate and do work in that language. This activity helps staff and students share the experience of learning in a second language.

Successful bilingual programs are featured in a school's educational agenda as an integral ingredient in the school's mission (Carter & Chatfield, 1986). While bilingual staff should understand the school's academic goals and incorporate them in their curricula, regardless of the language of instruction, the administration and other staff should also recognize the bilingual program's goals and support its approach to education. This occurs when the bilingual program curriculum is planned together with the whole school's curriculum, where bilingual program staff are active members of the school faculty, and where bilingual students are the responsibility of all the staff. When a middle school in Massachusetts formed interdisciplinary clusters, they included the bilingual students in their plan. They staffed one of the clusters with bilingual teachers from various disciplines and included a bilingual faculty member in each of the other clusters. In this way the needs of bilingual students are considered in all school clusters while students in the transitional bilingual program are fully served by the bilingual cluster.

Integration of the bilingual program is not complete without bringing the students together in academic and social contexts. This can be accomplished in a variety of ways.[3] In schools with bilingual programs, bilingual and mainstream students can come together daily or weekly to work on academic projects (such as a hands-on science project) or special activities (such as math games or a bilingual play). Regardless of the model, the integration of students must be bilingual and bicultural, that is, both languages are used and the status of the students and their cultures are equal (Brisk, 1991).

Conclusion

Research and experience demonstrate that there are ways to create good schools for bilingual students and that such schools do exist. Successful bilingual programs emerge in schools that have made an unconditional commitment to all of their students, including bilingual students. The challenge to schools is to secure informed and supportive leadership that drives goals, establishes respect for languages and cultures, integrates the program, and welcomes parents as partners in their children's education. Building the blocks of the pyramid for success takes time. Most successful schools have worked hard for more than five years to reach their major goals. Such schools continue to improve constantly and adjust to changing circumstances.

Many conditions are needed for quality bilingual programs. Such programs need to be housed in good schools. Good schools with strong leadership retain quality personnel, allow consistent curriculum development and instructional innovation, and closely monitor the academic progress of all students in order to improve themselves. In such schools, language and cultural diversity become a social reality; children grow and learn while respecting each other and their own identity; bilingual and mainstream staff work together to achieve the academic mission of the school; and families collaborate with the school, contributing their own knowledge and skills to the effort to educate their children.

Notes

1. For a complete analysis of all characteristics necessary for quality bilingual education, see Brisk (1998).
2. Some of the successful schools illustrated in this chapter are part of the database of the Bilingual Education: Portraits of Success project. The goal of this project is to identify, document, and disseminate information on successful bilingual programs. The project is a joint effort of the National Association for Bilingual Education, the Lab at Brown University, and Boston College (see http://www.lab.brown.edu/public/NABE/portraits.taf)
3. See Brisk (1998) and De Jong (1996, 1997) for descriptions of different integration approaches.

References

Brisk, M. E. (1991). Toward multilingual and multicultural mainstream education. *Journal of Education, 173,* 114–129.

Brisk, M. E. (1998). *Bilingual education: From compensatory to quality schooling.* Mahwah, NJ: Lawrence Erlbaum Associates.

Carter, T., & Chatfield, M. (1986). Effective schools for language minority students. *American Journal of Education, 97,* 200–233.

De Jong, E. (1996). *Integrating language minority education in elementary schools.* Unpublished doctoral dissertation, Boston University.

De Jong, E. (1997). School policy and learning in bilingual contexts. In J. N. Jorgensen & A. Holment (Eds.), *The development of successive bilingualism in school-age children* (pp. 43–70). Copenhagen: Royal Danish School of Educational Studies.

Faltis, C. J. (1993). *Joinfostering: Adapting teaching strategies for the multilingual classroom.* New York: Merrill/Macmillan.

Fern, V. (1995). Oyster School stands the test of time. *Bilingual Research Journal, 19,* 497–512.

Graham, C. R., & Brown, C. (1996). The effects of acculturation on second language proficiency in a community with a two-way bilingual program. *Bilingual Research Journal, 20,* 235–260.

Greene, J. P. (1998). *A meta-analysis of the effectiveness of bilingual education.* Unpublished manuscript, University of Texas, Austin, Department of Government.

Hidalgo, N., Bright, J., Sui, S. F., Swap, S., & Epstein, J. (1995). Research on families, school and communities: A multicultural perspective. In J. A. Banks & C. A. Banks (Eds.), *Handbook of research on multicultural education* (pp. 498–524). New York: Macmillan.

Kleinfeld, J. S. (1979). *Eskimo school on the Andreafsky: A study of effective bicultural education.* New York: Praeger.

Lucas, T. (1993). What have we learned from research on successful secondary programs for LEP students? A synthesis of findings from three studies. In *Proceedings of the third national research symposium on limited English proficient student issues: Focus on middle and high school issues, Vol. 1* (pp. 81–111). Washington, DC: U.S. Department of Education.

Moll, L. C., Amantin, C., Neff, D., & González, N. (1992). Funds of knowledge for teaching: Using a qualitative approach to connect homes and classrooms. *Theory into Practice, 31,* 132–141.

Ramirez, J. D. (1992). Executive summary. *Bilingual Research Journal, 16,* 1–62.

Valdés, G. (1996). *Con respeto: Building the distances between culturally diverse families and schools.* New York: Teachers College Press.

Valdés, G. (1997). Dual-language immersion programs: A cautionary note concerning the education of language-minority students. *Harvard Educational Review, 67,* 391–429.

Voices from the Basement: Breaking through the Pedagogy of Indifference

AMBRIZETH HELENA LIMA

Hush your mouth, child . . .

I went to jail when I was about eleven years old. I went with a group of other children my age who were also sent there by the government. I clearly remember the hot, square, windowless room, with a few desks and chairs scattered around to accommodate our thirty restless little bodies. We were allowed to go home to our families at the end of the day. In the morning we would happily resume the long walk to the little jailhouse, as we played with each other in the carefree manner characteristic of many eleven-year-olds. When we arrived at the narrow door of the little room, we would trip over each other, so eager were we to get inside. We would find Mr. A. already there, leaning precariously against the shaky table in front of rows of desks that had seen better days. He would stare at us as we came in, with this uncertain look, as if he had no idea why we were all there; or perhaps it was the fact that he was no more than twenty-five years old. I remember sitting in the front desk, transfixed, staring at his big Afro and wondering why he always tried to chew on the speck of hair under his bottom lip. He would then take out the tools that we would need to do the day's work, as we turned to each other to discuss who would play defense or left wing at break time.

I do not remember hearing Mr. A. yell to get our attention. Perhaps it is because we were always afraid he would keel over if he exerted himself, since he was so thin. Or perhaps we knew he had the key and we wanted it. We wanted it of course because it would help us escape; it would buy us freedom for a few hours at least. And he gave us the key — not the whole key, mind you, just pieces of it, little by little, like sweet candy to entice and tempt us.

In our little jailhouse, Mr. A. gave us a voice when he handed us pieces of literary works to read and critique. He "picked" our brains as he debated religion with us. I remember a particular story, "The Death of Nha Candinha Sena," that depicted the daily happenings in a Cape Verdean village. I remember crying when we read "My Sweet Orange Tree," the story of a poor little boy whose mentor ended up dying. Every time he took the pieces out of his battered bag, we would wonder where he got the material since there was no machine around to make them. As he gulped in the hot air that circulated in the crowded room, he discussed the shape, the content, the makeup of the pieces; he disagreed, he challenged, he explained . . . he cared.

You see, in that little jailhouse that served as our classroom, Mr. A taught us to read. *"And then I went to school . . . and this harmony was broken. The language of my education was no longer the language of my culture."* These words from Ngugi (1986, p. 11) express clearly how I felt when I came to U.S. schools: I felt different. But again, I was fifteen, an age when everyone feels different, especially if one is experiencing culture shock, language shock, and every other kind of shock one might think of. But it seems to me that, because I did not speak English, I was special — special in an isolating, humiliating sense of the word.

A part of me died in my new school. I became mute — or perhaps people around me became deaf. I became invisible, or maybe people lost their sight. An active teenager involved in social and community-oriented activities, I now became disabled. You might think that my experience on my home island was tragic. After all, how many people go to school in a jailhouse because there are no schools (and no criminals) on the island? When it rained we practically had to wade into our classroom, and when the only car in the village drove by we had to shake off the spider webs and dust that would fall all over us. Surprisingly, through all the difficulties that characterized education in my poor African country, there was a feeling of oneness that is impossible to put into words. There was a blessed sense of oblivion to our plight because there was nothing to which we could compare ourselves. The resources were the same for everyone: nonexistent. We all seemed to have the same overused books that had gone from one generation of students to another. The people who had money did not find school supplies on the island to buy for their children. Unless they moved to another island, they were condemned to the same jailhouse where we all went to school.

In the bilingual program at my U.S. school, on the one hand, they provided us with necessary supplies and a sense of belonging within the program. Our native language was spoken in the classroom and we had a teacher who really cared about us. Most of us did well academically, even graduating with honors. On the other hand, I have always felt that I could have been or done so much more. I could have joined the choir, gone to spring dances, or joined track if I had known that those options were available to me. In hindsight, I realized that perhaps too many changes were taking place simultaneously and perhaps nothing could have been done differently: I was fifteen, faced with a new culture and, most of all, a new language. As I write about my experience, I can almost hear some readers saying, "Well, then you do agree that bilingual children are segregated by the program." In response I'd have to point to gifted high school students who are in self-contained classrooms because they are considered gifted. I am not judging this fact but, rather, pointing out that what determines whether these gifted students are segregated or not is the way that people view the program and how they relate to the students in those classes. They are viewed as smart children who are on their way to college, and they are perceived to be part of the school in a positive way. Bilingual students, however, are viewed as "limited English proficient," and there is a sense that they should not "rock the boat." After all, they are "lucky" that they have a program for themselves. I have heard many teachers say, "They come here and they want to take over. They even want to be taught in their own language! They are lucky they have a school to go to!"

I can imagine how bilingual students might feel today when they hear such comments. I still remember my urgent desire to get rid of the stigma of being a bilingual student, of not being American. I guess I wanted to be just a "regular" student. While taking some mainstream classes, I worked diligently every day to do my English homework. Then I realized that the homework the teacher assigned for me was much less than what he assigned to the rest of the class. I felt embarrassed and asked him to give me the "regular" homework, since I felt that I could do it. And I did it.

I once asked my bilingual teacher, whom I still love and respect, why we did not participate in school activities like the other students. She became upset and did not say much. Perhaps she felt as helpless as we students did. Perhaps she felt as different as we did because she was a bilingual teacher who spoke three languages. It was not until I went to college and studied literature that celebrated other cultures and languages that I regained my voice, that I saw the clear connection between the language I spoke and who I was as a Cape Verdean, as an African. And when I reflect on the impact that this realization had on my life, in shaping the human being that I am today, I can corroborate Gloria Anzaldúa's eloquent statement: "So if you really want to hurt me, talk badly about my language. Ethnic identity is twin skin to linguistic identity — I am my language. Until I can take pride in my language, I cannot take pride in myself" (Anzaldúa, 1990, p. 207).

Whispers in the "Basement" of Indifference

I wish I could say that my dream was always to become a teacher, to give of myself to others, but I cannot. I did not set out to be a teacher, but looking at my life in retrospect, I should have known that I was "destined" to join the vocation. I started tutoring my playmates when I was around twelve years old. My stepmother set up a "classroom" in our kitchen and I would "teach" every day after school for a small fee. The only drawback was that I would hurry through the lessons so we could play with our dolls. Throughout my high school years in the bilingual program I met wonderful teachers who encouraged me to persevere, in spite of many problems that came my way. However, I had no wish to emulate them, since I was thinking of careers that would give me a position of prestige and respect. In those days I think I wanted to be a flight attendant. During my college years I tutored at the university and taught English to factory workers, but I wanted to go to law school. I shunned the Future Teachers of America Club in favor of the Pre-Law Association.

Nevertheless, after teaching in Cape Verde for one year right after graduating from college, I decided to give teaching a try. I told myself that I would teach for a few years until I finished law school. Does it sound familiar? Finally, after teaching for two years and enjoying every minute of it, it dawned on me that I had become a teacher. A bilingual teacher by profession, but most of all by devotion and ideology. I mention ideology especially because not everyone who teaches or works in a bilingual program shares the ideological principles that motivate others to passionately advocate for and defend the bilingual movement. This realization forced me to examine my role as a teacher, and to understand that this role gives me the responsibility not only to teach my students, but also to ensure their well-being in and out of the classroom. I look at it this way: I have power over the lives under my care. When I shut my classroom door, few people know what really goes on in there. I must deduce, therefore, that the system I work for, the society in which I live and teach, trusts that

> the educator, believing in the worth and dignity of each human being, recognizes the supreme importance of the pursuit of truth, devotion to excellence, and the nurture of democratic principles. Essential to these goals is the protection of freedom to learn and to teach and the guarantee of equal educational opportunity for all. The educator accepts the responsibility to adhere to the highest ethical standards. (Soltis, 1992, p. ix)

What often confuses me is that when teachers start advocating for students who are not being treated fairly by the system, that trust is no longer of any consequence. The system begins to question the judgment of the person who is doing only what the profession or vocation asks of him or her. Then the teacher, by advocating for these children, becomes the enemy and finds himself or herself in direct conflict with the "system" because he or she dares to question circumstances that place children, especially bilingual children, at a greater disadvantage than other children.

When did it all begin? When did the ability to speak another language become such a stigma? Is it when our children were being placed in "compensatory" programs because they spoke a language other than English? Is it when not being proficient in English became the equivalent of being mute and deaf?

I do not want my students to have to ask me what I asked my teachers when I saw that we were treated differently. And if they do, I never want to look at them and admit that they cannot be or cannot do things because they are bilingual or not American. I want to fulfill my moral and ethical obligation, and see that all children get a fair shot at a good education. One may ask, "Why does the responsibility of educating these children fall on us Americans?" The "us" includes me as well. I embraced this country as my own the minute it opened its doors for my family and me. I no longer feel that I am a guest in this country: I participate fully as a citizen when I vote and pay my taxes. I want to shed my "alienness" so that when I open my mouth to advocate for bilingual education I will not have to hear the voice saying, "You are ungrateful. Why did you not stay in your country?" If in fact I contribute by voting and paying my taxes in this society, then I must make sure that I am contributing to its future by ensuring that my students become productive members of the same society. I have a moral obligation to shape America's future, and I believe that America's future is also in a bilingual classroom. Yes, America's future is Latino, Cape Verdean, Asian, Haitian — you name it! As I wrestle with my conscience, as I weigh my responsibility to the children under my care, I let the voice of experience add some common sense to the urgency and anger that sometimes can blind the best of us. I have come to realize that I do not have to risk my job or yell at people (although I have done both) to advocate for my students. In my search for a "rational" way to advocate effectively, I have realized there are many strategies and three major areas of advocacy that I can use to be a more effective advocate: advocacy in the classroom, advocacy in the school, and advocacy beyond the school.

Advocacy in the Classroom

I have realized in recent years that I cannot fight my students' battles all the time. I must give them the tools that will enable them to advocate for themselves beyond the classroom. Consequently, I try to design units that teach them about their rights so that they can empower themselves. I try to convey to my students the fact that they have rights as we study ethnic and racial identity, the civil rights movement, laws related to immigration, etc. People can only have a conviction about something that they know about. Knowing their rights gives them the strength and confidence to fight for themselves as they regain their voices.

I encourage them to participate in student government because that is where they are represented and can exercise the power that comes with voting. Furthermore, my students must break the cycle of passivity that permeates their existence, not only in their school, but also in their community. They often participate in "mock elections" by voting for actual candidates in their district. By examining the candidates' platforms, they become aware of the issues that surround them. Every year they go to the State House to rally in favor of bilingual education in Massachusetts. With these activities, I hope they understand that as the "future of America" they have a political role to play in their school and society.

I encourage my students to explore their own culture and share it with the school population through publishing in their own language in the school newspaper and organizing cultural events, such as Cape Verdean independence week. At my present school, the headmaster is an exceptional person who respects bilingual students and teachers. Perhaps because of his own experience as an African American male within a racist society, he is receptive to events that promote the students' culture or ensures their participation in the school community. For example, in my first year at the school, my students wanted to present their research papers orally. Since the project entailed comparing a Cape Verdean feast called *Sinza* to the Thanksgiving celebration, we decided to invite American students to our class. Other teachers brought their mainstream students, who listened to the presentations, ate Cape Verdean food, and listened to Cape Verdean music.

The opportunity to have such cultural interactions within the school enables me to guide my students through the process of integration, not only in their school, but in the community and society at large as well. I especially encourage them to become bicultural in the sense that they retain elements of their culture that they brought with them and gain other cultural values from their host country. I do not encourage assimilation by insisting they do away with their language and learn English as soon as possible. I mention language because it is an integral part of their cultural identity. Since they are in a transitional program, the tendency is to attempt to "fill them up" with English because "that is the only way they will become successful in this society." But how many people do we know who speak fluent English but are nevertheless "relegated to the margins?" (Macedo, 1991, p. 264). Therefore, I must deduce that it cannot only be facility in the English language that makes a person successful. If a student has the capacity to think critically, he/she will acquire English in time. Should the student be limited to "baby language" until he/she can speak fluent English? I do not think so. After all, "bilingual education should be a vehicle by which linguistic-minority students are equipped with necessary tools to reappropriate their history, culture, and language practices" (Macedo, 1991, p. 270). When they maintain their native language as they acquire English, when they identify with their own culture as they are incorporating aspects of the American culture, then bilingual students can speak for themselves, share their culture with others, and live comfortably in two worlds that define their experience as immigrants.

Advocacy in the School

Sometimes I feel that I do not have any right to "complain" because I do not participate in running the school as much as I could by joining the school site council and other organizations. I think I am still part of the culture of passivity that permeates some bilingual programs. Perhaps I share with my colleagues that relentless feeling of being an "alien," of not being part of the whole. Will we ever regain our full speech instead of continuing to whisper in the forgotten corners of the "basement"? Perhaps we can regain our speech when we advocate for a true multicultural education. By multicultural education I mean a "humanizing pedagogy that values students' background knowledge [and] culture" (Bartolomé, 1994, p. 182), not the pseudomulticulturalism that encourages students to dance a few token dances and urges the parents to bring a few "ethnic" dishes to school, giving the administration the feeling it has fulfilled its obligation to be "tolerant" of cultural differences. Multicultural education for me is antiracist education. Its purpose certainly does not include "tolerating" other people, but rather helping others "deal equitably without the cultural and racial differences that you find in the human family. It is also a perspective that allows us to get at explanations for why things are the way they are in terms of power relationships, in terms of equality issues" (Miner, 1991, p. 174). I hope that some day we bilingual teachers will become assertive teachers who are not merely "tolerated," but are respected by others as valued participants in school operations and as advocates for true multicultural education.

I know that I can educate other teachers about my students by establishing working relationships with them and vice versa. In many schools, however, it seems that the first task is to convince the other teachers that the bilingual students are actually part of the school, rather than temporary visitors or intruders. These same teachers do not seem to feel that the bilingual children are part of their responsibility. They are not aware of cultural nuances that a bilingual student may bring to the classroom and, worst of all, they do not modify their teaching strategies to accommodate these students. Should not all teachers know their audience? Would that not help eliminate many preconceived notions that one might have about a particular group? One monolingual teacher at my school said that Cape Verdean students did not do well in her class because they did not have a written language in their country of origin. I almost fell off my chair. I corroborated the statement by saying that I in fact communicated with my family back home through telepathy. Needless to say, not too many people were very happy with me.

If my colleague didn't think these students had a language, did she know that they had a history? Would she have been able to include these students' history in her curriculum? I believe she could have; I believe she must. In our schools there is often dissension between groups of students because they really do not know each other. If these students could get to know each other's history, see the commonality between them as fellow human beings, they would learn to communicate with each other.

I co-taught a class of Cape Verdean and African American students with a mainstream teacher at my present school last year, in spite of our trepidation about its success. The objective of the class was to document the school's history. Although some of the Cape Verdean students did not speak English fluently, the African American and Cape Verdean students worked side by side without a sense of having to "tolerate" each other. Instead they worked together as they interviewed people within the school community on different issues, including the school's bilingual program and the presence of a Cape Verdean community in their neighborhood. We did not have any problems related to race or ethnicity. This collaboration between bilingual and mainstream students helped all of us to change preconceived notions about each other and learn from each other's experiences.

Advocacy beyond the School

I feel that something is escaping me, that I am not advocating for bilingual education beyond my school. Does my mission as a bilingual teacher end the minute I leave the building? What am I doing outside of the school to make sure that bilingual programs continue to exist and improve in quality? I should not just concentrate on teaching, although that is what I often hear from my superiors. I do not intend to be the next Jaime Escalante, but I do envision becoming part of the union, for example, to have a voice in decisions about bilingual program class size. I can also see myself and other teachers holding conferences to share best practices, and writing responses to published attacks on bilingual education. With these presentations and articles we will aim to earn the respect that we deserve. Bilingual teachers are often deemed incompetent because our modesty doesn't allow us to "brag" about what we do. I have wonderful colleagues who do wonderful work in their classrooms. However, they are so quiet that no one takes a second look at them. It is time we promote ourselves by showing what we are capable of in conferences and newspapers and educate the public about the bilingual movement. Finally, I can see myself attending hearings, being aware of changes in policies or laws, voting for the "right" person — that is, becoming "a shaker and a mover" to guarantee that we will have people in the government who share our ideology and will defend the bilingual movement and dispel the perception of powerlessness that people associate with immigrant communities.

I have been considering the terms that define bilingual programs, and I think we have adopted jargon that fuels arguments against the bilingual movement. For example, we use the term *compensatory* to refer to bilingual programs, although many students in these programs already speak two languages. In contrast, when students take foreign language courses they are perceived as intelligent, multifaceted citizens of the world, although they might not be able to say more than a dozen words in that language. The foreign language teachers are also viewed as cultured authorities in the language they teach, even if they have a heavy American accent or have never lived in the country whose language they teach. Just what are bilingual programs compensating for, I ask? For already speaking more than one language? When we accept the term *compensatory*, I feel that we are agreeing with the hegemonic classification of languages. *Multilingual* or *multicultural* would be a much more accurate term for what a bilingual program is truly about.

Another bothersome term is *regular program*, which is used to designate the monolingual program. This term implies that the bilingual program is, well, *ir*regular. Why not call them *monolingual* and *bilingual* programs, terms that accurately reflect the nature of the programs? Another term that is now being used to designate bilingual students is *English-language learners*, rather than *limited-English-proficient students*. My students are more than that. They are not empty vessels that have to be "filled" with English, but young people who bring with them a wealth of life experience. My goal as a teacher is not only to teach them English, but also to enable them to express themselves in the language they know best. Is the goal of the bilingual program to shut them up until they learn enough English? Is their worth measured by their proficiency in English? Does the fact that they do not speak English eradicate every other facet of their lives? This is where the humanizing pedagogy comes in, one in which we value students' experiences and see them as whole people. If we have to label our children, let us find more humanizing terms.

The Power That Can Be

I believe that it is my ethical and moral responsibility to advocate for my students. As a former bilingual student and current bilingual teacher, I would be remiss if I remained quiet. I no longer want to whisper in the "basement" of indifference; I do not want to feel that my students or I should be happy with what we have. I recently heard a colleague refer to members of the bilingual movement as "poor people who need our help" in deciding what to do "for their children." This same person would never consider telling middle-class parents how to educate their children. And yet, the parents of bilingual children are deprived of their dignity, viewed as simple, childlike adults who need to be told what to do.

Nevertheless, I sense hope growing within the immigrant community as its members recognize that they do indeed have power. This power comes from the realization that our cause is a just one. We have community leaders and parents who can be a strong source of support for us. Most of all, we have our students who are our inspiration: it is because of them and for them that we continue to struggle. As Anzaldúa states, we are "stubborn, persevering, impenetrable as stone, yet possessing a malleability that renders us unbreakable. . . . We . . . will remain" (1990, p. 211).

References

Anzaldúa, G. (1990). How to tame a wild tongue. In R. Ferguson, M. Gever, Trinh T. Minh-ha, & C. West (Eds.), *Out there: Marginalization and contemporary cultures* (pp. 203–211). New York: New Museum of Contemporary Art.

Bartolomé, L. I. (1994). Beyond the methods fetish: Toward a humanizing pedagogy. *Harvard Educational Review, 64,* 173–191.

Lee, E. (1994). Taking multicultural, anti-racist education seriously. In F. Schultz (Ed.), *Annual Editions: Education* (pp. 174–177). Guilford, CT: Dushkin Publishing Group.

Macedo, D. (1991). English only: The tongue tying of America. *Boston University Journal of Education, 173,* 263–272.

Ngugi, W. T. (1986). *Decolonizing the mind: The politics of language in African literature.* London: J. Currey.

Soltis, J. (1992). *The ethics of teaching.* New York: Teachers College Press.

About the Authors

Cynthia Ballenger is a Project Director at TERC and a staff member at the Chèche Konnen Center for Science Education and Linguistic Minority Children — a group of teachers and teacher researchers who come together to explore their classroom practice in science. Her major professional interests focus on teacher research, bilingualism, creole languages, and science education. She has recently published her first book, *Teaching Other People's Children* (1999).

Lilia I. Bartolomé is an Associate Professor in the Graduate Teacher Education Program at the University of Massachusetts, Boston. Her research interests center on home/school cross-cultural language and literacy practices, and on oral and written classroom discourse acquisition patterns of language-minority children in U.S. schools. Her publications include *Dancing with Bigotry: The Poisoning of Culture* (with D. Macedo, in press) and *Misteaching of Academic Discourses* (1998).

Berta Rosa Berriz has taught in public schools for the past eighteen years. She is currently a Bilingual Staff Developer in the Boston Public Schools and an Adjunct Professor at Lesley College in the Creative Arts and Learning Program. Her professional interests include teacher research in urban classrooms, cultural arts and bilingualism, and multicultural and antiracist education. As a teacher researcher, Berriz has examined the role of arts in identity and literacy development of children in two-way bilingual classrooms.

Maria Estela Brisk is a Professor in the Lynch School of Education at Boston College. Her professional interests center on bilingualism in school contexts and the education of language-minority students. Her most recent publications include *Literacy and Bilingualism: A Handbook for All Teachers* (with M. M. Harrington, in press), *Bilingual Education: From Compensatory to Quality Schooling* (1998), and *The Transforming Power of Critical Autobiographies* (1998).

Jim Cummins is a Professor at the Ontario Institute for Language Studies. His professional interests focus on educational equity issues, second-language acquisition, and bilingualism. His recent publications include *Negotiating Identities: Education for Empowerment in a Diverse Society* (1999) and *Brave New Schools: Challenging Cultural Illiteracy* (with D. Sayers, 1997).

Mohamed Hassan Farah is a Somali bilingual teacher in the Boston Public Schools. His primary professional interests include literacy and academic development in the first and second language and best-teaching practices in bilingual high school classrooms accommodating Somali refugee students. Actively involved in educational issues concerning the Somali community in the United States, Farah is currently studying the integration of instructional technologies into bilingual classrooms.

Katy Mei-Kuen Kwong is a Chinese bilingual teacher in the Malden (MA) Public Schools. Her professional interests center on issues of bilingualism, identity development, and barriers to access to high-quality programs in urban high schools. An active community organizer, she is chairperson of the Massachusetts Asian American Educators Association, a statewide organization that advocates for equity in education for the Asian American and Pacific Island community in the United States.

Ambrizeth Helena Lima is currently an English-as-a-Second-Language (ESL) teacher in the Boston Public Schools. Her professional interests center on bilingual and ESL studies, and political and educational issues concerning the Cape Verdean community in the United States. An active community organizer, Lima's publications include "Tomorrow I'll Eat My Carrots" (1998), "Creolinglish: The New Language spoken by Cape Verdean Creole Speakers" (1997), and "The Ethics of Teaching 'Limited English Proficiency' Students" (1997) — all published in *Cimboa: A Journal of Letters, Arts and Studies*.

Donaldo Macedo is a Distinguished Professor of Liberal Arts and Director of the Graduate Program in Applied Linguistics at the University of Massachusetts, Boston. Macedo has published in four languages in the areas of critical literacy, bilingualism, and creole studies. His publications include *Dancing with Bigotry: The Poisoning of Culture* (with L. I. Bartolomé, in press) *Ideology Matters* (with P. Freire, 1999), and *Literacies of Power: What Americans Are Not Allowed to Know* (1994).

Sonia Nieto is Professor of Language, Literacy, and Culture at the University of Massachusetts, Amherst. Her professional interests include multicultural education, the education of Latinos, immigrants, and other culturally and linguistically diverse students, and Puerto Rican children's literature. Her publications include *Puerto Rican Students in U.S. Schools* (forthcoming), *Affirming Diversity: The Sociopolitical Context of Multicultural Education* (3rd ed., 2000), and *The Light in Their Eyes: Creating Multicultural Learning Communities* (1999).

Dennis Sayers is a Teacher Researcher at the Ann Leavenworth Center for Accelerated Learning and editor of *Computer Assisted English Language Learning*. He is a cofounder of De Orilla a Orilla, a telecommunications network that connects classrooms throughout the world. His research centers on teacher research, two-way immersion programs, and technology mediated literacy learning. He is coauthor of *Brave New Schools: Challenging Cultural Illiteracy* (with J. Cummins, 1997).

Heloisa Souza is a bilingual parent liaison in the Boston and Somerville public schools. She is cofounder of the Brazilian Women's Group — an advocacy organization that provides leadership to the Brazilian community in the Greater Boston area on political and educational issues. As a journalist, Souza has published on issues concerning Brazilian immigrants, including *Associaçoes Brasileiras em Boston [Brazilian Associations in Boston]* (1999) and *Retrato em branco e preto: Uma história oral da mulher brasileira imigrante na área da grande Boston [Black and White Portraits: An Oral History of Brazilian Women in the Greater Boston Area]* (1997).

Evangeline Harris Stefanakis is a Senior Program Associate with Programs in Professional Education and an Instructor in the Learning and Teaching area at Harvard University Graduate School of Education. As a researcher and teacher educator, she focuses on issues of bilingualism, special education, and assessment of children from diverse linguistic, cultural, and national backgrounds. Her most recent publications include *Whose Judgment Counts? Assessing Bilingual Children* (1998) and *The Power in Portfolios* (1997).

About the Editor

Zeynep F. Beykont received a doctoral degree in Human Development and Psychology from the Harvard Graduate School of Education and conducted postdoctoral work as a Community Fellow at MIT's Urban Studies and Planning Department. Her professional interests center on identifying language policies and programs that support the cultural, linguistic, and academic development of minority youth. Over the past twelve years, she has worked as a researcher and consultant in many school-, museum-, and community-based educational programs. Her forthcoming book, *Achieving Linguistic Democracy: The Role of Research,* focuses on the role of research in addressing issues of equity, access, and cultural and linguistic democracy in educational institutions.